MONUMENTS FOR POSTERITY

MONUMENTS FOR POSTERITY

SELF-COMMEMORATION AND
THE STALINIST CULTURE OF TIME

ANTONY KALASHNIKOV

CORNELL UNIVERSITY PRESS
Ithaca and London

Publication of this book was made possible, in part, by a grant from the First Book Subvention Program of the Association for Slavic, East European, and Eurasian Studies. Additional funding from the Society of Historians of Eastern European, Eurasian and Russian Art and Architecture was generously provided.

Copyright © 2023 by Cornell University

All rights reserved. Except for brief quotations in a review, this book, or parts thereof, must not be reproduced in any form without permission in writing from the publisher. For information, address Cornell University Press, Sage House, 512 East State Street, Ithaca, New York 14850. Visit our website at cornellpress.cornell.edu.

First published 2023 by Cornell University Press

The author and the publisher have made their best endeavors to contact the copyright holder for Figure 13, a still from the film *Spy* (© 2012, Rossiia-1). The publisher welcomes communications from the copyright holder, so that the appropriate acknowledgments can be made in future editions.

Library of Congress Cataloging-in-Publication Data

Names: Kalashnikov, Antony, 1991– author.
Title: Monuments for posterity : self-commemoration and the Stalinist culture of time / Antony Kalashnikov.
Description: Ithaca : Cornell University Press, 2023. | Includes bibliographical references and index.
Identifiers: LCCN 2022019493 (print) | LCCN 2022019494 (ebook) | ISBN 9781501768637 (hardcover) | ISBN 9781501768651 (pdf) | ISBN 9781501768644 (epub)
Subjects: LCSH: Memorialization—Social aspects—Russia (Federation) | Monuments—Social aspects—Russia (Federation) | Socialist realism in art. | Socialist realism and architecture. | Soviet Union—History—1925–1953.
Classification: LCC DK510.52 .K35 2023 (print) | LCC DK510.52 (ebook) | DDC 937.084/2—dc23/eng/20220527
LC record available at https://lccn.loc.gov/2022019493
LC ebook record available at https://lccn.loc.gov/2022019494

We cannot build cheap, awkward things in Moscow, for what we build in Moscow is for the centuries, for generations, and the point is . . . that we create a genuine monument to the epoch.
  —Iosif Stalin, releasing additional funds for the reconstruction of Gor'kii Street in the late 1940s

Contents

Acknowledgments ix

Introduction: Beyond Totalitarian Monuments 1

1. Stalinist Monuments in Context 16
2. Historicist Aesthetics: Developing an Enduring Architecture 30
3. Synthetic Composition: Anticipating Posterity's Gaze 49
4. The (Un)contested Politics of Stalinist Monument Building 71
5. The Cultural Foundations of Stalinist Monument Building 97
6. Self-Commemoration and the Interwar Culture of Time 113

Epilogue: Posterity's Monuments 130

Notes 145
Bibliography 175
Index 197

Acknowledgments

This book represents a highly interdisciplinary project, but this was not my original intention. Rather, the richness of my sources—and, eventually, the demands of my argument—forced me to become a dilletante in several previously unfamiliar fields. For this reason, the advice, feedback, and support that I received from several individuals was all the more indispensable. Above all, my sincere gratitude goes out to my mentors, Heather Coleman, Dan Healey, and Polly Jones. Their guidance with the intellectual shape of the book, as well as their assistance with practicalities, cannot be understated. Their generous commentary, steady encouragement, and unfaltering willingness to help undergirds this entire manuscript. I am also thankful to Steve Smith and Jan Plamper, as well as to the participants of the University of Alberta East Europeanists' Circle and the Mid-Western Russian History Workshop, for their incisive reading and invaluable advice on earlier drafts. Importantly, I am grateful for feedback from two anonymous readers, as well as the reviewers of *Slavic Review*, in which an earlier version of the second chapter appeared, under the title "Stalinist Futurity and Historicist Architecture" (fall 2020 issue).

I am also thankful to colleagues—too many to list—at my various academic homes over the years: the University of Oxford, the University of Alberta, and the Institute for Advanced Soviet and Post-Soviet Studies (Higher School of Economics). Not least, I would like to acknowledge the assistance of the staff of the archives indicated in the bibliography, as well as the employees of the Bodleian, Harvard, University of Alberta, Russian State, and British libraries. I also want to recognize the Clarendon Fund, the Government of Alberta, and the Social Science and Humanities Research Council (SSHRC) of Canada for their financial support throughout my work. Funding for fieldwork and conference participation while writing this book was generously provided by Nuffield College, the Arnold Bryce and Read Fund, the Ilchester Endowment, the Royal Historical Society, and the British Association of Slavonic and East European Studies.

Lastly, I would like to express my gratitude to my immediate family. To my parents, for a childhood steeped in Russian music, literature, and cinema, and for their uncompromising commitment to passing down the language (despite my not infrequent tears). To my wife, Elana, for her steadfast support of my pursuits, her flexibility in balancing our respective academic commitments, and her insightful "outsider perspective" on my research. And to little Elsie and Lydia, for helping me keep this book in proportion, and for bearing with a "papa who writes stories about what happened a long time ago."

MONUMENTS FOR POSTERITY

Introduction
Beyond Totalitarian Monuments

My first visit to Moscow as a teenager was a profound experience. The overbearing magnificence of the capital was a stark contrast to my Canadian prairie hometown, primarily distinguished by its large shopping mall. In Moscow, empires had been founded, broken, and reforged, with this history memorialized in the city's sculptural and architectural monuments. As I admired this seductive iconography of grandeur, I knew that Moscow's character developed largely in a period of monumental "socialist construction" under Stalin's leadership. Over the years, as I processed these impressions, I wondered if these monuments were fashioned precisely to ensure that future generations looked back on the Stalin period with awe and adulation. Officially, after all, the grand boulevards and ornate metro stations, towering high-rises and imposing statues had all been built to "immortalize the memory of the era" (*uvekovechit' pamiat' epokhi*). Indeed, this notion—that Stalinist monuments were built to impress posterity—had been voiced periodically, although never systematically explored. As the dissident historian Aleksandr Solzhenitsyn suggested long ago, Stalin desired to "leave a great monument to his reign of the same general sort as the pyramids."[1] However, limiting the focus to the dictator's hubris is misleading. As I argue in the chapters that follow, the state's extravagant program of monument construction merely harnessed and institutionalized the *widely shared* desire to be remembered. This collective striving to self-commemoration is, above all, a unique and intriguing *cultural* phenomenon, and its investigation takes one beyond the dictator's psychopathology—and, indeed, beyond the dominant "neo-totalitarian" approaches to Stalinist monuments (which treat the latter as instruments of official propaganda).

My focus here is on changing visions of the future: the displacement of utopian hopes by the fantasy of an enduring Soviet nation, secured and embodied in the succession of remembering generations. In effect, the construction of monuments for posterity assuaged popular anxieties within the context of a modern temporal order severely strained by declining confidence in a better future. This development echoed across ideological divides in the darkening interwar world; exorbitant monument-building programs were not the sole preserve of "totalitarian" dictatorships like the Stalinist Soviet Union and Nazi Germany. In societies reeling from economic and social breakdown, the carnage of the First World War, and the looming threat of its repetition, imagining and working to ensure that posterity gratefully remembered one's era shored up hopes of collective survival.

Monument building as a compensatory response to waning faith in progress is an unexpected conclusion, particularly when applied to the Soviet context. After all, it is often presumed that an optimistic striving toward communism was central to the Soviet project and its official culture, from the Bolshevik Revolution onward. Yet the resonance of communist utopianism fluctuated greatly and was in abeyance for most of the Stalin period. Initially, on consolidating his preeminent position in the party, Stalin proclaimed a "Great Break" in the pace of revolutionary transformation. The radical policies introduced by the accompanying First Five-Year Plan (1928–1932) fed hopes of an imminent breakthrough to paradise, an attitude the regime encouraged in its bid to mobilize labor.[2] With the construction of communism now linked to the achievement of measurable production targets, overfulfilling the plan would bring the millennium forward. However, as the First Five-Year Plan foundered, and high hopes turned to disillusionment, the regime quietly retired its promises. In 1931, it openly signaled its displeasure with utopian "hare-brained scheming."[3] Henceforth, the theme of the communist future was marginalized in Stalinist political discourse.[4] Tellingly, not a single utopian novel was published for the next twenty-five years.[5] In a marked reversal, utopian dreaming, previously a mainstay of Bolshevik culture and politics, was no longer likely nor welcome.

It was precisely at this point, in early 1931, that the political leadership unveiled its plans for building the phantasmagoric Palace of the Soviets—the central construction project of the decade. Disregarding the chaos besetting its industry and the unfolding debacle of forced collectivization, the regime embarked on the creation of the tallest and largest edifice in the world. This was to be the seat of the Soviet government, the headquarters of its ruling All-Union Bolshevik Party, and the central hub of the world communist movement. On the surface, the palace appeared to be a classically utopian endeavor, and its eventual inglorious failure suggests no small measure of hare-brained scheming. However, this project marked a watershed in changing attitudes toward the future. Rather than preempting and showcasing the marvelous prospects of tomorrow, the palace was envisioned as a lasting monument to the Stalin era that would memorialize the present to edify future generations. "Many centuries will the Palace of the Soviets stand," prophesied one widely circulated commentary, "people will be born, grow old, generation after generation, but the Palace of the Soviets . . . will remain the same as we will see it in the next few years. The ages will not leave their mark, we will construct it so that it stands without aging, forever."[6] Alongside promises of radical utopian transformations, this description presented a different future, one made appealing and familiar through the enduring presence of today's monuments, and the mnemonic connection between contemporaries and posterity that they ensured. After 1931, self-commemoration efforts came to dominate the Stalinist relationship to the future.

The new temporal outlook was materialized in a massive monument construction program that was no longer limited to traditional, stand-alone sculptures. The definition of what constituted a monument broadened significantly;

FIGURE 1. Perspective drawing of the Palace of the Soviets design, Boris Iofan and others, 1935. Canadian Centre for Architecture. Gift of Howard Schickler and David Lafaille.

the hypertrophy of the Palace of the Soviets signaled, but hardly contained, this shift. On the one hand, the monument-building agenda expanded to include the design of civil constructions (public and residential buildings), infrastructure (bridges, waterways, and metro systems), and urban spaces (squares, parks, and thoroughfares), all of which were now expected to stand perpetually as testaments to the era. On the other hand, "synthesis"—the fusion of architecture, sculpture, and decorative art into vast monumental complexes—became the dominant compositional principle. The Palace of the Soviets project illustrated these new precepts effectively. According to 1939 projections, the palace was to have 31,500 m^2 of wall paintings, 3,800 m^2 of mosaics, 4,800 m^2 of majolica, 11,000 m^2 of interior bas-reliefs, seventy-two large sculptures, 650 busts and smaller sculptures, and nineteen monumental sculptural groups standing ten-to-fourteen meters tall—which together would memorialize the glorious Stalin epoch.[7] The enormous palace would ultimately act as a centerpiece of a "new, Stalinist Moscow," a city which would itself become an "unprecedented monument of stone and sky" through the total reconstruction of its built environment.[8]

As it happened, the Palace of the Soviets was never completed. Construction froze in the wake of the German invasion in June 1941. Later that year, with the enemy at Moscow's doorstep, the palace's rising steel foundations were hastily cut up and welded into hedgehog antitank barriers. Even so, the Stalinist regime largely made good on its promise to transform Moscow into an unparalleled "monument of stone and sky." These included dozens of squares redesigned around sculptural monuments, the sumptuous pavilions of the *All-Union Agricultural Exhibition*, scores of resplendent metro stations, the adornments of the new Moscow-Volga Canal, and seven record-setting high-rises. These and other projects, primarily centered on the capital, visually embodied the regime's memorial program (and form this book's empirical bedrock). The extravagance of these projects, set against the backdrop of extreme poverty and a succession of crises that characterized the period, testify to the centrality that self-commemoration assumed for the Stalinist regime in the years 1931–1954.

Although scholars have only addressed the theme of self-commemoration in passing, the decline of utopianism and the accompanying rise of monument building, in contrast, have received much attention, not least because the changing architectural agenda of the time captured this shift so starkly. Indeed, the monument-building drive inspired by the Palace of the Soviets competition almost immediately displaced a decade of state-supported avant-garde experiments. These modernist projects centered on prefiguring and accelerating the birth of the new world, through the design of social condensers (domiciles which would nurture the progressive habits of the "new Soviet person") and disurbanist planning (which would erase the distinctions and inequalities between town and country). Like the following chapters, extant scholarship also analyzes the abandonment of such schemes in favor of monumentalism by reference to fundamental shifts in Soviet temporal culture. However, in the existing interpretations, these shifts are in the last instance treated as the outcome of the Stalinist regime's changing strategies of domination.

One approach treats monumentalism as heralding the return of the past to Soviet culture. Proponents note that the resurgence of monumentalism coincided with a wider conservative restoration that enveloped various spheres of cultural and political life following the First Five-Year Plan. This "Great Retreat" saw the regime abandon revolutionary emancipatory projects in favor of greater wage and status differentials, conservative educational and gender policies, and a partial rapprochement with organized religion. Crucially, the regime reverted to a traditional, nationalist strategy for popular mobilization and legitimation, positioning itself as heir to the Russian imperial project. This backward-looking narrative of continuity was disseminated, in large part, through new sculptural and architectural monuments. These resurrected a (partially modified) pantheon of national heroes, and restored the styles and forms associated with former imperial grandeur.[9] Ultimately, in this view, Stalinist monuments presented the idealized present as the culmination of a glorious national past, thereby expressing a fundamentally backward-looking outlook and the revival of traditional Russian authoritarian politics.

This perspective, which foregrounds the return of the past, hinges on the supposed identity between commemoration and conservatism. However, the (invented) past can be and historically often was employed to legitimate programs that were fundamentally forward-looking. Mythologized national origins can consolidate faith in a shared destiny, putative ancestral lands can legitimate irredentist programs, and heroic histories can inspire posterity's emulation.[10] In short, the past is often constructed in view of its value to the future. By applying these insights, some scholars (including proponents of the "neo-traditionist" school who foreground the hybridization of long-term Russian developmental patterns with Bolshevism) have challenged the chronotopic metaphor of Stalinism's "Great Retreat." Rather, they maintain, Stalinist temporal culture was better characterized by a shift to a gradualist, evolutionary model of progress, in which certain Russian imperial traditions and historical narratives were rehabilitated and adapted to the service of a radically different future.[11] Monuments, regardless of their subject or stylistic embellishment, remained trained on the regime's stated mission of constructing a communist society. When utopia failed to materialize with the revolution, Bolshevik leaders realized that they would henceforth be playing the long game. Monuments performed the function of heterotopia—miniaturized ideal worlds, which publicly showcased the communist future and kept the utopian flame alive.[12] Proponents of this view point to the dictums of socialist realism, the mandatory artistic method that the design of Stalinist monuments self-avowedly followed. A key tenet was the depiction of reality "in its revolutionary development," that is, pregnant with the communist utopia.[13] In this schema, opulent and alluring monuments (even those dedicated to the memory of past events) acted as islets of the future, demonstrating the rewards of loyalty toward the cause and providing temporary reprieve from the miseries of the present. The steady expansion of these monumental spaces throughout the period actively demonstrated the inevitability of communism's advance. In this view, monuments ultimately expressed Stalinism's enduring, future-oriented utopian impulse.

A third, competing tradition of thinking about Stalinist temporality, which is increasingly gaining ground, points to a new, eternal experience of time. Scholars of this suasion do not deny the enduring salience of utopianism in this period, but rather point to its subtle restructuring. As Lars Blomqvist contends, "totalitarianism [was . . .] its own utopia": the Stalinist regime claimed to have already constructed the fundamentals of an ideal society. This rhetorical strategy neutralized the search for political alternatives—being already perfect, the present order could not be changed for the better.[14] This implied the end of history: the future could not (by definition) hold anything new, and thus effectively disappeared from temporal culture in favor of eternity. Proponents of this argument see the Stalinist regime as having "introduced a new temporality: the concluded future (a kind of future pluperfect)." With the utopia "already having been built, the future . . . already arrived . . . the only thing that remained was to experience utopia," as Evgenii Dobrenko puts it.[15] In this context, distinctions between past, present, and future became blurred—Stalinist monuments anachronistically presented both former glories and future achievements as contemporaneous features of the eternal, utopian status quo. Furthermore, monuments' permanent appearance was intentionally inflected to imbue the Stalinist order with an aura of timelessness and immutability, thereby shoring up the regime's legitimacy and authority.

Despite their differences, all three perspectives share the basic premises of the old, "totalitarian" approach to the history of Stalinism. This scholarly tradition, born at the dawn of the Cold War, foregrounded the unconstrained might of the Stalinist regime and its fundamental logic of power accumulation. The "neo-totalitarian" historiography that I describe above developed later, but continues to uphold these original precepts. Specifically, cultural phenomena in the neo-totalitarian model (the monument-building program and the temporal visions that it incarnated) act as instruments of political domination. Whether resurrecting past imperial glories, showcasing the vistas of the communist future, or demonstrating the perfection of the eternal status quo, monuments (which the impoverished country could scarcely afford) served the interests of Stalinist leaders. The regime infiltrated every stage of production: from supplying commissions to intervening in artistic design, managing construction, and finally orchestrating the applause to which it unveiled its monuments. These dynamics were reproduced in other interwar dictatorships, especially Fascist Italy and Nazi Germany, reinforcing the connection between totalitarian power and the valences of monument building. Indeed, even while totalitarian approaches have generally fallen out of favor since the 1970s, neo-totalitarianism remains dominant in histories of the Stalinist temporal and built environment.

In the following chapters, I aim to move beyond the political reductionism implicit in neo-totalitarian treatments of Stalinist monuments, to reconsider the actors involved and the strivings that animated them, and ultimately to situate the monument-building program within a broader interwar context.[16] To begin with, the notion of monuments as propaganda of official temporal culture is complicated by the peculiar character of these objects. After all, a regime that was candid about the agitational aims of Soviet cultural production ostensibly vested quite a different function in its monuments, which were to "immortalize the memory of the era" for the benefit of future viewers.

In the early stages of the Palace of the Soviets competition, the former People's Commissar of Enlightenment (minister of culture) Anatolii Lunacharskii underscored that the edifice had to be "an extremely durable monument to the epoch and a witness to posterity."[17] Rejecting earlier experiments with impermanent, propagandistic monuments, Lunacharskii suggested that Soviet industry was now powerful enough to create more lasting constructions.[18] Within a few years, at the very first congress of the Union of Soviet Architects, Politburo member Vlas Chubar' generalized this requirement and charged architects with "creating great historical monuments, which would show posterity the glory of our epoch," a slogan thereafter endlessly reiterated.[19] Henceforth, the press dubbed all major constructions "monuments to the era," the "stone pages of a monumental chronicle," a "bequest" to future generations, and contributions to the "treasury" and "gold reserve" of Soviet culture. In so doing, the Stalinist regime embraced a more prosaic understanding of monuments as prospective (that is, future-oriented) objects: "creation[s] erected for the specific purpose of keeping single human deeds or events ... alive in the minds of future generations."[20]

More uniquely, Stalinist monuments were tasked with immortalizing not the past, but the idealized present. Indeed, the lacquered character of these self-representations has predisposed scholars to see mere regime propaganda, but their underlying commemorative function is crucial. As David Arkin, a leading art critic of the time, explained, "in fashioning a monument, the artist usually looks to the past, sometimes to one quite far removed [. . . but] we create monuments not to bygone times, but to our glorious present."[21] To be sure, smaller sculptures commemorating the more distant past were also constructed throughout the Stalin period.[22] Yet the grandiose, synthetic monumental complexes, which absorbed unparalleled resources and commanded the close attention of political leaders, memorialized the past only as a frame to the illustrious present. The Palace of the Soviets serves as a prime example, as it was originally dedicated to the memory of Vladimir Lenin, erstwhile Bolshevik leader and founder of the Soviet state, who had died some seven years earlier. By the time construction was underway, however, the design foregrounded contemporary content, smuggled in under the guise of commemorating Lenin. For instance, the columns fronting the grand entrance were to be inscribed with Stalin's six oaths made at Lenin's funeral, the palace's second-largest chamber would be named the Hall of the Stalin Constitution (and decorated accordingly), and the planned Museum of Soviet Socialist Culture, located on the upper levels, allocated half of its proposed exhibition space to "the implementation of Lenin's ideas and complete triumph of socialism in the USSR under Stalin's leadership."[23] Unsurprisingly, the palace designers began to refer to the building as a monument "to glory of the great Stalin era" and "to our epoch of victorious socialism."[24] Later, amid the raging Great Patriotic War (as the East European theater of the Second World War was known), the design was once again updated to reflect and commemorate Soviet battlefield triumphs. New features included murals depicting the Battle of Stalingrad, a Memorial Hall to the Heroes and Heroic Feats of the Soviet Era, and fifteen-meter statues of soldiers to grace the palace's facade.[25] In a similar way, the most important Stalinist monuments (and even those ostensibly dedicated to the individuals and events of the past) were fundamentally tasked with self-commemoration.

Fantasies about being remembered by posterity—what the philosopher Hermann Lübbe terms "pre-ception"—are by themselves unexceptional.[26] Only infrequently, however, has this yearning been invoked to justify collective undertakings, like the mass construction of prospective monuments. Similarly, and despite common assumptions, monuments themselves are rarely vested with the goal of collective self-commemoration. Egyptian pyramids, Greek *heroa*, Roman mausoleums, and medieval cathedrals, while built to withstand the ravages of time, expressed prevailing eschatological conceptions more than the pursuit of undying earthly glory. This pattern was broken in the long nineteenth century, when secular monuments first began to represent and immortalize the nation. Even so, this nascent function remained at cross-purposes with commemorating sovereign power. As observed in prerevolutionary Russia, for instance, monuments were overwhelmingly dedicated to members of the ruling tsarist family, rather than to the empire at large.[27] Only following the First World War, when the modern nation-state came into its own (through the breakup of multiethnic empires and the universalization of popular sovereignty, embodied in broad enfranchisement) did monuments begin to truly commemorate the collective. Even then, however, monuments did not always focus on immortalizing the present for a distant posterity.

The purported self-commemorative mission of Stalinist monuments stood out markedly from both preceding and succeeding Soviet monument-building practices, as chapter 1 demonstrates. These either lacked a pronounced prospective orientation, or gravitated toward memorializing the increasingly distant past. To be sure, the rhetoric of self-commemoration reveals little about political leaders' real motives. Yet the Stalinist regime pursued the goal of self-commemoration earnestly, and it did more than verbally recodify its construction projects as "monuments to the era." Rather, the regime put forward a broad set of requirements: that these objects be constructed durably, while remaining understandable, distinctive, and appealing to future viewers. Responding to these demands, art professionals began to develop the theory of prospective monument design, the outlines of which I reconstruct from their writings in trade journals and key pronouncements at conferences and meetings. Surprisingly, as chapter 2 recounts, the new compositional solutions pushed the style of Soviet architecture in a decidedly traditionalist direction. Specifically, Stalinist architects selected supposedly timeless historical styles to ensure that their monuments remained understandable to posterity, rather than to evoke a glorious past or an eternal, totalitarian status quo. Furthermore, they employed time-tested materials, architectonic forms, and decorative mediums to ensure monuments' physical durability, further biasing the latter toward a traditionalist composition. This logic reflected transnational trends, as interwar architects in both fascist and liberal democratic contexts, tasked with immortalizing the era, also gravitated toward historicist aesthetics, and did so for similar reasons.

The regime was also concerned about how posterity would distinguish stylized Stalinist monuments from their historical models, and whether Stalinist monuments would remain attractive and relevant, rather than become stuffy or antiquated. As chapter 3 reveals, monument builders proposed synthesis—the partnership of architecture, sculpture, and art in monument design—as the principal solution to these problems. By means of figurative representations and epigraphy, synthetic monuments could express the specificity of the Stalinist era on the canvas of a powerful, timeless, but ultimately indistinctive architecture. Further, sculpture and art could imbue monuments with a romantic, emotional character that would ensure their enduring appeal. Once again, these compositional devices, which substantiated key features of Stalinist monuments, broadly paralleled design practices beyond Soviet borders. However, synthesis presented its own dilemmas—solutions to the problem of indistinctiveness threatened to semantically overload a monument, potentially repelling future viewers. Conversely, romanticizing the memorialized subject in order to heighten aesthetic appeal could dissolve the monument's historical specificity. Such tensions remained unresolved, opening the way for the regime's interventions in monument composition. Ultimately, political leaders endorsed an architecture of excess, but this stemmed more from the specific problems of prospective monument design than from an innate totalitarian extravagance. Altogether, the genuineness with which the regime pursued self-commemoration problematizes the neo-totalitarian reduction of monuments to the propaganda of official temporal culture.

That is not to say that the regime did not have ulterior motives behind its quite earnest attempts to immortalize the era—decidedly, it did. However, understanding these considerations requires a look beyond the neo-totalitarian model of an all-powerful regime freely and proactively choosing to embark on a massive program of monument building. Inadvertently, the neo-totalitarian model not only reifies a Stalinist regime directed by leaders with competing visions and interests, but also sidelines the context in which these political functionaries constructed their goals and reacted to wider developments. Recovering this context requires engaging with a broader set of actors implicated in monument-building processes, whom the regime could not ignore when crafting its commemorative program.

From a purely institutional standpoint, the overwhelming power and centrality of the regime is uncontestable. Art professionals staffed independent studios and workshops, but the state held a total monopoly on proposing projects and awarding contracts. Various ministries commissioned architectural monuments, coordinating their projects through municipal planning boards and after 1943, through the All-Union Committee for Architectural Affairs and its successors. For their part, sculptural and or artistic components of monuments were typically commissioned by the All-Union Committee for Arts Affairs. As a further instrument of control, all art professionals were licensed through their membership in mandatory, state-controlled unions, established following the notorious April 23, 1932 decree of the Politburo (the communist party's highest governing body) "On the reconstruction of literary-artistic organizations." Importantly, through their trade journals and conferences, the Unions of Architecture, Sculpture, and Visual Art (as well as their regional subsidiaries) disseminated the regime's agenda; they were "a medium for communication with the government; an organizing and, above all, an evangelizing entity," as Matthew Bown explains.[28] The USSR Academies of Art and Architecture played a similar role through their pedagogical and research activities. Both the unions and academies were monitored by internal "party groups" (professional members who doubled as party activists) and by the departments for propaganda and culture under the auspices of the party's Central Committee. Clearly communicating its demands, the regime was able ensure compliance through the threat of professional and even criminal consequences for those art professionals refusing to adapt.

Moreover, being one-off projects of key significance, large-scale monuments received even more attention from regime leaders outside the established bureaucratic channels. Typically, ad hoc monument-building committees were led by eminent political functionaries, who managed these projects directly. The Palace of the Soviets construction council, for instance, included Politburo members Kliment Voroshilov, Lazar' Kaganovich, and Viacheslav Molotov, with their superior always in the background.[29] Thus, in the course of the design competition, Stalin informed the three of his preferred entry (which promptly received first place), demanding along the way that several modifications be implemented in the design.[30] As the chief architect Boris Iofan testified, in the years that followed Stalin continued to intervene in the design of the palace: "with clear directions and advice, he suggested the direction our artistic research should take." Among other recommendations, the supreme leader proposed the dimensions and proportions for the palace's tiers, limited the facing to only two types of stone, suggested colossal architectural sculptures dedicated to the Communist International, and approved the decorative themes of the main hall and foyers.[31] Indeed, Stalin did not confine his interventions to the Palace of the Soviets but frequently toured works in progress, commenting on them orally.[32] This close level of attention was made possible by the concentration of major monuments in Moscow, the country's symbolic focal point. As Igor Golomstock concludes, none of the capital's monuments would have been possible without Stalin's personal approval.[33] In a narrow sense, therefore, it was the regime that orchestrated the shift to monument building in 1931, and later abruptly ended this program soon after Stalin's death in 1954.

Notwithstanding the preponderance of institutional power, however, I argue in the following chapters that wider cultural processes stood behind the turn to self-commemoration, conditioning the political leaders' turn to the mass construction of prospective monuments. Specifically, this period saw the emergence of a broadly shared cultural value—the yearning to be remembered—a crucial variable determining the (un)contested politics of monument building. Chapter 4 demonstrates that from the perspective of the regime, individual and collective immortalization represented a symbolic reward with which to incentivize labor, loyalty, and military valor. However, the success of this policy was predicated upon the preexisting and widespread desirability of being remembered. This assumption was unsurprising given that commemorative honors were not only bestowed on deserving citizens, but were also appropriated by political leaders, who sought fame everlasting and curated monument design accordingly.

Even so, the regime also attempted to involve the masses in the self-commemorative project. It framed the construction of these monuments—representations of which circulated widely in posters, films, book illustrations, postcards, and postmarks—as a heroic, pan-national project. Intriguingly, despite the overrepresentation of "great men" in Stalinist monuments, the public remained genuinely enthusiastic about the prospect of indirect, collective immortalization through these objects. As visitor books testify, Soviet citizens participated widely in design exhibitions. They inundated art professionals and party-state institutions with letters proposing more monuments. Private citizens even tendered their submissions to monument design competitions restricted to professionals. In fact, this enthusiasm—which ultimately devolved into significant grassroots monument-building initiatives during the Great Patriotic War—overtook and even conflicted with regime priorities, prompting hostile responses from the authorities.

The shared cultural value of being remembered structured both the instrumentalization and the negotiation of the monument-building program—a dynamic vividly exemplified in the relationship between the regime and Soviet art professionals. Exhorting artists and architects to uphold quality standards in works built for the centuries, the regime underscored that monuments would immortalize their creators as well. While enticed by such prospects, artists and architects could also turn the tables, petitioning political leaders for commissions and superior resources necessary for fashioning such lasting works of art. The shared value of being remembered thereby acted as a cultural foundation to which the regime's monument-building program, and its negotiation by various actors, responded.

Chapter 5 investigates the cultural impulse to self-commemoration and demonstrates how its materialization in prospective monuments undergirded the fantasy of an enduring national collective, whose links were to be forged through intergenerational memory. This hope responded to the anxieties induced by the extreme social dislocations accompanying rapid modernization and the devastating experience of the Great Patriotic War. After all, despite the contrived optimism of official rhetoric (including the ritual affirmations of progress toward the bright communist future), the regime's increasingly vague and distant promises rang hollow. Change, while accepted as inevitable, fueled insecurity and unease in the wake of the disasters of the First Five-Year Plan. Amid such disillusionment, an alternative and compensatory model of the future, focused on deep continuities, gained traction. This fantasy foregrounded not the endurance of the Stalinist political order, but rather the survival of the national collective. The nation's identity would be secured and stabilized through an intergenerational chain of memory, in which both the commemoration of the past and the immortalization of the present would play vital roles. Importantly, this narrowly conceived national imaginary did not promise a restoration of former glories and cannot be reduced to the regime's political machinations. Rather, this alternative vision of the future represented a cultural response to the crises of the period. It galvanized the impulse to self-commemoration and, ultimately, created the context for the regime's sudden turn to monument building. After the death of Stalin, political liberalization, rapidly growing standards of living, and relative stability once again buoyed up confidence in a better future. The regime, searching for alternative models of legitimation, attempted to channel these hopes into a revival of communism utopianism. In this context, self-commemoration and prospective monument-building quickly fell by the wayside.

Neo-totalitarian accounts typically liken the Stalinist monument-building program to that of its political cousins, most notably Nazi Germany. Indeed, there are compelling similarities, even when appreciating the self-commemorative aims of this program (which neo-totalitarian treatments sideline). After all, Hitler's regime also envisioned a plethora of lasting edifices: grand boulevards, public buildings, museums, solemn memorials and pantheons, and expansive parade grounds. Berlin's central construction—the gargantuan Volkshalle (People's Hall) for 150,000 people—was designed consciously as a foil to the Palace of the Soviets (ironically, like the palace, it too was fated to remain uncompleted). As an infrastructural monument, the autobahn network (and its numerous bridges, viaducts, and sculptural adornments) was comparable to Soviet canal megaprojects.[34] Hitler, like Stalin, was personally involved in these undertakings (which often followed his own amateur designs) and waxed eloquent on these monuments' self-commemorative mission in his annual addresses at the Nuremberg party rallies. Mere months after seizing power, Hitler was already warning that "a people that has not placed the construction of its own monument among the values of its culture is deemed by history to be hardly worthy of mention."[35] As the monument-building program gained momentum, he promised that new constructions "shall satisfy the requirements of eternity . . . these buildings of ours should not be conceived for the year 1942 nor for the year 2000, but . . . shall stretch into the millennia of the future."[36] The Nazi regime's ambitions were most infamously expressed in Hitler's dictate that monuments be constructed with a view to their so-called ruin value. As his court architect Albert Speer later recounted: "buildings of modern construction were poorly suited to form that 'bridge of tradition' to future generations which Hitler was calling for." However, "by using special materials and by applying certain principles of statics, we should be able to build structures which even in a state of decay, after hundreds or (such were our reckoning) thousands of years would more or less resemble Roman models," still picturesque in their ruination.[37]

Such overblown monument-building ambitions, however, were hardly exclusive to Stalinism and its fascist cousins, as chapter 6 reveals. Certainly, the Stalinist regime pursued monument building with a singular ruthlessness, heedless of its staggering economic costs. Nonetheless, the Stalinist case was only one radical presentation of a global phenomenon. In the darkening interwar years, the fantasy of an enduring nation largely displaced more optimistic visions of national destiny, prompting a fascination with prospective monument building that bridged the authoritarian-democratic divide. After all, the ubiquitous culture of self-commemoration shored up the fantasy of national survival, rather than the strength and immutability of any given political order. The monuments inaugurated in Depression-era America, for instance, did not lack in grandiose scale and in ambitions to outlast the centuries. From record-breaking infrastructure like the Hoover Dam to modest but capitally built post offices, the Works Progress Administration framed its projects as everlasting monuments to an American spirit undaunted by the ongoing crisis. Effectively, by shifting the emphasis to an alternate (but fundamentally compatible) vision of the future, self-commemoration stabilized the temporal order of modernity at a time of widespread disillusionment with the progress narrative. For various reasons, this dynamic did not revive in the 1970s, when progressive expectations foundered yet again, giving way to a "presentist" culture of time, indifferent to posterity. By then, the national imaginary was itself hobbled, and the future-oriented, modern temporal regime gave way to a presentist order of time, within which immortalization had no place. Discussions around today's newly unveiled monuments rarely refer to future generations (and still less to immortalizing our inglorious present); instead, they commemorate past injustices in order to better transcend them.

Yet although the culture of collective self-commemoration has faded, its material legacies remain. Intriguingly, as the epilogue demonstrates, the Stalinist regime's concerted attempts to ensure posterity's adulation were not entirely in vain. Stalinist monuments have weathered iconoclastic campaigns, retaining their visibility, aesthetic appeal, and close associations with the regime that spawned them. Although the meaning and significance of these objects has shifted in the intervening decades, aspects of the historical narratives originally vested in them linger on, in however adumbrated a form. At least in Russia, Stalinist monuments continue to resonate with contemporary nationalist and statist discourses. In so doing, these monuments play a unique and important role, engaging contemporary viewers' emotions and obscuring the more repugnant aspects of the Stalinist experience. True to their design, Stalinist monuments continue to actively immortalize their era—a troubling conclusion that underscores the abiding need to contextualize and critically reframe these dangerously alluring objects.

Chapter 1

Stalinist Monuments in Context

The Bolsheviks' first foray into monument construction came on the heels of the October Revolution. Mere months after seizing power in Petrograd, on April 12, 1918, the Council of People's Commissars (the wartime Bolshevik-controlled government of the Russian rump state) issued the decree "On the monuments of the republic". This law ordered the destruction of tsarist sculptural monuments and their replacement with statues and memorial plaques dedicated to progressive cultural and political figures. Vladimir Lenin, the force behind the decree, had been inspired by Renaissance utopianist Tommaso Campanella's novel *City of the Sun*. In this ideal community, monuments and murals edified citizens, "participating in the task of education, of nurturing [*vospitanie*] new generations."[1] Similarly, the Bolshevik initiative pursued immediate, didactic aims, and came to be known as the Lenin Plan for Monumental Propaganda. For decades, Soviet monument builders referred to Lenin's plan as the inspiration and lodestar for their work, and neo-totalitarian accounts have seized upon such open admissions of the propagandistic nature of Soviet art. Such assessments are not incorrect—monuments were always invested with didactic functions—but these were sometimes secondary to other goals. Fundamentally, Soviet monuments were protean objects; only in the Stalin period did the regime imbue them with a distinctly self-commemorative function, channeling unparalleled resources into their construction.

Indeed, a review of Lenin's plan brings into relief the unique character of Stalinist monument building, in terms of its target audience, the subjects of commemoration, and the importance accorded to it by the regime. For one, monuments constructed in the early days of the Revolution lacked a pronounced prospective orientation: they spoke to contemporaries, rather than posterity. As Lenin himself clarified: "do not think that I . . . imagine marble, granite, and gold letters. For now, we must make everything modestly . . . for the moment I am not even thinking in terms of eternity or permanence."[2] The objects commissioned by the plan were to "serve precisely the task of extensive propaganda, rather than immortalization," seconded the Commissar of Enlightenment Anatolii Lunacharskii.[3] Amid the unfolding civil war, Bolshevik leaders hoped that monuments of revolutionary heroes would inspire popular emulation in the defense of the embattled workers' state.

In further contradistinction to Stalinist monument-building practices, the Lenin plan fashioned the new pantheon primarily out of the "great men" of the past, not the present. In a list of subjects slated for sculptural rendering, which was formalized in late July 1918, figures of the eighteenth and nineteenth century predominated. Only two had been active during the heady days of the Revolution (the recently deceased Menshevik philosopher Georgii Plekhanov and the Bolshevik leader V. Volodarskii, assassinated a month prior).[4] Admittedly, the decree did call for some "monument designs to mark [*oznamenovat'*] the great days of the Russian socialist revolution."[5] In fact, the avant-garde artist Vladimir Tatlin's famous design of the Monument to the Third International was originally conceptualized as a Monument to the Russian Revolution, and was commissioned as part of the plan. Tatlin's creation was to straddle the banks of Petrograd's Neva River and rise to an astounding 300 meters. A fantastic pyramid of upward-spiraling steel girders supporting three rotating glass volumes, the edifice was to house the headquarters of the Third International (the recently founded alliance of communist parties). Accordingly, the monument was to be outfitted with powerful radio transmitters, figure projectors, a telegraph exchange, and a printing press.

On the surface, the monument appears to have foreshadowed the Palace of the Soviets project; both fused the functions of a government center with an ostensibly commemorative mission. Yet Tatlin himself saw his creation as a programmatic challenge to the traditional understanding of monuments.[6] The futurist poet Vladimir Maiakovskii hailed it as "the first monument without a beard," and scholars still wonder whether, given its functionalism, hyper-modernist aesthetic, and "monumental antimonumentalism," it was more of an object "commemorating the future," shot through with Bolshevik utopian expectations.[7] After all, rather than historicizing and commemorating

FIGURE 2. Draft design of the Monument to the Third International, Vladimir Tatlin, 1920. Image from El Lissitzky, *Russland: die Rekonstruktion der Architektur in der Sowjetunion*. Wien: A. Schroll, 1930. Beinecke Rare Book and Manuscript Library, Yale University.

the Revolution, the Monument to the Third International expressed the hope of a global communist transformation (per the project's name change), and the limitless technological possibilities of tomorrow.

Regardless, Tatlin's tower—which was never seriously expected to be built—remained a pipe dream. The fledgling Bolshevik regime, which had inherited a country at war and an economy in tatters, diverted only meager resources to commemorative sculptures, to say nothing of the type of costly architectural monuments that eventually came to dominate Stalinist practice. Only a few dozen statues of yesteryear's "progressives" (along with a handful of memorial plaques) were ultimately constructed under Lenin's plan. Even these were executed in cheap, temporary materials and soon fell apart or were demolished. Considered a resounding failure even by its proponents, the plan was abandoned by 1921. Over the next decade, monument construction stagnated. Between 1922 and 1931, only eight stand-alone sculptural monuments were commissioned by central decree.[8] If inspiring contemporaries was the paramount objective of Lenin's plan, the regime evidently realized that truly ephemeral media (such as film, radio, and print) were significantly more cost-effective than near-ephemeral mock-ups of sculptural monuments. In architectural practice, similarly, Tatlin's project remained an outlier. Eschewing monumentalism, the regime concentrated its scant resources on functional constructions and, more rarely, bankrolled utopian avant-garde experiments in the hopes of showcasing the progressive and revolutionary qualities of socialist architecture.

Rather, it was Soviet mortuary culture that kept the monumental tradition alive in this period. Before the Revolution, Bolsheviks had put on "red funerals" in honor of deceased Party members and other radicals. These had upheld customary burial rites, if only as a cover for mass political rallies (which were generally illegal).[9] Following this tradition, work on the "Memorial to the Victims of the Revolution" in the Mars Fields of Petrograd and the "Kremlin Wall Necropolis" in Moscow began as early as the final months of 1917. Both were to house the remains of the first revolutionary martyrs, fallen in recent street fighting. Nonetheless, with the dead already buried, and a civil war on their hands, the Bolsheviks soon lost interest in constructing elaborate tombs. The Kremlin Wall Necropolis remained uncompleted and disorganized (and was redeveloped only under Stalin, in the late 1940s), while the more ambitious memorial on the Mars Fields soon fell into disrepair.[10] Similarly, although the Bolshevik regime began to issue decrees immortalizing the memory of recently deceased notables, sometimes even ordering the construction of monuments in their memory, these projects typically remained unrealized.

By contrast, Lenin's death in early 1924 elicited a much more energetic and future-oriented response. Within days, the legislative Second Congress of the Soviets, which was then in session, passed the decree "On the construction of monuments to V. I. Lenin," commissioning statues in all major cities, and proclaiming that "the image of our great leader must be immortalized for all future generations."[11] A funeral commission was immediately set up; but rather than burying Lenin at the Kremlin Wall Necropolis next to his comrade-in-arms Iakov Sverdlov (as originally planned), Lenin was eventually embalmed and put on permanent display in a series of mausoleums on Red Square. Evidently, the commission was surprised by the mass outpouring of grief: in the dead of winter, tens of thousands queued outdoors to pay their respects to Lenin's body. Capitalizing on this, the regime moved to engineer a permanent cult of Lenin's memory. The funeral commission was soon reconstituted as a standing Commission for the Immortalization of Memory of V. I. Ul'ianov (Lenin), which oversaw the leader's embalming and the construction of his final resting place. Commissar of Foreign Trade Leonid Krasin, placed in charge of the mausoleum's design, demanded that it be "planned and executed to last for centuries, for an entire eternity."[12] In the ensuing years, the commission also tended to Lenin's memory by commissioning (and censoring) photo albums, death masks, phonograms, documentaries, postcards, exhibitions, busts, and paintings of the leader.[13]

The measures enacted following Lenin's death strengthened the commemorative aspects of Soviet mortuary culture and presaged important aspects of the Stalinist turn to self-commemoration. If only for narrowly political reasons, the regime attempted to systematically immortalize the memory of a contemporary—its recently deceased leader—for the benefit of future generations, rather than contemporaries. Nevertheless, in the context of the mid-1920s, Lenin's immortalization was exceptional in several respects. Not only did it remain a singular event, the Lenin cult and its permanent material incarnations ran up against significant opposition from both popular and elite quarters. Hostility to Lenin's embalming, and to the wider monumental program, was voiced openly in the press.[14] For instance, on the pages of the party's official mouthpiece, *Pravda*, Lenin's widow Nadezhda Krupskaia admonished: "do not make him monuments, palaces in his name, pompous celebrations in his memory—he gave all of these so little consideration, they were such a burden to him. Remember how impoverished and chaotic the country still is."[15] Other high-placed opponents maintained that both the Lenin monuments and the leader's embalming were un-Marxist: frivolous and individualist, with strong overtones of mysticism to boot.[16] Thus, the influential art journal *LEF* opposed creating "icons" of a person "who fought various cults his entire life."[17]

In the context of a still-palpable utopian enthusiasm, key actors remained caught up by the prospects of tomorrow and were relatively unconcerned with legacy fashioning, even of an individual of Lenin's symbolic stature. In thrall to such sentiments, the artistic avant-garde was disinterested and unprepared for monument commissions. Their research program, which focused on designing impermanent, flexible, and mobile constructions (perceived as temporary way-stations in the race to communism) necessarily precluded a static monumentalism.[18] Representative of this outlook was Maiakovskii's poem "Aloud and

Straight:" "The hell I care / for bronze's weight memorial, the hell I care / for marble's frozen slime! / We're comrades all- / so let us share our glory, / one common monument / let's have / to tell our story / in socialism, / built in battle for all time." Similarly, in his poem "Vladimir Il'ich Lenin," Maiakovskii explicitly condemned the "rituals, / mausoleums / and processions, / the honeyed incense / of homage and publicity," accruing around the memory of the leader.[19] Ultimately, the funeral commission itself was largely divided on the appropriateness of keeping Lenin's body on permanent display, and the measure passed only by a narrow margin.

Even while prospectively oriented, monuments and the embalming of Lenin's remains reflected the specific problems of regime succession more than a concerted striving to immortalize the era. Fundamentally, the Lenin cult was promulgated by a regime bereft of its charismatic leader, desperately searching for ways to shore up its legitimacy and to continue to draw from Lenin's popularity. In this sense, the closest parallel is the immortalization of Stalin's memory on his own death on March 5, 1953. The very next day, the regime commissioned the "Pantheon—A Monument to the Immortal Memory of Great People of the Soviet State" to house his embalmed body (as well as the transferred remains of Lenin and others buried in the Kremlin Wall Necropolis).[20] As with the Lenin cult, this measure was at least in part a calculated response by a regime whose legitimacy had been rooted in Stalin's person. Once the succession had stabilized, and the leadership began to perceive the former dictator's legacy as a liability, the initiative was quietly shelved.

By contrast, when the Stalinist regime inaugurated its monument-building program by announcing the construction of the Palace of the Soviets in 1931, it went significantly beyond immortalizing the memory of a recently deceased leader. Rather, the regime now called for commemorating the entire epoch, a much more ambitious undertaking for which sculptural monuments of great men would not suffice. Only "synthetic" monuments—those which fused grand architecture with commemorative sculpture and art—could hope to leave the Stalin era's mark on history. That same year, the regime unveiled its plans for several more such edifices in the capital city, in addition to the Palace of the Soviets: the Moscow-Volga Canal, the country's first metro system, and numerous bridges across the Moscow River.[21] To some extent, the functional aspects of these projects remained in line with the earlier Bolshevik modernizing agenda. However, the new demand that they be embellished with art evocative of the Stalin era constituted a radical departure, and it signaled more than the widening of commemorative functions to architecture. Now, despite the specific subjects of their sculptural adornments (which could still be historical), synthetic monuments to the era would above all commemorate the times in which they were built—the glorious Stalinist present, rather than the past. Further, by infusing capital constructions with memorial content, the regime made sure that its self-representations would survive the ages, that they would not fall apart like the modest sculptures of Lenin's plan. Thus, the immediate, didactic objectives of earlier Soviet monuments (which tended to commemorate the past for the benefit of contemporaries), while never negated, were now overlayed with a future-oriented, self-commemorative mission that had fully come into its own.

Equally significant was the unprecedented importance now vested in commemoration, previously only a peripheral concern to Bolshevik leaders (the Lenin cult aside). Above all, this is demonstrated by the regime's willingness to foot the eye-watering bill of its expanded monument-building program. Expenses—on a completely different order of magnitude—stemmed not only from the enlarged scale of monumental architecture and its lavish embellishments, but also from heightened structural demands. Lunacharskii's call that the Palace of Soviets be built to last was soon taken up by art professionals and applied generally. As early as 1933, artist and art historian Nikolai Chernyshev was reminding his colleagues that the "very definition of a monument can be derived from its [etymology, which underscores the concept of memory], i.e. a work that it is slated [to stand] for a sufficiently long time, outliving many centuries and sometimes even millennia."[22] At a later conference of the Moscow branch of the Union of Soviet Artists, Chernyshev illustrated this point by suggesting that Michelangelo's murals would not be considered monumental had they been executed in aniline paints or in pastel, or if *Moses* had been sculpted out of snow.[23] Chernyshev's ideas were transplanted to the architectural field and treated as a given at the 1946 conference of the Union of Soviet Architects. There, his colleague Aleksandr Gabrichevskii concurred that "monuments and commemoration [*memorial'nost'*] are effectively synonyms," necessarily requiring superior durability; the architect Sergei Toropov seconded the notion that "memorial constructions are designed for an eternal existence."[24] By the end of the period, the 1954 edition of the *Great Soviet Encyclopedia* (Bol'shaia sovetskaia entsyklopediia) authoritatively intoned that monuments are "usually made of long-lasting materials."[25]

In practice as in theory, new monuments embodied the striving to maximal longevity, evincing their genuinely prospective character. In the interests of durability, architects deployed marble, granite, and labradorite facing in the first stations of the Moscow metro, unveiled in 1935—a costly compositional approach soon transposed even to mundane residential constructions.[26] Unsurprisingly, the regime also demanded durability from its monuments' sculptural adornments, as well as from stand-alone statues (which were to act as the new nodes of reconstructed neighborhoods). The 1935 Plan for the Socialist Reconstruction of Moscow, which guided the capital's redevelopment, ordered "the creation of monuments to outstanding revolutionaries . . . to leaders in science, technology, art, to fighters for the liberation of mankind—on public squares, embankments and parks."[27] Design competition requirements specifically demanded that these monuments be long-lasting, thereby officially forbidding cheap plaster or cement castings.

Such an ambitious program would have been deemed prohibitively expensive only a few years prior. After all, even when it had come to immortalizing Lenin in 1924, many institutions had rushed to rename themselves in his honor, in order to preempt the more costly expectation of putting up Lenin statues.[28] The shift to the construction of massive, perdurable synthetic monuments, however, testified less to the country's expanded economic capacity than to the high priority which the regime now accorded to self-commemoration. While the Soviet Union's industries had indeed grown rapidly in the intervening years, its standard of living had stagnated or even declined. In 1932, as the regime held its competitions for the design of the Palace of Soviets, the country was struck by a devastating famine that claimed millions of lives. Yet despite this and other humanitarian crises of the Stalin period, the extravagant monument-building program proceeded apace and even gained momentum. This is doubly impressive given that the regime's building ambitions nearly always outpaced their practical realization: shortages of funds, raw materials, facilities, and equipment were endemic. These challenges were compounded by the dearth of skilled labor and bureaucratic disorganization, both exacerbated by the wave of terror that swept the Soviet political establishment and creative intelligentsia in the late 1930s.[29]

Despite these travails, the regime largely succeeded in changing the face of the capital by the end of the decade, through a combination of ruthless measures (which included the use of forced labor on projects such as the Moscow-Volga Canal and the metro) and priority funding (Moscow was given extraordinary political and economic advantages vis-à-vis other Soviet cities at the party plenum of June 1931).[30] Particularly significant were new squares, bridges, and monumental thoroughfares that transformed the formerly chaotic and unregulated city into a modern metropolis. Infusing the socialist capital with a memorial character, a plethora of "monuments to the era," sumptuously adorned with sculpture and decorative art, were unveiled in full splendor: twenty-two metro stations, the Moscow-Volga Canal complex, the pavilions of the *All-Union Agricultural Exhibition*, and several major public buildings (including the House on the Embankment, the Lenin Library, the Council of Labor and Defense complex). All of these edifices paired practical functions with a commemorative mission. Thus, for instance, the architects of the Red Army Theater designed it not only as an entertainment venue, but also as an "architectural monument to the Red Army . . . which with the help of sculpture and monumental art would become a distinctive museum of [its] history and life."[31]

"Moscow is covered in scaffolding!"—this popular slogan of the late 1930s encapsulated the promise of still further imminent transformations.[32] Surprisingly, and very revealing of official priorities, the tempo was only slightly set back by the German invasion in June 1941. As the country reeled from military disasters, with Hitler's armies quickly overrunning its western reaches, the regime was forced to suspend most of its monument-building projects. Yet as with the challenges of the previous decade, the immortalization of the Stalin era was only temporarily and partially frustrated by wartime frugality. In practice, the moratorium on the construction of stand-alone sculptural monuments held for less than two years.[33] While they waited, artists and architects developed the techniques and theory of monument building and perfected their designs for future projects. Sculptors immortalized military heroes and political leaders in smaller busts and statues (several of which were later enlarged as full-sized monuments). Moreover, work on priority projects had never really stopped. The regime resumed construction of new metro stations in Moscow in early 1942, as soon as German forces were dislodged from the capital's immediate environs. The decoration of these six stations (the theme of which was swiftly revised to commemorate the Great Patriotic War) was carried out "through bombing raids, with frozen hands, and on rations consisting of a potato, at best" as one of their architects later reminisced.[34] Further exemplifying the regime's priorities, mosaics for these metro stations were airlifted at great peril from the blockaded and starving city of Leningrad.[35]

By 1943, even as vast swathes of the country remained under German occupation and the war was far from over, monument building was once again on the agenda, as prominent as ever. Moscow saw the unveiling of the six metro stations, as well as the Triumph of Victory bridge-side monument on the Leningrad Highway (which commemorated a war not yet won). Work began on a record-breaking monumental stairway in the city of Gor'kii, memorializing the Battle of Stalingrad. This project required enormous inputs of capital (a projected five million rubles), materials in short supply (1,500 tons of cement, 350 tons of iron, and 3,000 m^3 of gravel), and significant "volunteer" labor—all in a city beset by urgent reconstruction needs and struggling to sustain the war effort.[36] Nonetheless, reaffirming the official position, the Soviet head of state Mikhail Kalinin called on architects to rebuild devastated cities "for the centuries," even if this "would delay construction, and cost a lot."[37]

Furthermore, monument building was hardly the sole preserve of the central government. On the initiative of local authorities and various military units, hundreds of improvised war memorials went up across the country. Even so, unsatisfied with these haphazardly built objects, and anxious that they would not stand the test of time, the All-Union Committee for Arts Affairs proposed mandating that these monuments be executed only in "long-lasting materials—granite, marble, and other natural stone, as well as bronze, cast iron, and the like," notwithstanding their cost and unavailability.[38]

Following the hard-won victory over Nazi Germany in May 1945, postwar devastation in no way dampened these extreme monument-building ambitions. The regime commissioned scores of war memorials and organized the planting of victory parks. Initially, the reconstruction of entire cities largely revolved around the concept of war commemoration.[39] Their new urban plans envisioned "monuments, triumphal arches, public memorial buildings, museums, panoramas, pantheons, commemorative spaces, squares and alleys of heroes, monument-installations, and Victory parks. Non-memorial buildings were also imbued with monumental features. Grand staircases, colonnades, embankments, lighthouses, and bridges all acquired the character of memorials," as Tat'iana Malinina relates.[40] The redevelopment of Minsk and Kiev, the ravaged capitals of the Soviet Union's most important national republics, evoked these compositional principles on a particularly grand scale. In Moscow, the regime ordered the construction of eight high-rises in early 1947, at the height of the postwar famine (in the course of which hundreds of thousands starved to death). These buildings were designed to memorialize the triumph of victory, and thereby bolster the grandeur of the first city of the newly formed socialist bloc, as their architects later attested.[41]

The mass construction of prospective monuments crested in the early 1950s. Even as the regime downgraded the prominence of war commemoration, it commissioned ever more ambitious monuments to immortalize the transformation of the Soviet Union into a global superpower. Constructions that failed to do so were censured; Moscow's Serpukhovskaia metro station (1950), for instance, received a negative review on the pages of the Union of Soviet Architects' flagship journal *Arkhitektura SSSR* because "it did not tell of even one heroic event in the history of our people, did not immortalize it."[42] To keep up with the unprecedented volume of work, the All-Union Committee for Arts Affairs was forced to recommend the creation of a new Main Directorate for Monumental Sculpture; it also considered relocating sculptural workshops to be nearer to railway stations, to put the delivery of stone on a truly industrial footing. A string of megaprojects was completed in these years, including seven of the aforementioned Moscow high-rises, another line of ornate metro stations (opened in 1953), and a resplendent, reconstructed *All-Union Agricultural Exhibition* (opened in 1954). Beyond the Soviet capital, the Volga-Don Canal, an enormous infrastructural monument in its own right, was unveiled as a commemorative ensemble of stately architecture and sculpture in 1952. Thus, from a position of marginality, monument building emerged as a central focus of the regime's construction agenda, commanding vast resources even in moments of acute strain. Furthermore, and unlike their precursors, Stalinist monuments embodied a markedly prospective orientation, memorializing the present for the benefit of posterity.

To be sure, at no point did the Stalinist regime deny the immediate, didactic functions of monuments, as they were once envisioned in Lenin's plan. Intriguingly, however, the target audience shifted from contemporaries to future generations. Posterity was not to stand in passive adoration of the Stalin era, but was to be inspired and transformed through its illustrious example. Monument builders frequently lyricized on this theme. The sculptor Vera Mukhina referred to monuments as "a call-to-arms to future generations," through which "the government [makes] vivid and long-lasting role model[s]" of immortalized individuals, whose example would teach posterity the meaning of "valor and civic duty."[43] "It is natural for people not only to bow before the great, but also to seek to emulate them," she explained, and this desire "is the engine that [will drive] humanity to progress and to light."[44] Similarly, her colleague Evgenii Vuchetich argued that monuments should use "the example of the best people to nurture in contemporaries and future generations a great love for and loyalty to the motherland" and, "stepping over the ridges of the centuries, awaken in the future individual the same feelings which filled the hearts of our heroes, who sacrificed their ardent lives for the homeland."[45]

A good example of how such didactic considerations informed the commissioning of prospective monuments is the Pan-Slavic Committee's lobbying efforts in the immediate postwar period (this group initially had been formed to mobilize East European emigres for the Soviet war effort). Following the committee's visit to Bulgaria, its Chairman Lieutenant-General Aleksandr Gundorov reported that old Russian monuments, built by the tsarist regime after the 1877–1878 war of liberation, had positively predisposed Bulgarians toward the Soviet army. Inspired by this supposed effect, Gundorov called on the party's Central Committee to initiate a similar program of monument construction all over Eastern Europe, in order to secure goodwill toward the USSR in the future—a proposal which was eventually carried out.[46] Indeed, the first major war monuments were constructed in Eastern and Central European capitals (such as Vienna, Warsaw, and Berlin) rather than in the USSR proper. By the

1950s, hundreds of such memorials (commissioned by both the Soviet army and the newly installed communist regimes) dotted the urban centers of the Soviet satellites.[47] At the same time, while didactic considerations were, in theory, hybridized with the goal of self-commemoration, they remained largely secondary. As later chapters demonstrate, the regime focused far more on the *act* of immortalization than on its reception by a vaguely defined future audience. The specific narratives to be transmitted to posterity, the way in which the Stalinist era would appear with the passage of time, and how its remembrance would affect future generations were rarely defined precisely.

Just as monument construction reached new heights, the regime pulled back from such commitments soon after Stalin's death in the spring of 1953. True, one the first decrees of Stalin's heirs was the construction of the aforementioned pantheon, in which the leader's body would be laid to rest. But the pantheon was never meant to be a grandiose capstone to the project of immortalizing the Stalin era. By the time competition guidelines had been hammered out, in early 1954, the political impetus behind the project had become redundant. The building was relegated to the capital's outskirts, and its dimensions were restricted to a rather unassuming 80,000 m^3 (members of its architectural council were themselves taken aback by this minimalism, "given the scale of country, the longevity of this construction, and the burials that ought to be made within it").[48] These guidelines reflected not only the diminishing usefulness of Stalin's memory (after all, the pantheon was also to display the embalmed body of Lenin, whose eminence remained unquestioned), but the subtle demotion of self-commemoration generally. Ultimately, even a modestly conceived pantheon was not to be; the project was axed later that year.

Indeed, even though the capacity of the Soviet state had only strengthened over the previous decades, the leadership again reassessed prospective monument building as economically unjustifiable. The rising First Secretary Nikita Khrushchev personally intervened at the December 1954 "All-Union Conference of Builders, Architects, Workers of Construction-Materials, Equipment, and Road-Building Industries, Project-Management and Research Organizations" to signal the regime's new architectural agenda. There, Khrushchev raged: "on the example of master architects many young architects, who are barely out of college and haven't yet found their feet, want to design only one-off buildings and hurry to build monuments to themselves."[49] An orchestrated media campaign was immediately launched against the "excesses" of Stalinist monumentalism and the "vanity of architects, who attempt to immortalize their art even in mundane constructions."[50] Such early signals were confirmed by the Council of Ministers' November 4, 1955 decree "On the elimination of excesses in design and construction," which definitively stripped civil constructions of any monumental or commemorative functions. Eventually, the Academy of Architecture was disbanded, and architects themselves were demoted to the sidelines of the building process (due to standardization and the allocation of greater powers to construction bureaucracies), to the point where they faced "virtual professional extinction."[51] Several unfinished Stalinist monuments were quietly abandoned or were fundamentally redesigned. For example, the bottom tier of Moscow's eighth high-rise (which was projected to become the capital's tallest) was converted into the modernist, box-like Hotel Rossiia. "Monumentalism and triumphalism were out and function was in," as Graham Gill aptly summarizes.[52]

In a narrow sense, Soviet architecture's reversion to an austere utilitarianism freed significant resources urgently needed for Khrushchev's signature mass housing campaign. Yet the shift also expressed deeper changes in the official relationship toward the future. Specifically, the regime expected that the provisioning of private apartments (to a public largely confined to barracks and communal apartments) would revive floundering faith in the communist utopian project. In some sense, as Steven Harris observes, the regime's 1957 pledge to eliminate housing shortages within ten to twelve years prefigured its promise in 1961 to achieve communism "in the main" (*v osnovnom*) by 1980.[53] Soviet leaders hoped that the wider availability of housing (as well as of consumer goods and entertainment) would actively demonstrate society's steady advance to the communist future, one that was increasingly defined by material plenty.

Revealingly, in this context, the languishing foundation pit of the Palace of the Soviets was transformed into the world's largest open-air swimming pool. The palace project itself—now relocated to another site—underwent two more rounds of competitions in 1957 and yet another in 1958. Competition regulations called for a low-rise composition, a size decrease by a factor of fifteen, and greater simplicity. Although the project was eventually abandoned, its conceptual heir was the Palace of Congresses (1961). Constructed within the walls of the Moscow Kremlin, this multipurpose convention center hosted not only the Supreme Soviet and the party, but also cultural events like ballet performances and an annual children's New Year's carnival.[54] The design of this semisubmerged, rectilinear, glass and concrete building was largely functional, and the Palace of Congresses in many ways signaled and defined the new archetype for Soviet public buildings. In and of themselves, these new edifices were far from utopian, but they were harnessed toward a renewed utopian project, in the face of which self-commemoration fell by the wayside. The construction of lavish synthetic monuments vanished almost entirely from the regime's agenda.

Post-Stalinist monuments were henceforth confined to traditional, standalone compositions typically dominated by sculpture. For some time, even these were subject to belt-tightening: for instance, an immediate de facto ban on bronze monuments, promulgated in response to the shortages and high cost of the metal, held until the end of the 1950s.[55] Yet the point is not that decision makers now judged monuments to be an unaffordable luxury; after all, the absolute number of newly commissioned sculptural monuments had only increased in the post-Stalin years. What changed radically, however, were their functions, which reverted to those reminiscent of the Lenin plan's goals of inspiring contemporaries with historical examples of heroism and patriotic devotion. Even while sometimes continuing to use durable materials, they were no longer framed as gifts to posterity. Rather than memorializing contemporary events and individuals, the subjects of new monuments again became increasingly distant: above all the Great Patriotic War, but also the October Revolution, and even older events in the national histories of the Soviet republics. One late 1960s publication dedicated to new Soviet monuments still claimed that "contemporary subjects . . . are becoming in recent years one of the main themes in monumental sculpture." Yet the author was able to refer to only a handful of monuments to space exploration as examples of such.[56] Indeed, monuments to cosmonauts were few and most were constructed from the 1970s onward, when the great days of Soviet achievements in space were quickly fading into the past. The famous Iurii Gagarin monument in Moscow, for instance, was unveiled only in 1980 (in the lead-up to the Olympic Games), almost two decades after his momentous space flight. Thus, while the pre- and post-Stalin periods also saw the creation of a few prospective monuments immortalizing the present, these remained peripheral both to prevailing monumental practice and to cultural policy overall. Self-commemoration, and its material incarnation in the mass construction of synthetic monumental complexes, was a phenomenon largely unique to the Stalin period of Soviet history.

Chapter 2

Historicist Aesthetics
Developing an Enduring Architecture

The regime's turn to self-commemoration toward the end of the First Five-Year Plan was accompanied by an equally momentous stylistic shift in Soviet architecture, which saw the sudden and rapid revival of traditional aesthetics. Paradoxically, this retrospective turn stemmed at least in part from the prospective mission of the monument-building program: architects advocated for a return to time-tested compositional elements that would ensure the enduring vitality of Stalinist architectural monuments. Heretofore, Soviet architecture had gravitated to a different aesthetic. Seeking to prefigure and accelerate the birth of the new world, the avant-garde experimented with the architectonic possibilities of new construction techniques and materials (such as glass and concrete), and embraced an austere functionalism, eschewing embellishment and decoration. One of the most famous examples of such a project was Moisei Ginzburg's residential building for the People's Commissariat of Finances, unveiled in 1930. By means of socialized laundry, cooking, recreation, and childcare facilitates, this so-called social condenser was expected to emancipate individuals from patriarchal, petty-bourgeois habits and foster a collectivist spirit.[1] Aesthetically, the building's composition was strictly utilitarian: clean facades and streamlined, geometric forms.

Yet by the early 1930s, the regime abruptly ended its support for such utopian endeavors and their associated stylistic expression. Independent groupings of avant-garde architects were abolished in 1932, in favor of the amalgamated

FIGURE 3. Exterior view of Moisei Ginzburg's residential building for the People's Commissariat of Finances, unveiled in 1930. Photograph from *Arkhitektura SSSR* 1935, no. 5.

and centrally controlled Union of Soviet Architects. In a spectacular about-face, the authorities demanded that Soviet architecture limit itself to a more traditional program (in which monument building assumed an ever-greater prominence) and style. Following the international phase of the Palace of the Soviets design competition (in which all submissions were ultimately rejected, although Boris Iofan's design took first prize), the February 28, 1932 report of the construction council suggested that in the future, concept development "should focus on using . . . the best of classic architecture."[2] Given the attention that the palace received from high-placed political leaders (several of whom sat on its construction council), the significance of the edict was immediately appreciated. Even so, the "critical assimilation of the heritage of the past" (*kriticheskoe osvoenie naslediia proshlogo*) was an abstract slogan, and, as Richard Anderson notes, "what constituted classical architecture, and which classical techniques were desirable remained open questions" for some time.[3]

The initial answer to these was Ivan Zholtovskii's residential building on Moscow's central Mokhovaia Street (1934), which was widely touted as the concrete embodiment of the new official requirements. Heavily reliant on Palladian principles (of which Zholtovksii was a lifelong devotee), it boasted giant pilaster columns topped with composite order capitals, classical cornices, and elaborate balustrades. A triumphal arch marked the grand entrance of this monumental seven-story building, the façade of which was clad in sandstone-imitation ceramic. The project was generously funded, which was crucial given its eschewal of standardized components.[4] Following the building's completion, critics hailed it as a new model for Soviet architecture, and dubbed it "a nail in the coffin of

FIGURE 4. Exterior view of Ivan Zholtovsky's residential building on Mokhovaia Street, unveiled in 1934. Photograph from Viacheslav Shkvarikov, ed., *Sovetskaia arkhitektura za XXX let RSFSR*, Moscow: Izdatel'stvo Akademii arkhitektury SSSR, 1950.

constructivism" (the main avant-garde grouping at the time).⁵ Specifically, they lauded the "grand, *monumental* effect achieved through [Zholtovskii's] use of classicism."⁶ Henceforth, all new architectural monuments—notwithstanding their prospective orientation—were to be executed in a retrospective styles. Having signaled this requirement, the regime was able to force a speedy and relatively bloodless transition to historicist aesthetics through its monopoly on commissions, control over architectural education, and an obedient Union and Academy of Architecture.

To be sure, this new direction in Soviet architecture stopped short of the purism with which Zholtovskii employed Palladianism and was instead unabashedly eclectic. Many avant-garde architects initially accommodated their ongoing projects to the new requirements simply by overlaying the original designs with classical forms and embellishments.[7] Furthermore, the regime cast a broad net in its call for assimilating the heritage of the past. As a result, new designs not only evoked several acceptable historical styles, but often combined various elements of these within a single construction. The architectural palette of the time was so wide that scholars now have difficulty agreeing on a stylistic label, referring alternately to Stalinist neoclassicism, empire, baroque, and gothic. Very generally, however, Stalinist monumental architecture followed in a broadly conceived classical tradition (particularly in its Graeco-Roman, Renaissance, and neoclassical iterations) up to the late 1930s. The emphasis then shifted from classicism to vernacular (*narodnye*) elements. Monuments in the Soviet national republics evoked an Orientalist pastiche of their perceived architectural traditions, while projects of Union-wide significance gravitated to a specifically Russian neoclassicism of the eighteenth and early nineteenth century. Nonetheless, however one conceives of it, the historicism of Stalinist architecture was palpable and contrasted markedly with the preceding avant-garde aesthetic. It remained the only acceptable style for more than two decades, until the revival of modernism in the late 1950s.

At first glance, the turn to historicism seems to confirm Stalinist culture's conservative reorientation, its "Great Retreat" from the progressive, transformative agenda of the avant-garde. In this view, the philistinism of Stalin's coterie, and the equally "backward" preferences of the masses—both of which were modeled on prerevolutionary aristocratic tastes—undergirded the reversion to traditional, monumental aesthetics. As Frank Lloyd Wright wrote in 1937: "nothing pleases [the Russian masses] so much as the gleam of marble columns under high ceilings, glittering chandeliers, unmistakable luxury as they had to look up to it when it decided their fate, when they ate out of luxury's hand if they ate at all."[8] But more importantly than tastes (which the regime seemed ready to ignore in other spheres) historicist architecture allowed the Soviet Union to be "identified with images of imperial greatness," and created the "illusion of a 'noble past' . . . a magnificent, centuries-old world culture," promoting a nationalist and statist mythology.[9] After all, the historicist turn in Stalinist architecture was soon supplemented by a parallel push for heritage preservation and restoration, which brought imperial monuments, as objects of national pride, back into the public eye. In this view, therefore, the historicist revival in Soviet architecture was both expressive and constitutive of reactionary developments, a reversion to prerevolutionary tastes and a nationalist, authoritarian politics.

An alternate interpretation of aesthetic revivalism clusters around the aforementioned notion of Stalinism cultivating an aura of total perfection, of an already-achieved utopia. In this understanding, the revival of past architectural styles supported Stalinism's self-characterization as the apogee of world historical development. As Vladimir Paperny influentially argues, heritage was sifted for what would make it into the final "circle of inheritance."[10] "'Progressive' world culture [thereby] acquire[d] a superhistorical significance and eternal relevance," elaborates Boris Groys. It would be incorrect to see the revival of historical styles "as a mere regression into the past," Groys goes on, "because [Stalinism] insists that it is an absolute apocalyptic future in which distinguishing between past and future is no longer meaningful."[11] In this perspective, the eclectic revival of progressive heritage was instrumental to demonstrating the consummation of history in the utopian present. A "collage of historical styles," from classicism to art deco, was intended to evoke a sense of completion and eternity.[12] Thus, as Katerina Clark concludes, historicist architecture, which "transcended ordinary time and crossed into timelessness," conferred upon Stalinism "the status of an ontological ultimate."[13] In this perspective, architecture's eclectic use of the forms and styles of the past bolstered Stalinism's claim of having achieved an eternal, perfect present.

These two neo-totalitarian approaches share a fundamental assumption: that the regime independently sensed the political utility of imposing historicist aesthetics on the architectural community. True, in a narrow sense the regime *was* ultimately responsible for the traditionalist revival, forcing avant-garde architects to reinvent themselves, almost overnight. But the notion of political leaders independently deciding stylistic questions—encapsulated in Dmitrii Khmel'nitskii's quip that "each building had an official architect [but] the architect of all architects was Stalin"—is clearly hyperbolic.[14] Rather, the regime's endorsement of historicism stemmed at least in part from the arguments that architects *themselves* furnished, and it was largely *incidental* to the wider goal of self-commemoration. Paradoxically, Soviet architects deemed historicism particularly well-suited to prospective monument design; the fact that they were able to articulate this (convincingly, so it would seem) was a key consideration contributing to the official endorsement of traditional aesthetics. Intriguingly, it appears that this logic was echoed in the broader traditionalist turn in interwar architectural practice outside the Soviet Union.

As early as 1933, the architect Ivan Fomin argued that Graeco-Roman "classical architecture is the language understandable at all times and in all cultural epochs, to all peoples."[15] Fomin's views, which had been fringe just a few years earlier (along with his project of developing a "Red Doric" style that would fuse classicism and modernist, proletarian aesthetics) quickly became the doxa of Soviet architectural practice. Tasked with designing monuments that would remain understandable to posterity, Soviet architects quickly recognized classicism's suitability on account of its alleged universality. Importantly, unlike the international style of the architectural avant-garde, which also had pretentions to universality, classicism had a long historical pedigree to prove this quality. As Fomin's colleague Il'ia Golosov pointed out, in their search for monumental "big forms," Soviet architects could learn from classical architecture, for it had "survived several millennia."[16] At the first congress of the Union of Soviet Architects in 1937, architect and academician Aleksei Shchusev authoritatively proclaimed that "the basis of classical [architectural] culture, its laws, remain immutable. Whenever architectural thought became convoluted and overly complex, it always went back to the primary sources of classical culture." In the eyes of Shchusev and his colleagues, this enduring vitality made classical principles ideally suited for new, monumental "edifices on which people will gaze on for at least 100 years."[17]

Effectively, the fact that classicism had stood the test of time, and endured for centuries with little change, ostensibly demonstrated its truly timeless character. Soviet architects expected this artistic language to last into the indefinite future, remaining perpetually understandable and appealing to posterity. Accordingly, they proposed to carefully sift through classical heritage to discover its most stable and enduring elements. One prewar monograph, for example, promised to analyze "the reasons why this or that groups of constructions or a city as a whole became outstanding architectural monuments [and,] summating this analysis, to present conclusions applicable to city planning in the USSR."[18] Other works attempted to deduce the universal laws of proportion through a historical study of public statuary.[19] Soviet monuments, built for posterity, were to assimilate these time-hallowed elements. In 1940, the architect Georgii Gol'ts summarized this logic well in stating that "art has a future only when it relies upon the past."[20]

Soviet architects usually claimed to be recovering only the abstract principles of classicism, rather than mimicking its forms and style; after all, new monuments were also supposed to appear contemporary, in order to distinguish the glorious Stalin era from other epochs. But practice overruled theory, and Soviet architects could not resist embellishing their creations with forms considered timeless. Even Ginzburg, erstwhile avant-gardist and architect of the abovementioned People's Commissariat of Finances residence, listed the peristyle and peripteros as forms which had become firmly embedded in architectural practice and which could rightfully be called universal.²¹ Art historian Georgii Borisovskii went further, arguing that "for two thousand years architecture of various periods returned time and again to the extremely stable elements of Greek architecture. The order is a classic example of an architectural form [sic] that existed for centuries and never lost its importance."²² In 1939, the head of the Directorate of Visual Arts of the All-Union Committee for Arts Affairs seemed to sanction such views by also referring to the "ideal forms" of classicism.²³

Yet the historical record also revealed the limits to the ostensible universality of Graeco-Roman classicism. Indeed, the sheer variety of its local adaptations (from Ukrainian baroque to the Russian neo-Byzantine revival) demonstrated the existence of *multiple* classicisms, to say nothing of the alternative architectural traditions of the Soviet Union's non-Slavic peoples. Since the revolution, political leaders had become increasingly aware that Soviet multinational society demanded differentiated modes of cultural communication. At the sixteenth party congress in 1930, the authorities confirmed that henceforth, these were to be "national in form, socialist in content."²⁴ Retracting its previous predictions of an imminent "fusion of nations," the regime now assented that minority cultures would survive in the indefinite future. Applied to the design of prospective monuments, these tenets suggested that a more culturally sensitive approach to artistic language, beyond a one-size-fits-all timeless classicism, would be necessary for an enduring way of communicating with posterity.

Accordingly, by the mid-1930s, when the monument-building epidemic spread from Moscow to the capitals of the Soviet national republics, stable vernacular (*narodnye*) elements increasingly overlayed classical designs. The underlying logic was the same: history was the litmus test of truly timeless forms, vernacular traditions—their receptacle. Already in 1939, Ginzburg referred to vernacular art as "sets of artistic devices chosen by generations upon generations of people as most appropriate," a "'natural selection' of artistic elements which become models."²⁵ "Everything great continues to live not in the academies, but in life, in the language and culture of peoples, including in the language of architectural representations," the artist Nikolai Sokolov later echoed.²⁶ While such statements appeared to introduce a tension between popular, vernacular elements and the more elitist classical tradition, theorists were quick to dispel this misconception. "One must never oppose classic architecture (specifically, Graeco-Roman classicism) to the tradition of vernacular art, for the genuinely classical was at the same time genuinely vernacular," expostulated one 1937 editorial in *Arkhitektura SSSR*.²⁷ The incongruence between the two sources was further masked by the convenient slippage between "classical" and "classic" national architecture, both of which were denoted as *klassicheskaia arkhitektura*. In practice, from the late 1930s, Stalinist architecture revived local adaptations of classicism and, where absent, overlayed classical compositions with vernacular elements (filtered, to be sure, through the Orientalist perceptions of Russian or Russian-trained architects).

This hybrid style derived its "representations and forms [from the] consistent patterns ... of the culture of Soviet socialist nations," these being "directed not towards the past, but to the present and *future*."[28] It promised that Stalinist monuments would remain familiar and understandable even in the *longue durée* of cultural development. "The point ought not to be the [aesthetic] monumentality" of a given form, "but rather its eternity," explained Andrei Chaldymov, architect and former director of education at the Committee for Architectural Affairs, so "one ought not to shy away from national forms."[29] A good example of this logic was realized in Shchusev's design of the Uzbek State Opera and Ballet Theater House, in Tashkent (1940–1947). New theater houses, Shchusev explained, "are charged with describing our epoch in the coming centuries and should, undoubtedly, be marked with pronounced national architectural features."[30] Accordingly, local archetypes influenced the choice of ornamental motifs, the inclusion of decorative minarets, and the execution of the cornices, columns, and arches.[31] At the same time, the building's overall composition followed the traditional design of European theater houses, in its internal layout and external designs, which included such features as a classical portico and arcades. Altogether, Shchusev expected both

FIGURE 5. Exterior view of Aleksei Shchusev's Uzbek State Opera and Ballet Theatre House, unveiled in 1947. Photograph from Iakov Kornfel'd, ed., *Laureaty Stalinskoi premii v arkhitekture. 1941–1950*. Moscow: Gosudarstvennoe izdatel'stvo literatury po stroitel'stvu i arkhitekture, 1953.

the vernacular and classical elements to retain their understandability and appeal to future generations.

For their part, monuments of Union-wide significance increasingly mimicked *Russian* neoclassicism of the eighteenth and early nineteenth centuries, from the late 1930s on. Thus, for instance, the supporting statement for Leonid Pavlov's 1954 design of Stalin's resting place—the aforementioned pantheon project—argued that a building which "must stand for thousands of years ... cannot reflect the specific style of the moment ... [but] should be founded on Russian and Soviet traditions," which were more stable.[32] Yet Pavlov, in fact, was being tautological: "Soviet architectural traditions" had by then become synonymous with "Russian" ones. In effect, this dual function of Russian traditions—as an enduring architectural language of both ethnic Russians and other Soviet citizens—paralleled the role of Russian culture in articulating both a particularistic identity and, from the late 1930s, a pan-Soviet one.

However, even though official discourse tried to underscore the historical affinities between Russian culture and the traditions of other Soviet nations, the uncomfortable imperial and assimilationist overtones of the policy could not be avoided entirely.[33] To smooth over the edges, the regime initially enforced a de facto "taboo on recycling the imagery of medieval Muscovy."[34] Russian neoclassicism appeared to avoid these problems, at once evoking both a pan-Soviet, universal classicism, and a specifically Russian architectural tradition.[35] This style dominated the composition of the most significant monuments of the period, as well as of other minor constructions located in the RSFSR (the Russian territory of the Soviet Union). Only in the late 1940s, in the period of the *zhdanovshchina* (so named for the party's hardline ideology chief), did the regime prove increasingly unwilling to censure expressions of Russian chauvinism and the revalorization of previously "off-limits" heritage (such as church architecture). Even still, the pivot away from Russian neoclassicism was incomplete, and the unadulterated "Russian revival" style of the late nineteenth century remained a perennial whipping boy even at this time.

Seen in this light, traditional aesthetics served the future-oriented goals of self-commemoration, rather than cultivating retrospective associations with imperial glory or demonstrating the consummation of history in the timeless, utopian present. Rather, as discussions in Soviet architectural circles reveal, it was the forms and styles themselves that were considered inherently timeless, because of their empirically demonstrable, continuous usage throughout history. This enduring vitality made classicism and vernacular architecture artistic languages par excellence for communicating with posterity.

Importantly, the historicism of Stalinist architecture was expressed not only in its style and forms, but also in its penchant for traditional materials. Some neo-totalitarian scholars argue that these were used disingenuously, as mere "simulacra of permanence," to impart an illusory appearance of durability—and, by extension, of eternal existence—to the Stalinist political order.[36] Architects ostensibly achieved this effect by employing materials that were historically associated with robustness (thereby inadvertently bestowing, to an extent, a traditional appearance). Thus, Andrew Jenks argues that "monumental slabs of granite and marble reflected the durability and strength of the [Stalinist] order."[37] Similarly, Mikhail Yampolsky contends that monuments cultivated "a fundamental solidity . . . to express the idea of not being subject to time, of extrahuman temporality, of ahistoricity."[38] In support of this idea, scholars point to the Stalinist practice of imparting an appearance of permanence even to temporary constructions. Paperny and Evgeny Dobrenko, for instance, bring up the pavilions of the 1939 *All-Union Agricultural Exhibition*, which were variously embellished to appear durable, thereby "[symbolizing . . .] the strength and permanence of the entire Soviet order."[39]

This exhibition, planned and redesigned continuously from 1935, was to showcase the achievements of Soviet collectivized agriculture. The massive affair involved the development of 136 hectares in Moscow's suburbs, on which were constructed hundreds of pavilions and auxiliary structures dedicated to showcasing various branches of production, agricultural regions, and constitutive republics of the USSR. In 1939, the monumental ensemble finally opened after years of delays, and evoked vernacular and classical styles; indeed, even some cowsheds were adorned with columns and triumphal archways. At the same time, the exhibition's monumentality was largely fictitious. Pavilions' wooden columns and façades were plastered to resemble stone. Interiors were duplicitously decorated in ways reserved for permanent constructions, including paneling and decorative reliefs. Most sculpture was executed in plaster, while the central, twenty-five-meter Stalin monument was constructed of hollow ferroconcrete blocks (which began to crumble within a few years). In the above neo-totalitarian perspective, these "simulacra of permanence" imparted an illusion of structural durability, and, indirectly, lent an air of immutability and eternity to their ultimate author—the Stalinist regime.

But as with its historicism, the durability of Stalinist architecture was less a machination of state propaganda than a repercussion of the project of immortalizing the memory of the era. As demonstrated in the previous chapter, prospective monuments required a *real* permanence; the mock durability of the 1939 exhibition pavilions was exceptional and was not reflective of a devious use of "simulacra of permanence" in Stalinist architecture generally. Rather, it would be more accurate to see the constructions of the 1939 *All-Union Agricultural Exhibition* as situated in the liminal space between permanence and ephemerality that exhibition pavilions have historically occupied.[40] After all, the authorities had reconceptualized the exhibition in the middle of its construction (in 1937), suddenly demanding that the exhibition to remain open for five years, rather than a single season. Many completed pavilions had to be reconstructed; hence, in part, the contradictory crossbreed of wooden structures and durable surface embellishments and facing. Eventually, in line with the ever-greater centrality that self-commemoration assumed in Stalinist culture, the postwar exhibition was remodeled as a permanent exhibition and many pavilions were again rebuilt—this time as truly permanent structures.

Of course, it is difficult to disentangle the normal demands for structural integrity from the extraordinary demand that these objects stand as everlasting testaments to their era. However, the latter was suggested by the volume of experimental research into perdurable materials, architectonic forms, and synthetic decorations. One example of this research into longevity is the work carried out throughout the 1930s by the Palace of the Soviets' construction council. Together with the materials laboratory of the Academy of Architecture, it developed special cement mixes and metal alloys, eventually creating superior grades of cement and steel (which was 50 percent stronger than the common M-3 grade) for the Palace of the Soviets. Special anticorrosion lacquers, coatings, and enamels were also reportedly developed.[41]

The palace's quasi-classical architecture was to overflow with synthetic art, which was not spared from similar requirements of perdurability. The sculptor Sergei Merkurov calculated that the special corrosion-proof casing of the main Lenin statue would guarantee its service for one thousand years.[42] Researchers also claimed to have created a highly robust type of asbestos canvas ("which will preserve artwork forever") and promised to deliver nonelectrostatic paints (which would repel corrosive dust particles).[43] Hardier fabrics were also being developed for tapestries: wrinkle-free, moth resistant, and impervious to sunlight.[44] The 1930s also saw the creation of an experimental laboratory for monumental art under the auspices of the city planning department of the Moscow Soviet. This laboratory sought to develop new techniques for fresco and sgraffito painting to extend their longevity in colder climates. Monument builders claimed that experiments in applying frescoes to concrete and cement had yielded good results in terms of longevity, and to have reversed Lenin's pronouncement that "our climate will hardly allow us to make frescoes."[45] In 1945, the Academy of Architecture opened a laboratory for stone construction and facing.[46]

Nonetheless, as in their search for an enduring artistic language, architects often turned to the past in their quest for durability, further biasing their creations in favor of historicism. After all, the heightened significance of monuments, as objects built for the centuries, raised the stakes for the success or failure of innovations. Thus, at the very outset of the project, Anatolii Lunacharskii warned that "one cannot experiment on [the Palace of the Soviets], spending colossal resources and materials and dealing a blow to the proletariat's prestige."[47] As a later resolution of the Union of Soviet Architects expounded, "the Soviet architect should remember that . . . every architectural mistake, executed in concrete and stone, is almost impossible to fix."[48] Equally importantly, innovation was hampered by Soviet architecture's still-basic level of technical sophistication and by the endemic lack of resources. Given the regime's demand to build monuments rapidly, architects felt that there was simply no time for real experiments. Indeed, the day before the Palace of the Soviets construction council's momentous report, the government mouthpiece *Izvestiia* prepared the ground with an article by the writer Aleksei Tolstoi, who reflected on Soviet architecture's changing direction. "Whole epochs shaped architectural styles [and] generations of stonemasons built gothic cathedrals," expostulated Tolstoi, but the current socialist epoch "sets a different pace for art and its implementation."

However, Soviet monument builders, the writer explained, were to be "aided by all the cultural heritage of the past."[49] Tolstoi was no architectural theorist, but the "Red Count" was known to be close to the political establishment, and the article became a seminal reference point in subsequent discussions. Echoing this logic, the first edition of the *Great Soviet Encyclopedia* stated that "the creation of our classics, our style of monumental-decorative sculpture, would take too long if we did not look back at classical works in all their breadth. This will be of vital importance for the creation of gigantic edifices, particularly the great construction projects of communism."[50] Designs of the Palace of the Soviets vividly exemplified the conclusions drawn from such circumstances and demands. The final design was approved in 1934, with the end of the Third Five-Year Plan (1943) set as the expected completion date for all substantial construction. As time ran out for lengthy experiments with perdurable innovations, frustrated architects turned increasingly to the past to select hardy materials, architectonic forms, and artistic mediums which had, in retrospect, withstood the test of time. At a 1938 meeting discussing the palace's facing, the chief architect admitted: "We live in time and space, we cannot keep making laboratory experiments . . . which do not give us definitive results on the durability of materials. All of these experiments should be tested by life. Laboratory experiments are insufficiently advanced, they cannot take everything into account."[51]

Instead, palace designers extensively monitored and evaluated the condition of heritage buildings as a short cut to discovering true durability. As early as 1932, the Palace of the Soviets' deputy head of construction requested that the State Central Archive establish how extant Russian monuments had been built so robustly as to have outlasted the centuries. Landmarks to be investigated included the Bell Tower of Ivan the Great, the recently demolished Cathedral of Christ the Savior, St. Isaac's Cathedral in Leningrad, the Peter and Paul Fortress, and others. Palace designers were particularly interested in the type of materials and cements used, the techniques for mounting external facing, and the preservation measures carried out.[52] Similarly, a later commission studying the Marble Palace and other aristocratic estates near Leningrad reported on the unacceptable state of their centuries-old marble facing, which had fractured, chipped, and suffered from encrustation and discoloration in the harsh northern climate. By contrast, granite had successfully held together Egyptian pyramids for 5,000 years. Tufa (a variety of limestone) was also tentatively suggested, because a particular Georgian church made of it was well preserved after 500 years. In the end, the architects of the palace eventually decided upon granite facing, as this was "the only one guaranteed to last for centuries," with which "in 600 years the building will still be young."[53]

At points, this logic degenerated into a rather fantastic research program. In an effort to secure maximal longevity for the palace, art professionals suggested rediscovering the lost techniques of classical and ancient Russian fresco painting, and the paint composition used in 1,000-year-old Armenian miniatures.[54] Extra justification for the Palace of the Soviets' gigantic size was inferred from Egyptian sphinxes, whose colossal features could still be made out clearly, despite millennia of erosion.[55] To be sure, propagandists also saw opportunities for capitalizing on the romantic appeal of recovering the lost achievements of great civilizations. Thus, for instance, one popular commentary falsely claimed that the special make of cement developed for the Palace of the Soviets (DS-300) was based on Roman cement, "the best in the world . . . which holds up after a thousand years as after a day, never ages or weakens."[56]

Along with hardy materials, the past was scoured for durable architectonic forms. The sculptor Leonid Shervud, at a 1944 Moscow Union of Soviet Sculptors and Artists discussion, referred to Corinthian columns he had seen in Rome: "they are preserved, they stood for tens of centuries, and make up a form that demonstrates that the material is well-utilized and extraordinarily preserved."[57] Within a few years, this sentiment was echoed at the highest level. Aleksandr Gerasimov, president of the USSR Academy of Arts, noted that the "classical column represents a fine mathematical calculation in terms of durability;" even though some may say that classical columns are archaic, he explained, "may we have more of such 'archaism'!"[58]

Finally, the same logic influenced the selection of the mediums of decorative art, which would infuse architectural monuments with semantic content through figurative means. Accordingly, the Architecture Institute reactivated research into the material properties of monumental and decorative art by opening a specialized studio in 1935 (it was transferred to the Academy of Architecture in 1938). That very year, monument builders began to publicly affirm the perdurable qualities of mosaics.[59] And, indeed, very soon the construction of secular mosaics was restarted (after a century-long gap in Russian practice), being first applied in Maiakovskaia station of the Moscow metro (1938). In the supporting statement for his design, the chief architect of the station Aleksei Dushkin explained the significance of the medium: "What is a mosaic? Cobalt glass, pieces of which are fixed on a cement base to create a picture, the colors of which do not fade. The mosaic is eternal!"[60] Noting their water-resistance in Roman baths, the artist Aleksandr Deineka (who designed Maiakovskaia station's mosaics) also suggested using them in Soviet swimming pools, in outdoor stadiums, and on public squares.[61] With the newspapers praising the success of the Maiakovskaia mosaics, the medium, "conspicuous for its centuries-long permanence," was planned for the Palace of the Soviets where, as the artist Vladimir Frolov promised in one 1940 article, "the eternal material [would be employed] for highly artistic portraits of [the] epoch's political functionaries and of important historical events."[62]

One sees similar arguments for reviving the use of outdoor and indoor frescoes, also championed for their ability "to fix ... economic and cultural achievements ... for a long time."[63] Historically, artists used frescoes to tell epic stories, and the medium "live[d] for millennia," one reads on the pages of *Arkhitektura SSSR*. "With the passing of years, the fresco only gains in durability and [depth of] color," and, thanks to the thin film of crystals coating the surface, "it may be cleaned, washed, and disinfected."[64] Not coincidentally, designers of the Palace of the Soviets intended to extensively employ frescoes in interior decoration. While mosaics and frescoes were the main mediums dredged up from historical experience and revived by Soviet monument builders, the same logic was also applied to Roman murals, sgraffito, tempera and encaustic painting, and tapestries—all held up for their exceptional, historically proven durability.[65] Thus, sifting through the past to discover durable materials, architectonic forms, and decorative mediums biased Soviet monumental architecture toward historicism in significant ways.

To be sure, most claims of perdurability were vastly exaggerated. Hardiness in practice was diminished further by poor quality construction and the lack of adequate funding and materials. Granite's material properties, after all, would not affect a ferroconcrete structure's longevity, if the former was employed only for facing (which was typically the case). Yet it would be incorrect to treat the above declarations, alongside the overall "façadeness" of Stalinist constructions, as an intentionally contrived strategy for imbuing the regime with an aura of timelessness and permanence. After all, many of these discussions—revealing the genuine striving for durability—took place at closed meetings and conferences, or on the pages of professional journals with a limited public readership. Caught between the competing constraints of rapid construction, limited resources, and the demand to immortalize the era by building durable monuments, professionals were inevitably forced to cut corners and otherwise dissimulate. But, as in exaggerations of industrial output (*tufta*), the target of these deceptions was as likely the Stalinist leadership as the Soviet public. Genuine permanence was an official requirement for prospective monuments. Even the most outrageous claims to durability are, at a minimum, indicative of this demand, which architects strove to fulfill within their limited circumstances. Merely substituting simulacra of permanence was never enough, from the perspective of a regime intent on self-commemoration.

The prospective orientation of Stalinist monuments and their relationship to historicism can be brought together in the example of the Main Building of Moscow State University. Unveiled in September 1953, mere months after Stalin's death, the design was in many ways the epitome of postwar eclecticism and a go-to example of what was later pejoratively labelled "wedding-cake architecture" (*konditerskii stil'*). The largest of the (completed) Moscow high-rises, the tallest building in Europe until 1990, this was the key monument of late Stalinism. It eclipsed even the Palace of the Soviets project, then undergoing redesign, but whose construction directorate the regime had reassigned to building the university complex. Architects hailed the university building as "a new monument to our socialist epoch, the epoch of the genius architect of communism—the great Stalin," a building "fated to stand for centuries, [conveying] to the future the heroic labor of our days, the unparalleled glory of the era of the construction of communism."[66]

In fashioning this monument, designers claimed to have relied particularly upon those traditions of "Russian national art that had achieved fame throughout the centuries."[67] This resulted in a vertical, tiered composition, a façade patterned with red brick and decorated with stylized ceramic tiles (*izrastsy*), and vernacular ornamental motifs. At the same time, the complex also appealed to classical architectonic and decorative forms, particularly to those of an unequivocally memorial character (for instance, rostral columns fronting the porticoed grand entrance, and numerous rooftop obelisks). These historicist elements were expected to remain understandable and appealing to future generations.

Further, the goal of perdurability was vividly expressed in the building's constructive properties. One example was the use of a new type of ceramic facing,

FIGURE 6. Exterior view of the Main Building of Moscow State University, under construction. Photograph from Viacheslav Oltarzhevskii, *Stroitelstvo vysotnykh zdanii v Moskve*. Moscow: Gosudarstvennoe izdatel'stvo literatury po stroitel'stvu i arkhitekture, 1953.

dubbed "diapsidite," which the head of construction and the lead engineer described in the following way: "In the search for the 'eternal' construction material, we had an idea: to try to find it not in the earth's bowels ... but in a laboratory crucible. [The new material] was hit with a hammer, immersed in various solutions, subjected to heat and cold, and we concluded that nothing better could be found, that nature had been eclipsed! There is no known material which could compare in durability with the new artificial stone ... Even granite is destroyed by time, but time is powerless before [diapsidite]." While the two engineers presented diapsidite as an innovation in perdurable construction, it too hinged on retrospective evaluations of historical experience. Specifically, diapsidite was touted as a response to "the stern ... warnings of architectural history: once-elegant Venetian palaces and London churches [made of marble and granite] had become grey, washed-out buildings."[68]

Given the university's function "as a beautiful monument ... sculpture and art supplement[ed] that which architecture [could] not express on its own," explained the director of sculptural works Nikolai Tomskii.[69] Accordingly, the university complex was richly adorned with durable, synthetic monumental art. The building's four crowning colossal statues were encased in a ceramic cladding; chief architect Lev Rudnev claimed this would ensure that they stood "for centuries."[70] Yet more commonly, monument builders gravitated towards time-tested materials and mediums. Throughout the complex, scores of scientists were memorialized in bronze statues and medallions, marble busts, granite herms, and Florentine mosaic, which the chief engineers specifically praised for its historically documented resistance to fading and warping, "remaining unchanged in its original appearance for decades."[71] Altogether, these factors—stemming from the university's function as a prospective monument—pushed its composition in a decidedly historicist direction.

Thus, Stalinist monumental architecture embraced a timeless style not to present itself as an already-achieved, perfect utopia, but as an enduring artistic language for communicating with an imagined posterity. Similarly, architects did not focus on fashioning archaic looking simulacra of eternity, but genuinely strove to build durably, turning to time-tested materials, architectonic forms, and decorative mediums, further biasing their creations toward historicism. These considerations stemmed from the internal logic of building prospective monuments; historicism was championed by architects confronted by the regime's genuine goals of self-commemoration. After all, "in most situations . . . regime leaders were too busy to be able to give detailed instructions; architects, planners, and local officials, for example, had almost no such guidance," as Andrew Day points out.[72] Evidently, the regime accepted their arguments in favor of historicism. While the traditionalist revival was doubtless overdetermined, the above dynamic nuances the neo-totalitarian model in which political leaders independently selected historicism solely for its propagandistic qualities.

The regime's endorsement of historicist architecture as an effective vehicle for self-commemoration signals, paradoxically, historicism's capacity to express a future-oriented cultural impulse. Intriguingly, it appears that a similar logic may have been at play in the design of monumental architecture beyond Soviet borders, which was also typically executed in a quasi-historicist, stripped classical style, in both authoritarian and democratic contexts. Interwar stripped classicism revived the classical order and architectonics, a monumental scale, and traditional materials.[73] Evidence that these qualities were connected to the exigencies of self-commemoration is gradually emerging. William Rhoads recounts that in America, for instance, "the future was important to [President Franklin] Roosevelt; [he] was concerned that new buildings which he sponsored be durable—not only in materials and construction but also in taste." Wishing "to avoid anything which . . . was a passing fashion," Roosevelt promoted stripped classicism as the official style for public buildings in Washington, DC and others constructed under the New Deal's Public Works Administration.[74] Evoking a similar logic, architects of the Palais de Chaillot (the centerpiece of the 1937 Paris World Expo) justified their choice of stripped classicism as "well and truly belong[ing] to the French monumental tradition" and hence ideally suited for a monument "bequeath[ed] to future generations."[75] One can even see similar reasoning in the common predilection for time-tested materials. For instance, in designing the Senate House of the University of London (1937) with a view to its lasting 500 years, its architect Charles Holden specifically employed stone loadbearing walls instead of ferroconcrete.[76] Likewise, Adolf Hitler called for executing Nazi edifices in granite, whose qualities were proven by "vestiges of the German past [. . . remaining] scarcely time-worn." Granite, he proclaimed, would "ensure that [Nazi] monuments last forever. In ten thousand years they'll be still standing."[77] These demands were taken seriously: Germany's quarries were exploited at full capacity, and entire shipyards were founded to build an enormous fleet for carrying additional granite from Belgium, Italy, the Netherlands, and Scandinavia.[78]

Given the similarity of the self-commemorative goals to which these monument-building projects responded, their stylistic convergence is perhaps not coincidental. Indeed, interwar architects may have discovered the perceived advantages of historicism through transnational dialogue. Thus, for instance, Nazi architects in many ways looked to developments in Italy, not least for it being, in Hitler's words, "where Fascism immortalizes forces in monumental works."[79] Fascist Italy had indeed pioneered the stripped classical style that soon gained global dominance. For its part, in the aftermath of the Non-Aggression Treaty, the Soviet side requested a demonstration of German architectural models, which were exhibited in the Kremlin in late 1939. The monumental designs of Albert Speer, Hitler's court architect, evidently found favor with Stalin.[80] Like their German counterparts, Soviet architects also paid attention to developments in Italy, including, for example, the design and construction of the central headquarters of the Fascist party (the Palazzo Littorio), whose competition guidelines explicitly required that "the grand edifice should be worthy of handing down to future generations."[81] In 1935, after a decade of isolation, the Soviet Union even sent a delegation to the International Congress of Architects in Rome, at the invitation of the National Fascist Union of Architects.[82] Even more so than with fascist powers, Soviet architects remained in dialogue with their liberal democratic counterparts throughout the 1930s. Andrei Burov, Boris Iofan, Dmitrii Chechulin, Viacheslav Oltarzhevskii, Vladimir Gel'freikh, Vladimir Shchuko, and other Soviet architects traveled through Western Europe and the United States extensively in this period, with a view to gaining technical expertise and artistic ideas.[83] As Irina Azizian concludes, "the process by which solemn monumental forms came to dominate . . . was paralleled by a similar concomitant process in Western architecture. [Soviet] culture was not yet hermetically sealed."[84] Therefore, the logic by which prospective monuments gravitated toward historicism was not specific to the Stalinist context, but was paralleled by and entangled with wider interwar practices. Tasked with immortalizing the era for the benefit of future generations, monument builders sought an enduring architecture; many found it by looking to the past.

CHAPTER 3

Synthetic Composition
Anticipating Posterity's Gaze

At a public exhibition showcasing competing designs of the Palace of the Soviets, held in 1932–1933, one visitor book entry read:

> Unfortunately, ... most of [the sketches] are composed in the old-fashioned way, only touched-up with a few contemporary features, such projects cannot perpetuate the memory of the start of the construction of socialist society ... and therefore I do not think that the Palace of the Soviets should be the way many authors think it should. Its task is to tell posterity without words, without a book, about the struggle of two worlds, about those heroes on whom fell such a glorious responsibility of steadfastly guarding the achievements of the October [Revolution], so that in the future every person, young and old, could immediately understand in honor of what it was built and who built it, and in what heated struggle it was constructed.[1]

After Boris Iofan's quasi-historicist design was pronounced the winner, another visitor-book entry denounced it as "greatly reminiscent of the Tower of Babel, one in which, as a historic monument to socialism, there is nothing new."[2]

As such comments poignantly demonstrated, the heavy reliance on traditional, (supposedly) timeless aesthetics presented their own set of problems. After all, the project of self-commemoration did not simply seek to leave objects of enduring aesthetic value, but demanded creations that would distinguish Stalinist monuments as specifically Stalinist, immortalizing the events and individuals of the era. Historically stylized monuments, despite being executed in an enduring artistic language, risked blending in with the heritage that they were modeled on (heritage which was itself being restored and reconstructed, especially in the postwar period). Further, effective self-commemoration demanded that these monuments remain relevant and interesting to posterity; historicism, however, risked appearing boring, stuffy, and antiquated. Architectural monuments were thereby subject to competing and contradictory demands: they were to be at once timeless and contemporary. Official critics branded designs that merely imitated traditional archetypes as restorationist, academic, archaic, anachronistic, retrospectivist, and epigonic. Ultimately, commissioning bodies could demand modifications and even refuse to move forward with the project. Anticipating posterity's gaze was thereby fraught with difficulties.

Stalinist art professionals soon realized that solutions to this conundrum could be found only outside the compositional devices available to architecture. Instead, and similar to other interwar monument builders, they proposed "synthesis," an approach that integrated sculpture and decorative art on an equal footing with architecture. By means of figurative representations and epigraphy, synthetic monuments could express the specificity of the Stalinist era on the canvas of a powerful, timeless, but ultimately indistinctive historicist architecture. Further, sculpture and monumental art could render subjects in an emotionally charged, romantic way that would ensure the relevance and attractiveness of Stalinist monuments to future generations. Nevertheless, solutions to the two problems—distinctiveness and enduring relevance—sat in tension with one another. The ways in which Soviet art professionals and political leaders navigated these tensions substantiated key features of Stalinist monument design.

Indeed, the comments expressed by humble Soviet citizens in relation to the Palace of Soviets articulated a problem that architects themselves perceived all too clearly, from the moment historicism came to dominate architectural practice. How would posterity distinguish Stalinist monuments from the heritage of the past? Viktor Vesnin, former avant-gardist and soon-to-be chairman of the Union of Soviet Architects, warned that "the Palace of the Soviets should be a monument to our great epoch. The language of classical forms, however one deploys it, is the language of the past, it must not be used to express the present."[3] This line of criticism hardly abated with time. During the Great Patriotic War, monument designs were censured on the pages of *Arkhitektura SSSR* for failing to memorialize "contemporary heroism," as they could have "appl[ied] to any heroic event of the past, to any historical situation." Designs of memorial pantheons, for instance, were criticized for employing a rotundal composition and vast collonades (being modeled, as they were, on the Roman Pantheon and its Parisian neoclassical imitation).[4] At the 1946 conference on monumentalism hosted by Union of Soviet Architects, the art historian Mikhail Il'in pointed out that classical obelisks "can relate to any historical event," and that "something must be done to make columns our own, Soviet, contemporary" (a similar criticism was leveled at proposed triumphal arches, deemed inadequate for commemorating victory in the Great Patriotic War).[5] Such accusations were not inaccurate: the earliest designs of Soviet war memorials largely mimicked traditional forms, whether in their classical (obelisks, stellae, columns, and triumphal arches) or vernacular variants (burial mounds, elements of medieval military and church architecture).[6] At another conference late that year, the Presidium of the Union of Soviet Architects condemned "the grandeur of a false pathos [*velichie lozhnogo pafosa*] . . . the mechanical transposition of Roman arches, Egyptian obelisks and pyramids, Gothic spires into our reality."[7]

Ironically, this meant that a timeless, enduring aesthetic, while necessary for communicating with posterity, could also be attacked for its very universality and indistinctiveness. Indeed, the cityscape compositions of several postwar urban reconstruction projects were criticized specifically for their aura of timelessness.[8] Similarly, chief architect Lev Rudnev's idea of having sculptures adorning Moscow State University (themed on the "Eternal Youth of Science") appear ageless ("as though they were made a thousand years ago and as though they could stand for another thirty thousand years") was attacked for being "absolutely abstracted" from the present historical situation.[9] The near-impossible demand of being at once universal and expressive of contemporary content was perfectly encapsulated in Moscow's chief architect Dmitrii Chechulin's criticism of one residential building design: "it would be advisable that this building be sufficiently contemporary, and that it never go out of fashion."[10]

The problem of distinguishing Stalinist monuments was particularly acute after the Great Patriotic War, when stylized constructions risked blending in with older heritage, which was itself undergoing extensive restoration and reconstruction. This was not the case initially: the early 1930s saw a wave of demolition precipitated by the expansive demands of Stalinist urban renewal programs. Architect and author of the 1935 Plan for the Socialist Reconstruction of Moscow Sergei Chernyshev articulated this approach well: "Preserving all of the most valuable in historical-revolutionary and artistic respects, we do not stop before the demolition of this or that structure, when it becomes a hindrance to the living development of the city."[11] It was only toward the end of the decade that the regime's increasing support for new national imaginaries (discussed in the next chapter) translated into sporadic attempts at preserving the architectural heritage of the past. Although a few buildings were saved from demolition by relocating them, a systematic policy was neither developed nor enforced. This changed in the postwar period, when the regime made heritage preservation a cornerstone of its reconstruction efforts.[12] This revaluation culminated in policies like the September 16, 1949 Resolution No. 48/16 of the Executive Committee of the Moscow Soviet, which underscored that protected heritage had inviolable land rights, that neighboring constructions were subject to height restrictions, and that "all city planning organizations should factor in the necessity of preserving heritage when designing [new] construction projects."[13]

In fact, without mentioning it by name, the above resolution evoked the doctrine of "ensemble" construction, according to which new, Stalinist edifices were expected to stylistically harmonize with the preexisting urban fabric. Such ensembles were to imbue a given locale with a unified character (*obraz*), overcoming the alleged cacophony of individual constructions, old and new.[14] Mobilizing these toward a single purpose was thought to "ultimately increase the architectural means of influencing [the public], which would be greater than that of a single architectural monument."[15] Ensemble construction was first placed on the agenda by the 1935 Plan for the Socialist Reconstruction of Moscow, although, as demonstrated in Chernyshev's remarks, it remained secondary to the transformative objectives of urban renewal. The idea of a city-wide ensemble with no building left behind was articulated only in the postwar period, when the new emphasis on heritage preservation met the pressing need to rebuild devastated cities from the ground up. Ensembles in the new Stalinist city would demonstrate unbroken (national) architectural traditions and their glorious culmination in Stalinist architecture. This policy can be viewed in the context of what anthropologist Sergei Oushakine conceptualizes as "chronographical suturing": "by bringing the two separate time frames together, this chronographic suturing, this temporal montage of two autonomous time frames (past and present), simultaneously leaves out all traces of historical, political, or . . . ideological incommensurability of the two periods. The formal semblance . . . is presented as an indication of a more profound—substantive—similarity."[16] Effectively, new Stalinist edifices were expected to mimic their surroundings. As the eminent architect Aleksei Shchusev explained, "when designing new buildings that make up common ensembles with ancient monuments, it is necessary to give the modern buildings features that are related to the architecture of valuable historical buildings."[17]

The distinctiveness of new Stalinist monuments was inhibited still further by the complementary ensemble practice of reconstructing heritage buildings to harmonize with newer constructions. For example, in the postwar period, the height of the Moscow Soviet offices (previously the eighteenth-century residence of the governor general) was raised by two levels to correspond with the new scale of Gor'kii Street. The building was also outfitted with an extensive pilaster colonnade, bas-reliefs, a triumphal arch entryway, and wrought iron, bronze-gilded gates. Ensemble construction therefore sought to bring all individual compositions to a common denominator, to the point that art historian Iulii Savitskii warned that "a person without experience in architecture would be unable to notice the difference between old and new buildings."[18] If even contemporaries could hardly distinguish Stalinist additions to the cityscape, the problem would be further magnified for posterity. The doctrine of ensemble (re)construction thereby constituted a serious impediment to Stalinist architecture's task of immortalizing its era.

Superior dimensions could, in theory, distinguish stylized Stalinist monuments within any given ensemble. The architects of Moscow's postwar high-rises, for instance, attributed precisely such properties to their creations.[19] The two hotels, three elite residential complexes, the headquarters of the Ministry of Foreign Affairs, and the Moscow State University Main Building were built by various ministries and were designed by different teams, but their close curation by central authorities resulted in a highly coordinated product. Six high-rises ringed Moscow's city center, the university overlooked the entire capital from the Lenin Hills, while the tallest, 275-meter Zariad'e administrative building rose steadily on the Kremlin's doorstep. Any one of these easily dwarfed the eighty-one-meter Ivan the Great bell tower in the Kremlin, the city's next-highest building. Together with the completed Palace of the Soviets, the high-rises' massive dimensions and central positioning were expected to eventually "subdue and unify the city" and "radically change its overall character."[20]

Yet if similarly styled, but undeniably larger monuments could evoke the visual superiority of Stalinist monuments in the present moment, the long-term outlook that anticipated posterity's gaze remained pessimistic. In the future, construction dimensions were expected to increase still further, eventually surpassing the size of Stalinist edifices. In 1939, for example, the sculptor Vera Mukhina's proposal to fashion one of Moscow's new bridges as a monument to the October Revolution, through its embellishment with several sculptures on this theme, was met with opposition. Architect Pavel Aleshin explained that a monument that was designed for the centuries and would commemorate an event of such world-historical importance, called for truly massive dimensions, which the bridge restricted. "In many years, [this bridge] may look like a toy."[21] Likewise, Politburo member and deputy chairman of the Council of People's Commissars Vlas Chubar' criticized the insufficient dimensions of the (rather sizeable) Lenin Library. According to him, it did not account for the "grandiose opportunities of tomorrow": the buildings and boulevards that were going to be built next to it would eventually render the library a low-rise building.²² All things considered, purely architectural means of distinguishing Stalinist monuments in the eyes of posterity were highly limited.

Recognizing this problem, monument builders turned instead to the opportunities offered by synthesis, the practice of uniting architects, artists, and sculptors in concept development and design. Specifically, the figurative capacities of sculpture and other monumental art promised to make architecture more "understandable to the wider masses" and to allow it to develop a "full and multifaceted" theme.²³ To apply Vladimir Paperny's later characterization, synthesis followed the logic of "illustration, that is, the layering of different translations from the same verbal original one on top of the other[, which] resulted in a surplus of information, ensuring the correct reading of the genuine text."²⁴ While synthesis was a general feature of Stalinist artistic practice, it provided unique advantages for crafting distinctive and eye-catching prospective monuments. As art historian Il'ia Sosfenov explained, even though architectural constructions "become the main witness to one's epoch in subsequent centuries . . . the content of an architectural representation is highly circumscribed." Architects, he went on, "turn to art and sculpture [for] at the heart of synthesis . . . is the desire for development and specification of the ideal and representational content of architecture."²⁵ Similarly, as his colleague David Arkin stated, "the synthetic unification of art is necessary for the most complete, comprehensive coverage and realistic representation of an artistic idea, *with a large field of action [throughout] time*."²⁶

Although there were precursors to synthesis in the artistic practice of the 1920s, it began to be conceptualized explicitly with the unfolding Palace of the Soviets design competition.²⁷ As mentioned, the palace was to overflow with murals, mosaics, sculptures, and other decorations, and these were employed specifically as solutions to the problem of indistinctiveness, without which the building would remain only a "symphony of mute stone."²⁸ As the chief architect himself attested, the "subjects of sculptural groups and bas-reliefs [would] reveal the Palace of the Soviets to be a monument to the Great October Socialist Revolution, a monument of the Stalin era."²⁹ Art historian Boris Ternovets, referring to the several kilometers (sic) of planned sculptural friezes around the base of the Palace of the Soviets, waxed lyrical: "in this monumental chronicle [the sculptor] can tell of the epic events of the Lenin-Stalin epoch." He envisioned a narrative recounting of key historical events, which would be "full of internal meaning, unpacking the deep ideational content of the monument [and] the worldview of its epoch."³⁰ Altogether, in the words of the artist Evgenii Lansere, "the greatest synthesis of architecture, technology and fine arts" would be harnessed to "tell future generations about [this] great time, about the building of communism, about the indestructible power of the teachings of Lenin and Stalin."[31]

But the palace was only the showpiece of a general approach henceforth mandatory for all new monuments. In 1936, Aleksei Angarov, acting head of the party's department for cultural and enlightenment work, proclaimed that architects ought to draw upon synthesis in order to impart "a *specific* semantic content [*opredelennoe ideinoe soderzhanie*]," which was especially important given that "the work of an architect is slated for the centuries." "Our epoch will be judged by several attributes, of which architectural monuments will be one of the most important. That is why the epoch places great demands on [architects], of which the questions of synthesis take up one of the most important places."[32]

While sculpture typically "synthesized" with architecture by being directly integrated into the latter, monument builders also suggested that stand-alone sculpture could infuse the surrounding architectural ensemble with memorial content. Beginning in the 1930s, this became an increasingly important compositional device accompanying the reconstruction of major public squares and thoroughfares.[33] As one editorial of the Ministry of Culture's flagship journal *Iskusstvo* put it, "the monument should be the compositional center of the given square, the given street, organizing the surrounding space, dominating it, constituting the core content of the whole complex."[34] Placed at key nodes of the city, "triumphal columns and obelisks, which always have a memorial significance, become visual accents in parks and city ensembles," elaborated Mukhina. "A correctly placed obelisk nearly always defines the square or intersection."[35]

Nevertheless, the semantic capacity of even the most self-consciously mimetic monumental representations was itself circumscribed. After all, sculpture, frescoes, and mosaics could never match the level of detail afforded even by easel painting (to say nothing of the written word). Furthermore, these were traditional mediums and their execution also tended toward historical stylization (Stalinist sculpture, for instance, followed classical archetypes). Working within these limitations, one way in which synthetic monuments immortalized Stalinism as a distinct era was through the liberal use of contemporary props (*attributy*). These included representations of clothing, power tools, vehicles, weaponry, and other objects particular to the time, which were expected to distinguish Stalinist monuments as specifically Stalinist. As sculptor Evgenii Vuchetich and the architect Iakov Belopol'skii argued, props would "help transmit the spirit of the epoch."[36]

The Committee for Arts Affairs, which commissioned most sculptural works in this period, frequently recommended integrating such props into monument designs. For example, in 1939 its council of experts (*khudozhestvenno-ekspertnyi sovet*) reviewed the design of a memorial plaque dedicated to the much-celebrated test pilot Valerii Chkalov. One council member, the sculptor Dmitrii Tsaplin, suggested shaping the plaque in the form of an airplane. "Even if time erases [the inscription], they will still see the silhouette and will learn who Chkalov was."[37] Nearly a decade later, in turn, the council discussing the pedestal for his sculptural monument similarly agreed that Chkalov's achievements must be somehow evoked visually on it, either by means of a map charting his record-breaking overflights, or a mosaic illustrating his feats.[38] Similarly, the council of experts considering the graveside monument for the sculptor Nikolai Andreev recommended props at several stages of the review; these would "make it evident that this is a sculptor [being commemorated, and would] express the epoch, express Andreev," as well as "underscore the role, meaning, and tenor [of the monument]."[39]

Beginning in the wartime period, contemporary objects themselves (rather than their representations) sometimes became part of monumental compositions. A Committee for Arts Affairs memo from early 1944 recommended the construction of monuments into which "authentic contemporary weaponry, made from eternal materials, would be inserted."[40] Accordingly, in the next two years, decommissioned Soviet tanks were installed as part of the Monument to the Liberation of Simferopol (1944) and the Monument to Soviet Tank Crews in Prague (1945). Pairs of T-34 tanks and ML-20 artillery pieces flanked the Soviet War Memorial in Berlin's Tiergarten Park (1945). Indeed, the practice of integrating contemporary weaponry into monumental complexes continued throughout the remainder of the Soviet period.

In monumental sculpture, the utility of contemporary clothing as a marker of the Stalin era precluded nudity. To be sure, Stalinist anxieties surrounding the nude body were not reducible to the objective of immortalizing the era, stemming as they did from an atmosphere of prudery and anti-eroticism that dominated after the 1934 ban on pornography. Yet nudity in sculpture was never a closed question; at a minimum, the naked body could demonstrate the advantages of hygiene and Soviet sport.[41] As Mikhail Zolotonosov's study of Moscow's Gor'kii Park statuary contended, Stalinist representations of the nude body were intended to generate "sexual affect and energy [. . . channeling these] into childbirth [and] labor."[42] However, in discussions of its appropriateness, artists warned that nudity was disadvantageous to the demands of fashioning distinctive-looking prospective monuments. Clothes and drapery "express the style of the [given] epoch," argued the sculptor Sergei Merkurov.[43] His colleague Matvei Manizer similarly rejected "timeless clothing," and eventually, in a bout of self-criticism, denounced his older nude sculptures as lacking "historical concreteness."[44] Mukhina, for her part, reminisced that when the state commission approved her soon-to-be-famous Worker and Kolkhoz Woman sculpture for the Soviet pavilion at the 1937 Paris World Fair (later rebuilt as a permanent monument in Moscow) it required her to "clothe" her originally nude statues. "That will make it clear that he is a worker," the commission's representative allegedly explained.[45] The same situation arose again in 1951, when a Committee for Arts Affairs council of experts ruled that Mukhina's brigade should "work on the clothing of the figures [of the monument Young Transformers of Nature, designed for Moscow State University] [as] it is necessary to find costumes characteristic of our epoch."[46]

Along with figurative representations of contemporary subjects, epigraphy represented another avenue for lending an enduring, distinctive character to synthetic monuments. From the very beginning, the 1935 All-Union Creative Conference of Architects had proclaimed a "battle for the embodiment in architectural language of the great slogans of our epoch."[47] As a key technique of "architecture parlante," epigraphy spearheaded the broader push for linguistic analogies in Stalinist architecture. Inscriptions on monuments supplemented the construction of commemorative plaques, which also saw a steady upsurge throughout the period.[48] From the perspective of the problem of indistinctiveness, epigraphy allowed for specifying otherwise nondescript monuments and imparting particular content about the individuals and events that they memorialized. As a 1950 dissertation on monuments to the Great Patriotic War (the first systematic study of these) explained: "It is evident that epitaphs and memorial inscriptions on monuments to the Patriotic War play a large and important role in . . . reporting specific information about historical events to which this or that monument is dedicated. It is difficult to overestimate the . . . purely historical importance of these epitaphs and inscriptions that immortalize on stone tablets the details of events and individuals' statements." The author went on to criticize the standard design of monuments to two-time recipients of the "Hero of the Soviet Union" award, which featured a plaque bearing the state decree bestowing the order, for not "providing even the shortest description of the heroic feats," which could have increased their "historical value" to posterity.[49] Altogether, this logic suggested that if monuments themselves were insufficiently clear or specific, words "inscribed on stone . . . would tell posterity of the heroic struggle of the peoples of the USSR."[50]

Accordingly, Stalinist monuments were suffused with words. The Palace of the Soviets was to reproduce passages from the constitution and quotations from Stalin's speeches; both eventually made it into the design of the Moscow State University Main Building.[51] The Triumph of Victory bridge-side monument (1943) was a veritable billboard, displaying four lengthy slogans proclaimed by the Central Committee on the twenty-fifth anniversary of the

October Revolution and on the twenty-fifth and twenty-sixth anniversaries of the Red Army. Epigraphy was perhaps most extensively employed in the composition of the Volga-Don Canal. The regime explicitly conceptualized this massive infrastructure project, which connected the Caspian, Azov, and Black Seas, as a monument to the civil and Great Patriotic wars, journey through which "was intended as a memorial procession," in Alexei Tarkhanov and Sergei Kavtaradze's later characterization.[52] Nearly every canal lock, sculptural monument, triumphal arch, bust, and obelisk had a supporting inscription, whose text was approved at the highest level by a decree of the Council of Ministers.

Some inscriptions were clearly intended to evoke a strong emotional response. For example, the triumphal arch of Canal Lock One was inscribed with a passage from a late-1942 letter to Stalin from the soldiers, commanders, and political workers of the Stalingrad front: "Before our fathers, the greying heroes of the defense of Tsaritsyn, before the regiments of our comrades stationed at other fronts, before the entire Soviet land we swear not to besmirch the glory of Russian arms, that we will fight to the last. Under your leadership our fathers were victorious in the battle of Tsaristyn, under your leadership we shall be victorious in the great battle of Stalingrad today."[53] Other inscriptions memorialized events through chronicle-like narration, such as the one at the base of the Monument to the Unification of the Fronts, located near Canal Lock Thirteen: "By order of the Supreme Commander comrade I. V. Stalin, on November 19, 1942, Soviet forces in the Stalingrad vicinity moved to counterattack. The strategic plan, developed and carried out under the leadership of comrade Stalin, resulted in a brilliant victory of the Soviet Army. On November 23, 1942, the mobile strike units of the South-Western and Stalingrad fronts met in the outskirts of the city of Kalach, which concluded the encirclement and subsequent destruction of the 330,000 strong German-fascist force."[54]

More radical proposals for infusing Stalinist monuments with epigraphy abounded. Shortly after the War, the art historian Aleksandr Gabrichevskii suggested that Soviet architecture be inscribed with poetry, while his colleague Lev Kulaga called for "transposing" the wartime directives of the People's Commissariat of Defense into architecture and sculpture.[55] Mukhina, noting the wide-standing use of commemorative inscriptions on the cartouches, walls, and columns of historic monuments, proposed etching the names of construction workers onto Soviet canal locks and hydro-electric dams.[56] Artists and members of the public suggested mounting memorial plaques in Moscow's metro stations featuring the names of their engineers, architects, artists, and even construction workers, so that they might "enter history."[57] In late 1947, the Committee for Architectural Affairs even proposed affixing memorial plaques to all major buildings constructed in the Soviet period.[58]

Thus, synthesis became the chief means by which stylized, historicist architecture was to achieve a distinct monumental form and to immortalize the specific events and individuals of the Stalin era. Synthesis became official doctrine with the launch of the Socialist Reconstruction of Moscow in 1935; as mentioned, that very year saw the opening of the Studio for Monumental Art, under the auspices of the Architecture Institute. Even so, according to art historian Tat'iana Astrakhantseva, architects, artists, and sculptors began working on a truly equal footing only in the postwar era.[59] Nikita Voronov goes so far as to argue that by the early 1950s, the previous preponderance of architecture was fully reversed, with sculpture now "dominant, while the [architectural] construction itself became something of a secondary detail of the gigantic monument."[60] Nonetheless, if synthesis became especially pronounced in late Stalinist practice, monument builders employed it in at least a nascent form from the 1930s onward.

The progressively expanding role of synthesis is illustrated vividly in the evolution of the Moscow metro. The application of synthesis was somewhat limited in the stations and corresponding surface vestibules of the first phase of construction (the thirteen stations that opened in 1935). Komsomol'skaia station was exceptional for its use of fresco, sgraffito, and majolica depicting socialist construction projects. Sokol'niki station also made use of majolica; it also deployed decorative bas-reliefs featuring the metro's construction workers (*metrostroevtsy*), and, along with Okhotnyi riad station, sculptures of Soviet athletes. Yet nine of the thirteen stations had no figurative art or sculpture to speak of. By contrast, stations of the second phase of construction (opened in 1937–1938) saw important experiments with synthesis. Ploshchad' Revoliutsii station, for example, demonstrated the extensive commemorative opportunities offered by sculpture in narrating the first two decades of Soviet history. Eighty life-size bronzes were generously outfitted with props to reveal their corresponding ideal types: paramilitary Voroshilov sharpshooters, NKVD border guards, and various other Soviet professionals and social groups. The statues were sequentially arranged along the station's main concourse to tell the story of revolutionary upheaval, socialist construction, and the ultimate arrival in the Stalinist promised land of self-actualized labor and recreation.[61] For its part, the resplendent Maiakovskaia station's mosaics, constructed in the cupolas above the main concourse, depicted "One Day in the Life of the Soviet land." Many of the thirty-five mosaics included recognizable representations of the most up-to-date Soviet technology, including the TB-3 heavy bomber, ANT-25 monoplane, U-2 biplane,

FIGURE 7. Ploshchad' Revoliutsii metro station concourse. Photograph from Samuil Kravets, Veniamin Makovskii, and Mikhail Zelenin, eds., *Arkhitektura Moskovskogo metropolitena*. Moscow: Gosudarstvennoe Arkhitektunoe Izdatel'stvo Akademii Arkhitektury SSSR, 1941.

I-15 fighter biplane, the Tupolev airship, the record-setting Soviet stratospheric balloon (*stratostat*), and other contemporary machinery.[62]

Despite wartime pressures, stations constructed in the third phase (and unveiled in 1943–1944) developed synthesis even further. All stations were outfitted with sculpture, bas-reliefs, or mosaics commemorating the Great Patriotic War, a theme developed through copious representations of military heroes, rearguard industry, and contemporary weaponry. Importantly, these stations saw the first use of epigraphy, which was clearly intended for commemorative purposes. For example, all surface vestibules were inscribed with the words "Constructed in the Days of the Great Patriotic War." Quotes of Stalin's speeches and the constitution of 1936 made it to all but three stations. Every station had some representation of the Supreme Commander; most had several.

Stations of the fourth phase of construction, opened between 1950 and 1954, overflowed with sculptures, bas-reliefs, mosaics, and frescos on a scale soon to be branded excessive. Monument builders experimented with bronze medallions (Paveletskaia), high-relief multifigured compositions (Taganskaia), and stained-glass windows (Novoslobodskaia), all of which depicted party leaders or recognizably Soviet individuals engaged in labor, recreation, and military service. The use of epigraphy expanded similarly. Several stations (including some that had been unveiled a decade earlier) were now inscribed with quotations from Stalin's speeches, the new national anthem (adopted in 1944), and the constitution. Metro stations' decorative art was also helpfully labeled. A 1953 discussion of the frescoes of Kievskaia-kol'tsevaia station resolved that "there must be a text inscribed on marble . . . to make the painting understandable. As [Il'ia Repin's] 'Zaporozhtsy' is understandable with its inscription; even Michelangelo's monumental paintings have all the prophets labeled, to avoid any misidentifications."[63] Accordingly, inscriptions pedantically explained Kievskaia's commemorative artwork: "M. I. Kalinin and S. K. Ordzhonikidze at the Opening of the Dnepr Hydro-Electric Station, 1932," "The Liberation of Kiev by the Soviet Army, 1943," "Victory Day Fireworks Display, May 9, 1945." These compositional techniques—highly mimetic monumental art supported by epigraphy—were to become models for metro systems under construction or undergoing creative development elsewhere (respectively, in Leningrad and Kiev).[64]

Analyzing the development of metro stations' design, contemporary critics asserted that synthesis was largely what *made* the Moscow metro into a monument to the Stalin era. As art historian Iakov Kornfel'd argued in 1952: "confident and clear architecture, supplemented by eloquent, heroic statuary, bas-reliefs, multicolored mosaics, [made the wartime stations] epically expressive monuments to the epoch."[65] Moscow's first, decoratively bare metro stations were semantically mute, and only the later, synthetic stations "wholly reflected reality [and became] monuments to great historical events," seconded his colleague Margarita Tosunova.[66] Thus, monument builders used synthesis to mark their creations as specifically Stalinist, facilitating the memorialization of particular events and individuals of the era.

Nevertheless, making monuments distinctively Stalinist was only one consideration among others. An equally important demand was that traditional-looking monuments remain relevant and interesting to posterity. Such a concern was voiced, for example, by a representative of the construction directorate of the Palace of the Soviets at a 1938 conference on monumental art. For all the focus on centuries-long durability, he warned that there might be "a certain gap between the longevity of the material and the longevity of its artistic effect on viewers."[67] Once again, the supposedly timeless language of classical and vernacular-derived historicism exacerbated this problem. Historicism risked appearing old and stuffy, being associated with ruins and museums. At the 1946 conference on monumentalism, architect and art historian Mikhail Il'in argued that classical obelisks "leave us completely cold."[68] The following year, at a meeting of the Moscow Municipal Executive Committee's Architectural Council, the Greek-inspired peristyle of Kurskaia metro station's surface vestibule came under criticism for imparting "a museum-like impression."[69]

Just as in their response to the problem of indistinctiveness, monument builders appreciated the rich opportunities offered by synthesis as a solution to the problem of irrelevance. After all, synthesis also promised to magnify monuments' emotional resonance. Art historian Nikolai Chernyshev explained: "if we understand synthesis as a combination of different kinds of art in a single complex, to enhance the ideological and artistic impact on the viewer, the mutual influence of several art forms increases not as a sum of parts but grows in a geometric progression. This is the whole force and justification of synthesis."[70] Similarly, Mukhina extolled the ability of art to "transmit the spirit of our times so vividly."[71]

Even so, synthetic adornments were a double-edged sword: the very subjects that they memorialized, and the artistic means of rendering these, also risked limiting their appeal in the eyes of future generations. For instance, in seeking to overcome the problem of indistinctiveness, synthetic monuments could inadvertently repel future viewers by being semantically overloaded. With this in mind, art professionals frequently clashed on the net benefit of utilizing contemporary props. For example, some questioned the value of representing a modern airplane (in the Chkalov monument) or a stratospheric balloon (in the Monument to Hero-Stratonauts). Eventually, they argued, this technology would become obsolete, and "the future viewer would not be able to understand" these objects.[72] Mukhina, for her part, pointed to the problems of representing contemporary clothing, allowing it an "auxiliary historical role" at most. While acknowledging that it can "acquaint the viewer with the [epoch's] historical costume," she contended that clothing increases the aesthetic value of a sculpture when it is "not only a label of the time, but when it adds to the overall representation and has great value plastically."[73]

Mukhina's argument brought up a wider problem. In order to retain their relevance, the very *subject* of synthetic adornments could not be limited to individuals or events, but had to be elevated to broader themes (such as labor or freedom) to express more effectively the spirit and values of the Stalinist era. Only such "generalized representations," (*sobiratel'nye/ obobshchennye obrazy*) would remain interesting to future generations. Thus, Mukhina argued: "posterity will be uninterested in the petty detailing of faces. For the viewer, what is important is the generalized representation that he loves, which excites, agitates, and exhorts him. Protocol-like rendering is interesting only to contemporaries who are personally acquainted with the subject, or to a scrupulous historian, but this is in any case not the domain of art." Markers of the present moment, such as contemporary clothing and other props, "die with their allotted time," she argued, "but generalized representations—never."[74] After all, "generalized representations are the sum of all that is eternal, of [all] that survives an individual or a given social formation."[75]

Translating Mukhina's ideas into a more specific program, Lansere argued that in order to capture an event for the centuries, the memorialized subject "should be raised above the level of the ordinary, the everyday, it must be moved to some distance, so one can feel its significance."[76] The fact that monuments are made for centuries means that the "idea, theme and subject need to be truly universal," seconded the art historian Osip Beskin.[77] Thus, while the basic premises of synthesis remained unquestioned, many art professionals argued that the true subjects of representation, if they were to remain relevant, ought to be socialist culture and the new Soviet man, rather than the specific heroic achievements and the illustrious individuals of the era.

Nonetheless, while the authorities supported the creation of generalized representations as such, in calling for adjusting the subjects of commemoration, art professionals were clearly overstepping their remit. For instance, in the course of a late-1947 discussion on the statuary slated for the capital's Moskvoretskii bridge, one of the commissioned sculptors Zinaida Ivanova argued against Shchusev's proposal for sculptures commemorating victory in the Great Patriotic War. "Time moves quickly, and contemporary themes become a little outdated in the future," Ivanova argued. Instead of commemorating specific historical events, she suggested the "theme of peaceful labor, which, in its content, is eternal."[78] This was a rare and brave act of dissent, as Shchusev had the support of a commission chaired by Politburo member and unofficial patron of the arts Kliment Voroshilov himself. Unsurprisingly, Ivanova's proposal was unsuccessful. Not only did it threaten, once again, to revert the monument into a timeless indistinctiveness, the subjects of memorialization were set by official commissions chaired or indirectly controlled by political or bureaucratic functionaries, who followed a different logic (which is discussed more fully in the subsequent chapter).[79]

Because the subjects of monuments remained specific events and individuals, generalized representations could only *build* on these in practice. At times, this seemed to be an impossible task. For instance, art historian Nikolai Mashkovtsev proclaimed that monuments to the Great Patriotic War "[demand] an extremely generalized, figuratively expressed large idea. At the same time, the unique individual traits of a specific human character should not be erased or lost. The demands of portrait-like rendering should be firmly applied to such monuments . . . The necessary task of the contemporary sculptor is to render the images of the heroes of the Great Patriotic War on a strict portrait-like basis, glorifying them, and transmitting their features for the centuries. The artist has no right to sacrifice portrait-like resemblance. He cannot defend himself by pointing to the artistic success of the generalized representation."[80] Because of the demand that monuments remain distinctive, artists had to twist themselves into middle-ground positions. Thus, in an early 1945 article, Mukhina stated: "future generations will want to know the character of the heroes of our days. In all my sculptural portraits . . . I aimed to give not only individualized portraits of my distinguished contemporaries, but to create generalized representations of the people of our time."[81]

In fashioning synthetic monuments, according primacy to either individualized or generalized representations constituted respective responses to the problems of indistinctiveness and of irrelevance. In seeking to overcome this antinomy, monument builders proposed a different means of representation: retaining a basic faithfulness to the specific subjects of commemoration, but eschewing one-to-one renderings, pejoratively labeled "photographic" or "naturalistic." As Mukhina explained: "it is important for posterity to see the overall image of our era in portrayals of these times, ones which would agitate, excite them, make them follow our lead. Therefore, in creating the generalized representation, the artist should not slavishly reproduce his individual subject."[82] One technique for achieving this—without sacrificing distinctiveness—involved imbuing monuments with a greater emotional charge. Such romanticism was expected to generate generalized representations with greater appeal to posterity. For instance, in a letter to Army General Filipp Golikov (of whom he crafted a bust in 1944), Vuchetich explained:

> Centuries will pass . . . Numerous architectural constructions, monuments to heroes and events of our epoch will remain; they will 'tell' the descendants about the great deeds of their ancestors . . . And young people will have to read in these images all the passion of our time, great love and hatred, all the glory of the spirit of these people. There will be no question of congruence (which is necessary nowadays), many other questions will not arise, but our ardent epoch should breathe in these portraits, in their facial expressions . . . The more characteristic the representation, the more temperamental and passionate, the closer this representation to the spirit of its time, the longer it will live, and a true work of art lives forever, because even time is powerless against it.[83]

Vuchetich's colleague Merkurov similarly advocated for grandiose, romantic renderings, contending: "we must transmit generalized representations of [our] heroes to the ages. The passion of our epoch should sound through the centuries in granite and bronze. There is no room for chaff and chicks. The range of our creativity must have a huge scope: from the sound of trumpets bringing down the walls of ancient Jericho, to the victorious fanfares of our era."[84] Mukhina similarly emphasized emotion, even bombast: monuments "immortalize the past, but with a passionate appeal for future generations, and therefore these monuments do not lose their impact for centuries."[85]

These comments implicitly justified a certain poetic license: minor adjustments could be made to the realistic renderings of specific memorialized subjects. Mukhina argued that "the artist has the right to imagination, and the strength and persuasiveness of the images created by him depends on the power of his imagination. . . . Idealization is intrinsic to generalized representations in monumental sculpture."[86] Similarly, Rudnev spoke of the prerogative to make adjustments in line with "artistic imagination," and "a poetic realism." He referred to Michelangelo's alleged riposte, when the latter was pressed about why he depicted the hunchbacked [sic] Lorenzo Medici as handsome: "who will know this in 500 years?"[87]

Yet despite increasing the relevance of monuments to posterity, a departure from mimetic, realistic representation was always dangerous. While the authorities might turn a blind eye to "lacquering," or beautification, greater abstraction involved greater risks, and once again reflected the different priorities of art professionals and their political patrons. While, in theory, regime leaders supported the goal of making monuments relevant to posterity, they were concerned that more abstract, romanticized renderings could invite semantic open-endedness— and, inadvertently, ideologically inappropriate interpretations. For instance, in his murals at Moscow's Kazan' railway station, Lansere eschewed contemporary props in favor of enduring allegorical symbols, which he understood as "generalized representations acquired . . . through legacy," "transmitt[ed] from generation to generation."[88] These compositions immortalized the recent victory and postwar peace. The *Peace* mural depicted a peasant woman bearing laurels and a naked babe. Lansere originally envisioned Pallas Athena as the central motif of *Victory*, but bowing to official pressure, substituted a warrior of medieval Rus' (successfully resisting demands to furnish him with an assault rifle).[89] Despite such compromises, Lansere worried that his murals would be attacked for supposedly depicting "the Mother of God with baby Jesus and St. George with a lance"—a potentially devastating criticism in the context of the regime's still-palpable anticlericalism and atheist ideology.[90] Lansere's timeless allegorical compositions were indeed soon questioned on the pages of the main art newspaper *Sovetskoe iskusstvo*, with a later monograph criticizing the murals for a "certain abstractness" that "marks them with a certain archaism and somewhat reduces their artistic merits."[91]

To be sure, such criticism of allegorical and abstracted (even if emotionally potent) designs could be inconsistent and unpredictable. For example,

FIGURE 8. Design of Evgenii Lansere's mural, *Victory*, unveiled at Moscow's Kazan' Railway Station in 1946. Image from Nina Shantyko, ed., *Evgenii Evgen'evich Lansere*. Moscow: Sovetskii khudozhnik, 1952.

Vuchetich's monument of the warrior-liberator at the Soviet war memorial complex in Berlin's Treptower Park (1949) also anachronistically depicted a Soviet soldier wielding a sword. This time, the media universally praised the monument, and it went on to receive a Stalin Prize (first class). On the whole, however, romanticized renderings of immortalized subjects were a risky business. The very topmost political leaders frequently intervened as the watchdogs of realism. In 1949, for instance, the design of Moscow's monument to Maksim Gor'kii (by Ivanova, Mukhina, and Nina Zelenskaia) was explicitly censured by a Council of Ministers decree for "overly emphasized and exaggerated features [that] violate the requirements of realistic truth and resemblance to life;" the sculptors were subsequently ordered to rework it.[92] The authorities were even willing to go to the effort of replacing monuments deemed insufficiently realistic. For instance, in mid-1952, a former acquaintance of the martyred party boss Sergei Kirov complained to the party's Central Committee that his monument in Riga "distorts [Kirov's image] to the point of being unrecognizable . . . viewers [wonder] if it depicts [Latvia's pre-Soviet authoritarian leader Karlis] Ulmanis or a bourgeois kulak-woman [*zhenshchina-kulachka*]." The monument was immediately removed and those responsible investigated.[93] The authorities did not object *as such* to retouching and romanticizing representations of commemorated subjects. Yet they reserved the right to rule on whether any such rendering invited subversive interpretations.

As a result, both commissioning bodies and art professionals tended to err on the side of caution. The Committee for Arts Affairs' council of experts, which had final say on the composition of sculptural monuments, was always preoccupied with the "portrait resemblance" (*portretnoe skhodstvo*) of memorialized subjects.[94] In the case of those recently deceased, the council frequently invited relatives to attest to the representation's likeness. In 1944, the committee's Russian republican branch even excused delays in the construction of monuments to two-time recipients of the "Hero of the Soviet Union" award, because the subjects were still at the frontlines and hence unable to pose (mere photographs being inadequate models).[95] Unsurprisingly, in this context, most artists chose to accommodate such demands, despite other considerations related to the effective design of prospective monuments. "The monumental form is the realist monumental form and there can be no other in our art," unambiguously and dogmatically concluded the sculptor Nikolai Tomskii.[96] Given that a highly mimetic approach was not only politically expedient, but also strengthened the distinctiveness of prospective monuments, it ultimately achieved the upper hand over romantic tendencies (even if the latter could bolster the relevance of these objects in the eyes of posterity).

Recognizing both the political and compositional limitations of romanticized renderings, art professionals also proposed laconicism as an alternative means of heightening the appeal of synthetic monuments to future generations. Rather than idealize and exaggerate representations to imbue them with an emotional charge, monuments could achieve greater expressiveness by saying less. Commenting on his Lenin and Stalin monuments for the Moscow-Volga Canal complex, Merkurov argued: "poor would be the monument if, when one looks at it, the first thing one would notice would be, say, the eyes or the overly precisely captured age of . . . the leader." Rather, "the objective was to . . . convey the main thing—what their representations say to . . . the future," expressing these "in simple, laconic, and sharp forms."[97] After all, the semantic capacity of synthetic monuments was not limitless. At best, they "could commit to eternity a small time-slice, sometimes a single idea, a single moment." In the inevitable selection of what to represent, "everything transient, accidental, modish, and mannerist should be swept away," argued the architect Georgii Gol'ts.[98] Ivanova similarly contended that laconicism was necessary to concentrate all the expressive force on the public significance of the immortalized subject.[99]

The striving toward laconicism expressed an anxiety that anything specific (so important to dealing with the problem of indistinctiveness) would eventually become, by definition, outmoded. In an early 1954 meeting discussing the design of the pantheon, Stalin's final resting place, Rudnev proclaimed: "The pantheon should be modern now, in 100 years, in 200, in 1,000 years, etc. It must be terribly laconic . . . I restrained myself in not allowing a single sculpture . . . Some ascetic technique must be found, which would be acceptable both today and in the future."[100] Occasionally, this logic found favor in ruling circles. Thus, while it eventually repudiated this approach, the construction council initially demanded that the architecture of the Palace of the Soviets be laconic.[101] In the 1945 competitions for victory monuments, guidelines specifically called for "simple and clear architectural forms."[102] One can find other examples of artistic restraint in the corpus of Stalinist monuments. However, if art professionals proposed laconicism as a solution to the problem of irrelevance, then the preoccupation with indistinctiveness ultimately exerted a greater pull. After all, as other art professionals pointed out, "non-specific, conventional images of a person, things, nature . . . do not tell anything to our contemporaries or to our descendants" and abstract representations lower "memorial efficacy."[103]

Thus, given the impossibility of adjusting the subjects of immortalization, artists proposed representing these in romanticized and laconic ways. While they expected such techniques to bolster the enduring relevance of their creations, this approach sat in tension with both the regime's political anxieties and with corresponding solutions to the problem of indistinctiveness. With details sacrificed to aesthetic appeal, posterity could fail to recognize the specific events and individuals of the Stalin era. Conversely, marking out the uniqueness of Stalinist monuments by means of semantic suffusion risked overloading and repelling future viewers. Despite these internal tensions, art professionals and political authorities all agreed on the fundamental limitations of timeless, historicist architecture, which by itself would surely become indistinctive and irrelevant with the passage of time. All parties endorsed the need to integrate figurative art, sculpture, and ornamentation into synthetic monuments.

Appreciating these considerations, connected as they were to the artistic problems of self-commemoration, deepens our understanding of the composition of Stalinist monuments, and provides further evidence of the genuinely prospective mission vested in them by the regime. At its behest, Stalinist monument builders gave considerable thought to the aesthetic preferences of future viewers, and fashioned their creations accordingly. The need to distinguish Stalinist monuments and highlight their historical specificity further undercuts claims that these monuments were meant to imbue the Stalinist political order with an aura of timelessness. Even though timeless architecture was deemed instrumental for communicating with posterity in an understandable artistic language, it was subordinated to commemorative goals and endorsed only with severe misgivings. Indeed, timelessness was a *pejorative* label, applied to those monuments which were stuffy, featureless, and indistinctive, having failed to adequately integrate art and sculpture into a synthetic design.

In fact, these concerns, connected as they were to anticipating posterity's reception of contemporary monuments, were hardly unique to the Stalinist context. In the interwar era, monument builders were similarly conflicted about whether to embrace novel compositional techniques that promised to heighten emotional resonance. As in the Stalinist Soviet Union, it seemed "inappropriate for memorial art to be experimental and . . . abstract," given its task of "convey[ing] some generally recognized meaning about what is being memorialized," as Alan Borg summates. The risk that experimental forms would be viewed as outmoded with the passage of time was also an important consideration.[104] Even so, throughout this period, calls for reinvigorating monuments' emotional resonance by liberalizing their formal vocabulary became increasingly louder, heralding crucial changes in monument design that took place in the West soon after the Second World War.[105] All in all, as Sabina Tanović concludes, the "impossible balancing act" of having memorials "communicate . . . emotional tension and to stay objective, informative, and truthful" was universal.[106] Compelling reasons for preserving both dimensions meant that the design of synthetic monuments never swung entirely to either pole, in the Soviet Union as elsewhere. That said, the antinomy also facilitated a certain degree of variability in artistic practice. The design of monuments beyond Soviet borders tended toward "stripped classicism," a stylistic variant more austere (in terms of sculptural and artistic embellishments) and more open to modern forms.

While inhabiting the same paradigm, Stalinist monument builders at times made different compositional choices, responding as they did to unique circumstances. While sympathetic to the striving to make monuments emotionally compelling and relevant to future generations, Stalinist political leaders were apprehensive about the ideological ambiguities that could be introduced by excessive romanticism and laconicism. Pursuing their own rationale (discussed in the next chapter), they also resisted suggestions of amending the subjects of memorialization. By contrast, solutions to the problem of indistinctiveness were less politically problematic. Consequently, the regime's interventions in prospective monument design promoted a highly mimetic realism, and contributed to synthetic suffusion (or an "architecture of excess," as it was disparagingly termed by later critics). At the same time, the authorities' interventions in monument design remained just that. Art professionals were no mere conveyor belts for executing regime leaders' preexisting notions of what prospective monuments ought to look like. Architects, artists, and critics took the charge of anticipating posterity's gaze seriously, and raised important concerns about the capacity of historically stylized monuments to remain forever distinctive and relevant. At the end of the day, regime leaders proved receptive to these arguments, endorsing synthesis as a key principle of monument composition (broadly in line with prevailing practice elsewhere). As such, the richness of Stalinist monuments—grand architecture suffused with sculpture and decorative art—stemmed more from the artistic problems of prospective design than from an intrinsically "totalitarian" extravagance.

CHAPTER 4

The (Un)contested Politics of Stalinist Monument Building

The theory and practice of Stalinist monument design reveals that the regime and its art professionals approached the goal of immortalizing the era in earnest. But what motives stood behind the sudden turn to self-commemoration and the consequent explosion of prospective monument building? As noted, neo-totalitarian scholarship treats these monuments either as newfound *instruments* of domination or, more rarely, as organic *expressions* of official culture. Within the tradition of understanding monuments as testifying to the "eternal" character of the Stalinist order, these two approaches are typified by Lars Blomqvist and Anna Kutseleva. In Blomqvist's view, monuments propagandized the regime's claim of having constructed an eternal (and hence immutable) political order.[1] For Kutseleva, the construction of "eternal" monuments was less a calculated strategy than a spontaneous manifestation of the narcissism of Stalinist official culture. After all, "a culture which characterizes itself as . . . the concluding stage of world development," she writes, "expresses itself in the striving to imprint itself in matter, to escape into timelessness."[2]

These approaches run the risk of political reductionism on the one hand, and cultural reification on the other. At the root of both problems is the neo-totalitarian assumption that cultural phenomena under Stalinism can be understood solely by reference to the ruling regime. Of course, the centrality of the Stalinist party-state is beyond dispute, on account of its overwhelming institutional and coercive power. But acknowledging the Stalinist regime as the prime mover of the monument-building program is not incompatible with an analysis of the sociocultural underpinnings that guided its decision making and policies. Accordingly, in synthesizing a new model, I look beyond the regime to recover the wider cultural assumptions behind the construction of prospective monuments, without losing sight of their embeddedness in the dynamics of political domination. Specifically, the Stalinist monument-building program was situated on the terrain of a shared cultural value—the desirability of being remembered—which shaped its politics in crucial respects.

From the perspective of the authorities, the mass mobilization of Soviet society, in the service of forced-pace modernization, increasingly demanded a differentiated scale of incentives. This was particularly pressing given the dissipation of utopian enthusiasm toward the end of the First Five-Year Plan. In this context, the regime extended the prospect of being immortalized as a symbolic reward for self-sacrificial labor, loyalty, and military valor. Indeed, the chief institutional vehicles for commissioning sculptural monuments and memorial plaques were the decrees revealingly titled "On the immortalization of the memory of x," which were passed by the central government on the death of notable individuals. As mentioned, although such posthumous decrees originated in the immediate postrevolutionary years, initially, they were sporadic and rarely called for the construction of monuments (and even when they did, such initiatives usually came to nothing).[3] By contrast, the 1930s saw a marked increase in the number of individuals who qualified for memorialization, and an expansion of the measures that such immortalization decrees called for.

Aside from ordering the construction of dedicated sculptural monuments and memorial plaques, immortalization decrees made funeral and burial arrangements (on occasion bestowing such bizarre honors as transferring the brain of the deceased to the Moscow Brain Research Institute). They could commission plaster death masks and tombstones, order the translation or republication of major writings and biographies, endow legacy scholarships and prizes, establish house-museums, and rename institutions and locales. Furthermore, these decrees were often accompanied by provisions for one-off payments and special pensions (*personal'nye pensii*) for the family of the deceased, and could confirm their right to retain lavish residences, access to chauffeured cars, special shops, health care facilities, cafeterias, and other privileges. These decrees were published prominently in central and regional newspapers (although family benefits, beyond one-off payments and pensions, were redacted).

Immortalization decrees were typically drafted by the institutions in whose employ the deceased had been. These filtered upward through the commissariats (ministries) and were ratified by the government: the Council of People's Commissars (after 1946, known as the Council of Ministers), which had the power of the purse. Measures calling only for commemorative renaming could be passed by the Central Executive Committee (later, Presidium) of the Supreme Soviet. Sometimes, the party- or government-appointed funeral commission introduced its own proposals. The Politburo's involvement was irregular but palpable, signaling the importance that the country's top leadership vested in these initiatives. Specifically, the Politburo reviewed the commemoration of party functionaries, as well as of figures patronized by individual Politburo members (who could introduce immortalization decrees directly). Typically, these decrees were approved without changes, although the most extravagant proposals could be rejected or amended by the authorities at each stage of the process. On occasion, immortalization decrees could be reissued for the same individual. Thus, for instance, the Politburo considered and approved twenty such decrees within a year of Sergei Kirov's death (and each decree was already an amalgamation of several proposals).[4] Sometimes, new decrees were also promulgated on the anniversaries of their subjects' death or birth.[5]

The meaning of such measures was clear: deserving individuals could expect to be recognized posthumously for their achievements and political loyalty. Conversely, individuals and groups victimized by the regime were subject to a "double murder": not only physically annihilated but also consigned to oblivion.[6] Even former notables, fallen from grace, were subject to *damnatio memoriae*: their monuments destroyed, their associated toponyms renamed, and their identities wiped from the historical record. In effect, a veritable political economy grew up around such promises of perpetual commemoration, vividly exemplifying what sociologist Zygmunt Bauman refers to as "a most powerful disciplining effort in the hands of [modern] society. Like other socially allocated rewards, immortality could be awarded in larger or smaller quantities, depending on the deads' assumed possession of values whose dominance society wished to secure or perpetuate."[7]

Under Stalinism, of course, it was a specific group of regime leaders, rather than society at large, that determined which lives had been properly lived. In most cases, unsurprisingly, the deserving few were political functionaries and representatives of the technical and artistic elites. Stalinism's "hierarchy of commemorability," the criteria according to which some individuals were preserved in memory while others were relegated to oblivion, followed the wider, emerging patterns of social stratification.[8] To be sure, the central (Moscow-based) commemorative pantheon included some folk heroes like the test pilot Valerii Chkalov and the martyred informer and Young Pioneer Pavlik Morozov. Yet these cases were exceptional, requiring ad hoc initiatives and powerful patrons. The eminent writer Maksim Gor'kii, for instance, had proposed a monument to Morozov in 1933 and eventually secured Politburo approval in July 1935. However, as Catriona Kelly relates, following Gor'kii's death in mid-1936, "there was now no one with real power who backed the idea of a central-Moscow monument." Construction was held up for over a decade until, amid a partial revival of the Morozov cult, a somewhat diminutive statue finally went up in a suburban Moscow children's park.[9]

Relatedly, schemes to widen the commemorative pantheon were sponsored by mid-level actors and, as such, usually foundered. An early example was the so-called Alley of Shock-Workers, which opened in mid-1931 in Moscow's Central Park of Culture and Leisure (known from the following year as Gor'kii Park), at the behest of its art commission (*sektor iskusstva*). The Alley's sixteen busts, which were specifically commissioned as permanent monuments, commemorated leading shock-workers who had been awarded the Order of Lenin or the Order of the Red Banner of Labor.[10] Evidently, however, these busts were poorly executed, having been "constructed in haste, which decreased their quality," according to one contemporary account.[11] The busts were soon dismantled, and similar experiments were seldom repeated, despite art professionals' intermittent proposals to immortalize the memory of humble laborers in the synthetic decorations of new monuments. Thus, for instance, the sculptor Boris Korolev testified that the Palace of the Soviets interior design team envisioned a "huge number of portraits, busts, sculptural figures of our heroes, Stakhanovites [over-performing workers], important people of the land of socialism," but the initiative stalled together with the larger palace project.[12] Similarly, the prewar concept of Moscow's Elektrozavodskaia metro station involved busts of Stakhanovites in niches along the main concourse. Nonetheless, as the station's architect Igor' Rozhin recalled, "when it came to determine the 'list' of those to be depicted, the idea was abandoned, as the ratifying authorities could not agree on who specifically should be immortalized in sculpture."[13] It was only in the postwar period that all two-time recipients of the "Hero of Socialist Labor" award became routinely eligible for sculptural monuments.[14] However, even this scheme remained in the planning stage until it was abandoned soon after Stalin's death.

Nonetheless, the Stalinist hierarchy of commemorability was fluid; in the late 1930s, with the looming threat of war, the regime moved to broaden the pantheon to include military heroes, heretofore underrepresented. One such scheme, decreed in mid-1939, ordered the immediate construction of larger-than-life bronze busts to repeat recipients of the new, and now highest, military order, "Hero of the Soviet Union." Monuments to two-time recipients of the "Hero of the Soviet Union" award would be constructed in their birthplace

FIGURE 9. Bust of two-time recipient of the "Hero of the Soviet Union" award Lieutenant Colonel Petr Pokryshev, sculpted by Nikolai Tomskii, unveiled in 1948. Photograph from Anatolii Paramonov, *Nikolai Vasil'evich Tomskii: skul'ptor-monumentalist*. Moscow: Iskusstvo, 1953.

locale, while three-time awardees would have an additional bust unveiled before the Palace of the Soviets.[15] The pronounced prospective character of these monuments was clarified in a mid-1946 Council of Ministers decree, which mandated that these bronze busts could be placed only on pedestals of cast iron, granite, marble or other durable stone, and only on a similarly durable foundation.[16] The prospect of being memorialized within one's lifetime was expected to reward military valor and to incentivize further emulation. As the art historian Dmitrii Kolpinskii explained in 1950, this program played "an enormous educational role, because each compatriot of the Heroes of the Soviet Union . . . sees how the people, the Party, and the government value and lift up his labor, his loyalty, and his heroic efforts in serving for the good of the Motherland."[17] The sculptor Nikolai Tomskii seconded this: "For his military or labor feats, an ordinary Soviet person is honored by his fellow citizens and the government: his monumental portrait adorns the square of his native village or city . . . For his relatives, friends, fellow countrymen, and the younger generations, this living, concrete example confirms how the people and the Party appreciate selfless labor for the Motherland, they see and understand that everyone is given the opportunity to earn this high honor."[18]

The construction of over one hundred such monuments to two-time recipients of the "Hero of Soviet Union" award was completed by the mid-1950s. Even so, the political expedience of extending commemorative honors to military men was counterbalanced by political leaders' distrust of competing sources of authority. This was particularly true of popular wartime commanders, whose status the regime demoted soon after victory (instructive in this respect is the case of Marshall Georgii Zhukov, the erstwhile deputy Supreme Commander, relegated to obscurity in mid-1946). This development was also reflected in commemorative policy. For instance, in late 1943, with the establishment of the new "Order of Victory" for top military commanders, awardees qualified for a memorial plaque in an antechamber of the Great Kremlin Palace (which was to be duly renamed the "Hall of Victory").[19] Ultimately, eleven Soviet generals and marshals received the order, but the memorial initiative did not advance beyond the design phase and was quietly dropped in 1954.[20] In the last instance, memorial subjects were selected according to the regime's shifting hierarchy of commemorability.

Nonetheless, while enticing individuals with monuments that assured them of a grateful posterity, political leaders expected the appeal of the monument-building program to operate primarily on the collective level. After all, the most important and lavish monuments commemorated not individuals but the Stalin era generally. The "monument" designation was applied liberally to most objects of the built environment, be they public, residential, infrastructural, or industrial constructions. This explains why it became so important to publicize and underscore, often falsely, the perdurability of these new edifices (even as permanence was sought after genuinely). Thus, for instance, not only were the Moscow metro's august halls of marble and granite said to stand indefinitely, official media declared even its concrete caissons eternal: "In subterranean constructions, [concrete's] durability increases limitlessly with time. Concrete is not susceptible to corrosion . . . like iron, and putrefaction, like a tree. Research on concrete, carried out in the last 40–50 years, demonstrates that in the first year, concrete increases in durability by 50% compared to its first month. Over the next thirty-five years, durability increases by another 60%. Further, the curve gets steeper [sic], allowing us to assume that after 100 years the material increases in durability by another 100%, and after 1,000 years—by 250% relative to the original."[21]

Commentators waxed lyrical on how these collective monuments would pass down the glory of the current generation through the centuries. For example, Sergei Dinamov, head of the arts subdivision (*sektor iskusstv*) of the party's department for propaganda and culture, intoned on the pages of *Iskusstvo* that through these projects, "the builders of our country will appear as titans to future generations. [Posterity] will be jealous of the current Soviet generation."[22] Evidently, the regime fundamentally believed that such fantasies would appeal to the Soviet public. Official discourse and propaganda never demonstrated *why* being remembered was desirable, but merely *showcased* the regime's efforts to immortalize the achievements of the Soviet people. A case in point is Viktor Koretskii's 1952 propaganda poster "We Build for the Ages." The poster depicted three construction workers examining their blueprints, against the background of a hydropower station under construction. There was no explanation for why "building for the ages" was important. Koretskii simply assumed that such a claim would appeal to the millions of Soviet citizens engaged directly or indirectly in the massive postwar reconstruction projects.

Likely, political leaders inferred the wide appeal of immortalization from their own yearning for fame everlasting. From the very beginning, observers and historians speculated about Stalin's near-pathological desire to make his mark in history. Interestingly, Solzhenitsyn's assertions (with which this books opens), and other similar psychohistorical claims, were confirmed by the first biographers to work in the Soviet archives, when they opened in the early 1990s. Dmitrii Volkogonov contended that Stalin "did everything to ensure that his life story would be told in bright colors . . . people knew about him only what he wanted them to know."[23] Roy and Zhores Medvedev likewise attested that "Stalin was always concerned about how he would be remembered by future generations."[24]

Figure 10. "We Build for Centuries!" Viktor Koretskii, 1952. Poster image provided by PosterPlakat.com.

Nonetheless, these claims remained largely impressionistic, and have been increasingly disputed. Sarah Davies and James Harris, for instance, influentially argued that Stalin viewed his personality cult (and its monumental incarnations) as a political necessity (for regime legitimation). Possibly, the cult was even distasteful to the dictator; at the very least, it centered on Stalin as a political figure, being "minimally focused on the personality and personal life of the *vozhd'* [leader]."[25]

Even so, some fragmentary archival evidence has recently emerged to suggest that legacy-fashioning could have been a genuine concern for Stalin after all. For instance, Jan Plamper describes how Stalin's office carefully curated the way he would appear in the archival record, which would form the basis for posterity's evaluations. Documents were sent alternately to the (relatively) open archives of the Marx-Engels-Lenin Institute and the dictator's personally controlled, restricted Central Committee Special Sector—the former cultivating Stalin's image at least in part for posterity.[26] To be sure, the question of how the dictator related to his immortalization will likely never be settled definitively. But for the present purposes, what is important is that those who knew Stalin best assumed that immortalization would appeal to him. The prospect of self-commemoration was therefore employed not only as a symbolic incentive targeting the public, but also as a way for mid-level functionaries and institutions to curry favor with their superiors. Thus, for instance, in a desperate attempt to regain the good graces of Stalin on the eve of the Great Terror, the soon-to-be-executed Karl Radek penned the lengthy article "The Architect of Socialist Society." Radek's vision of the glorious Soviet future was framed as a 1967 lecture by a professor who points out Stalin's pivotal role in history. Radek's article was well-received and was published prominently in *Pravda*, as well as in stand-alone editions.[27] Similarly, secret police chief Lavrentii Beriia's greetings for Stalin's sixtieth birthday evoked the fantasy of undying fame: "only future generations will be able to entirely comprehend the full picture of the historical process of communist construction, which was inspired and organized by comrade Stalin."[28] Ten years later, in the lead up to Stalin's seventieth birthday, the Union of Architects proposed several measures for Stalin's memorialization, including: "the erection of a Monument to Victory in the war in honor of Stalin, the placing of a monumental statue to the leader in front of Moscow University . . . and the construction of a Stalin Museum to the great man's life and works."[29] All of these measures, in fact, were already being put into effect, in one form or another.

Statues and busts of Stalin were ubiquitous in Soviet cityscapes. As John Steinbeck recorded in his 1947 travel diary, "Everything in the Soviet Union takes place under the fixed stare of the plaster, bronze, drawn or embroidered eye of Stalin . . . Statues of him dignify the façade of every public building. His bust

FIGURE 11. Exterior view of the amalgamated Victory Museum of the Great Patriotic War and the I. V. Stalin Monument in Erevan. Photograph from *Sovetskaia Arkhitektura* 1952, no. 2.

stands in front of all airports, railway and bus stations... He is everywhere."³⁰ Indeed, Stalin statues dominated the composition of monumental ensembles: colossal sculptures of the leader were placed prominently at the *All-Union Agricultural Exhibition,* and on the banks of the Moscow-Volga and Volga-Don Canals. Artists and architects, and the political functionaries who staffed the commissioning bodies, made sure to foreground Stalin's undying glory even in collective monuments to the era. Erevan's 1950 Victory Museum of the Great Patriotic War exemplifies this approach well: the military museum was a effectively a twenty-nine-meter pedestal for Sergei Merkurov's enormous I. V. Stalin Monument. The Moscow State University Main Building avoided a similar fate only narrowly: the original idea of a crowning Stalin statue was ultimately abandoned, presumably in the interests of harmonizing with the other high-rises.³¹ However, in the university buildings as elsewhere, Stalin's image (frescoed, painted, sculpted, poured, and fired), as well as inscriptions from his speeches and writings, was ubiquitous. As Igor' Golomstock observes, "the depiction of any historical event or real situation [was] like an individual flourish in a splendid frame surrounding the portrait of the leader."³²

As mentioned, Stalin closely curated monument-building projects in Moscow, and likely approved of his own copious representations in them. At the same time, these were not the result of Stalin's intercessions, but rather of mid-level functionaries and art professionals signaling their loyalty and zeal by appealing to the dictator's perceived desire to be immortalized. This dynamic was likely reproduced in relation to other political grandees, who headed their own patronage networks. Corresponding to their status in the political hierarchy, their monumental representations were less prominent than those of Stalin (at least in the major Soviet cities), but were also a significant feature of the "memoryscape." From 1938 to 1941, for instance, the Monumentskul'ptura factory alone produced not only 2,647 statues and 4,096 busts of Stalin, but also 1,124 statues and 2,580 busts of Kalinin, and 754 busts of Voroshilov.³³ As demonstrated above, such monuments were not only instruments for propagandizing leader cults; these objects were also fundamentally prospective, expressly designed and built for future generations. In this respect, it is likely that regime leaders' own desire for immortalization fostered the belief that monuments (and the prospect of being remembered by posterity) would appeal to the public.

Was the regime justified in this assumption? How did the Soviet public (if such an aggregate category is permissible) relate to immortalization? Superficially, one sees a familiar picture: a unanimous and overwhelmingly enthusiastic response to all monuments proposed by the regime, even and especially those immortalizing the dear leaders and their illustrious exploits. An extreme example is the public outpouring of various initiatives to immortalize Stalin in the days following his death in the spring of 1953. In thousands of letters, Soviet citizens suggested various measures, ranging from renaming the capital to establishing an Order of Stalin to constructing a "fountain of tears." These initiatives appeared spontaneous but were modeled on commemorations of other regime leaders who predeceased Stalin.[34] Their scripted nature is apparent in frequent proposals to construct a pantheon: as mentioned, the government had in fact already announced the project the day after Stalin's death, and this was widely reported in the press. Considering the tendency of monuments (even those purportedly commemorating collective events in the life of the country) to degenerate into memorials to regime leaders, it is tempting to view the public performance of enthusiastic support through a neo-totalitarian lens. Ostensibly, these responses were no different from other panegyric rituals that the terror-stricken Soviet public was forced to enact. The brainwashed minority who genuinely approved of monument building supported the official line in any context, or so the narrative goes.

Nevertheless, the overrepresentation of "great men" did not necessarily preclude the possibility that the Soviet public could recognize itself and feel commemorated through these monuments. Official discourse took care to highlight the popular (*narodnyi*), folksy origin of regime leaders, heroes, and other memorialized notables. The hope was that Soviet citizens would identify these as representatives of the collective, and thereby be immortalized by proxy. This ideal response was vividly exemplified by one entry in a visitor book at Smolenskaia metro station, which was unveiled in spring 1953. "The new line of the L. M. Kaganovich Moscow Metro is yet another stone in the grandiose foundations of the building of Communism. We will build it [. . . as a monument to Lenin and Stalin]. Centuries will pass, but the glory of our heroic days will never fade. Posterity will be proud of us, simple soldiers, simple Soviet people who built [illegible] communism."[35]

Aside from establishing equivalence between the metro station as a monument to Stalin and a monument to "simple Soviet people," this response revealed another way in which these objects could memorialize the Soviet collective: through the physical act of monument building, independent of the latter's semantic content. This was less dependent on the public accepting official mythologies concerning the identity of the Soviet elite and the people. After all, even if monuments memorialized the regime and its supreme leader, the people would be remembered as the creators of these objects. To apply psychologist Ernst Becker's concept, Stalinist monuments acted as "heroic projects," through which ordinary individuals could "earn a feeling of primary value, of cosmic specialness, of ultimate usefulness to creation, of unshakable meaning . . . by building an edifice that reflects human value." Indirectly, these monuments offered "the hope and belief . . . that the things that man creates in society are of lasting worth and meaning, that they outlive or outshine death and decay, that man and his products count."[36]

Official publications affirmed this way of identifying with monuments: less for what they memorialized than through the act of creating lasting objects. In a volume of reminiscences devoted to the construction of the first phase of the Moscow metro, one tunneller proclaimed: "when this wonderful, eternal monument to our young and ardent epoch is fully completed, each one of us will proudly and happily say of oneself: I worked for Metrostroi!"[37] In a similar-style publication on the construction of the Moscow State University Main Building, a crane operator also waxed eloquent: "The golden star of the Palace of Science . . . will glitter in the sunlight for many centuries, as a symbol of the labor-glory of the people of the Stalin epoch."[38] Hoping to capitalize on such sentiments, official discourse framed ordinary construction workers as fully legitimate "authors" working alongside architects.[39] Initiatives immortalizing their exploits included the handsome volumes referred to above: canonized historical accounts by ordinary workers involved in monument construction, published soon after the projects' completion. These were likely related to the project of workers writing the "histories of [their] factories and plants," up to the present day. Although Maksim Gor'kii's original call, which touched off the campaign, did not refer to future generations as a potential audience, this may have been inferred by the Soviet public.[40] Between 1931 and 1938, more than thirty such history books were produced as part of this venture.

Furthermore, despite the precedence of the Stalinist hierarchy of commemorability, anonymous, ideal workers and other professionals could also be reflected in monuments' iconography. For example, prewar stations of the Moscow metro were replete with representations of the *metrostroevtsy*, the heroic pioneers of underground construction. Another strategy involved museumification. In early 1933, one letter writer lobbied the director of construction of the Palace of the Soviets to record "all the smallest details of the construction of the world's first socialist colossus, the Palace of the Soviets . . . because it will serve as a beacon for the proletariat of all countries and for the oppressed peoples of the whole world, and the history of its construction in many, many years will represent a most valuable and most interesting chronicle of immortality."[41] Evidently, authorities recognized the potential appeal of such initiatives. For instance, in 1939, calling for the construction of a model of the Palace of the Soviets foyer, Aleksei Shchusev attempted to assuage concerns about the extra effort involved by promising that the model would be donated to a museum in due course.[42]

To encourage the widest collective identification with its monuments, the regime always trumpeted the size of the labor force involved in these building projects: the hundreds of thousands constructing the canals, the Moscow metro, the capital's high-rises, and other megaprojects. Authorities took care to source (or claim to be sourcing) the materials and workforce from various parts of the country, to foster the image of a national undertaking. For example, the construction of the Moscow metro involved "miners from the Ukrainian and Siberian coalfields and construction workers from the iron and steel mills of Magnitogorsk, the Dnepr hydroelectric power station, and the Turkestan-Siberian railway. Further, materials used in the construction of the metro included iron from Siberian Kuznetsk, timber from northern Russia, cement from the Volga region and the northern Caucasus, bitumen from Baku, and marble and granite from quarries in Karelia, the Crimea, the Caucasus, the Urals, and the Soviet Far East."[43] Propaganda similarly cultivated the image of the Palace of the Soviets as an all-Union project, emphasizing its wide sourcing of labor, materials, and specialist knowledge. "The entire country is building the Palace of the Soviets" (*Dvorets Sovetov stroit vsia strana*) was a popular slogan of the time. The pooling of labor not only encouraged collective identification with such national monuments, but in some sense, worked to create the Soviet collective as such. As archaeologist Colin Renfrew observes, "the very process of constructing [. . . a] monument in a sense calls that community into being."[44]

Beyond physical construction, the regime also opened indirect avenues for public participation in monument building, encouraging wide public discussions and constructive feedback. Urban planners responsible for the Socialist Reconstruction of Moscow organized public consultations on which monuments to decorate the new face of the city with.[45] Responsible institutions also organized frequent viewings of models and designs of architectural and sculptural monuments; a 1941 Committee for Arts Affairs decree went so far as to *order* design competition organizers to hold public exhibitions of all models of sculptural monuments of "significant social-political interest."[46] The 1943 resolution of the All-Union Conference on Sculpture widened this mandate to even include sculptures slated for mass production.[47] These events usually offered the opportunity to comment in visitor books. Visitor books were also available, on occasion, at newly unveiled architectural monuments, such as at the stations of the Moscow metro. Soviet newspapers republished some of the comments recorded in them, along with letters sent by engaged citizens.

The public's agency, of course, was negligible, but the appearance of official responsiveness played an important role. As Plamper argues, through "the publication of visitor comments in the newspapers [. . .] the act of commenting in a comment book was generally endowed with the meaning of participation or even empowerment."[48] One visitor to the *All-Union Art Exhibition* of 1950 not only affirmed his belief in the importance of public discussion but was confident that this input would be appreciated by posterity. He exhorted his fellow commentators: "Comrade viewers! More genuine, honest, and cultured critiques! The people's visitor comment book is a document of our times, not a joke."[49] Clearly then, the preponderance of "great men" selected for immortalization did not *necessarily* preclude the Soviet public's identification with Stalinist monuments. Monuments were employed as symbolic incentives, and as tribute to the vanity of regime leaders, but authorities went to significant efforts to ensure that these monuments would also be perceived as commemorating the Soviet collective as a whole.

Gauging how Soviet citizens responded to such efforts is difficult, to say the least. Direct public criticism of the monument-building program was, as a matter of course, unthinkable. Citizen letters to institutions and political leaders were self-censored (as they could be traced back to their authors). Visitor books at exhibitions were often signed under the watchful eye of guards posted nearby; critical comments could also be redacted.[50] If sustained hostility to the monument-building program existed, it cannot be found in the public record (nor, very likely, in later private testimony). And yet, owing to the pliancy and contradictions of official discourse, opposition could be voiced indirectly.[51] Overzealous monument building could be criticized as impeding the achievement of other objectives. For instance, at a late-1944 architecture conference, while affirming the necessity of building lasting monuments, city planner Viktor Baburin meekly suggested that such functions be vested only in public buildings. The planning and design of residential buildings, he contended, should be focused on cheapness and functionality.[52] Alternatively, indirect opposition could be voiced within the paradigm of immortalization, by reference to posterity's judgement (and the bad witness that overspending on monuments would supposedly give). As the eminent art historian Ivan Matsa proclaimed in 1946:

> We, the contemporaries of the Stalin era, will be asked not only about which Parthenons of our own we erected... Along with this, we will be asked about what built environment architects created for the everyday life of the builders, fighters, and heroes of this era. What kind of streets, squares, parks, houses, and everything that is prosaically called "mass constructions," were built for them? By the kind of answer that we will give to these questions, it will be possible to judge whether architects understood fully the tasks of their era, whether they were able to reflect its greatness.[53]

86   CHAPTER 4

Curiously, however, these avenues of indirect opposition were used surprisingly rarely. Be that as it may, this is far from a definitive answer to the question, so it is necessary to approach the problem from the other end, examining instances of support rather than opposition.

Support for and interest in the monument-building program, and its mission of prospective commemoration, was palpable. It emanated from visitor books at exhibitions of monument designs, these being "one of the few material records we have of Soviet society representing itself, talking to itself, and articulating its identities and divisions without the intervention of an editor," in Susan Reid's words.[54] It was evident in letters to newspapers, party and state institutions, and art professionals, which were "as close to a public sphere as one is likely to get during the Stalin period," in the opinion of Sheila Fitzpatrick.[55] These expressions were voluntary (a few organized campaigns aside), which already testifies to a certain level of genuineness and spontaneity.[56] Crucially, they were not a case of "speaking Bolshevik": the tactical mobilization of official ideology to advance individual goals.[57] Affirmations of support for monuments did not promise their authors any tangible gains beyond the feeling of participation in the process of immortalizing the memory of their era.

The genuineness of such sentiments is illustrated effectively in amateur proposals for building more monuments and for specific monument designs. Initially, the regime welcomed the latter by holding well-publicized, "open" design competitions for amateurs, alongside "closed," professional competitions (amateur projects were never executed, regardless of the results). In this way, the second, open phase of the Palace of the Soviets design competition in 1932 attracted over 150 submissions from the public.[58] In 1935, the youth newspaper *Kolkhoznye rebiata* solicited designs for the Pavlik Morozov monument, receiving over 500 from Young Pioneers.[59] But while the practice of open competitions disappeared from the second half of the 1930s, a deluge of unsolicited proposals continued to make its way to newspapers, individual artists, architects, political leaders, and various branches of the party and government. In fact, these proposals often presented monument projects that the regime was not even considering.[60] They revealed frustration with the pace of monument construction, such as one 1951 collective letter to *Izvestiia* expressing outrage over the lagging construction of the monument to the poet Gabdulla Tukai in Kazan'.[61] They also interposed in closed competitions (for instance, over 1,500 unsolicited submissions were received during the first, closed phase of the pantheon competition in 1954).[62]

The sincerity of these proposals was further evidenced by their occasional, unintentional political unorthodoxy or naiveté. In 1937, for instance, one letter writer to *Izvestiia* suggested constructing collaboratively designed, matching monuments to Chkalov's polar overflight, in the Soviet Union and United States.[63] A similar, wartime monument proposal called for the erection of matching "Pillars of Friendship, Victory, and Peace," in Moscow, London, and Washington.[64] Needless to say, Stalinist internationalism never extended quite so far. Furthermore, these amateur proposals exhibited a strikingly naïve confidence that any idea could be implemented, regardless of technical feasibility. For example, the 1937 public discussion of a monument to the epic rescue of the SS *Cheliuskin* icebreaker's stranded crew yielded dozens of the most ambitious proposals. These included a monument next to and at least as high as the Palace of the Soviets, a model ship (containing a museum and library) suspended by chains from a model airplane, a ten-storied iceberg-building (doubling as a polar research institute and residence for the *Cheliuskin* crew), and others.[65] The wartime period saw equally impressive suggestions. One proposal called for a giant mound on Red Square formed out of monoliths transported from each Soviet republic, under which their respective national chronicles would be buried.[66] Another envisioned memorial plaques, placed in every city, town, and village, which together would immortalize not only the names of all Soviet veterans, but also of their respective mothers, who reared them to heroic patriotism.[67]

In fact, party and government institutions, political leaders, and art professionals were frequently overwhelmed by the volume of such proposals and suggestions, which nearly always pled that the addressee acknowledge receipt and reply with their impressions. While working on the gargantuan Lenin monument that was to top the Palace of the Soviets, Merkurov was so exasperated by the copious correspondence from amateurs that he even complained to Kliment Voroshilov.[68] Nevertheless, recognizing the benefit of such collective identification with the monument-building program, the regime tried to appear attentive to amateur monument proposals and to public discussion. In one case, the Committee for Arts Affairs formed a full expert review council, which met *three* times to consider an amateur proposal for a 150-meter pyramidal victory monument with a spiraling staircase, topped by a sculpture of Stalin holding a globe. However, because the council's report rejected the design (noting that the structure was unstable, its architectonic composition "constructivist," and its concept of the Stalin sculpture "naïve and conducive to unwelcome associations"), the committee was forced to disappoint the author.[69] In another instance, the Committee for Arts Affairs also held a formal review of a war monument proposal submitted by group of veterans; its representatives met with the authors, giving them a positive response but explaining that without sanction from the Council of Ministers, their hands were tied.[70]

In 1944, another group of veterans petitioning Stalin to construct a commemorative theme park (provisionally named "Heroism of the Patriotic Wars") was met with a similar response. Their fantastic ten-page proposal called for monuments, museums, memorial halls, panoramas, trophy weapons (including German steamships and submarines), movie theaters, lecture halls, shooting ranges, parachute towers, equine parks, ski hills, ice rinks, circuses, dance floors, officer clubs, beaches, amusement rides, a library, publishing house, art gallery, sanatorium, military college, stadium, airfield, a "Pioneer's Palace," its own hydro-power station, and a thirty-to-fifty-meter raised monorail. Clearly, designers of the Heroism of the Patriotic Wars theme park had assimilated Stalinist gigantomania and bombast, but misread the chronic lack of capacity that such rhetoric all-too-often masked. Stalin's secretary Aleksandr Poskrebyshev forwarded the letter to Politburo candidate member and head of the army's political directorate Aleksandr Shcherbakov (note the high level of involvement). Shcherbakov tersely commented that "it is necessary to explain (politely) to the letter's authors that currently and in the near future the country faces more pressing issues"; the order was promptly carried out.[71]

The pleas that amateur proposals be acknowledged, and the efforts occasionally expended to receive a reply, testify to a strong emotional investment in the monument-building program—at least on the part of some individuals. An early 1940 complaint from one amateur designer of a Chkalov monument relates his odyssey through the Kafka-esque labyrinth of Soviet bureaucracy in the quest for a reply. Having sent his proposal a year earlier to the newspaper *Krasnaia Zvezda*, the author followed up with the editorial office after a lengthy silence. He was informed that the project had been forwarded to the Committee for Arts Affairs. The latter, however, denied having received it. An approach to the Secretariat of the Council of People's Commissars yielded nothing beyond a demand for the date and case number of the original submission acknowledgement from *Krasnaia Zvezda*. The author duly forwarded these to the Secretariat, to no avail. He therefore felt compelled to write to the Presidium of the Supreme Soviet of the USSR.[72] An analogous story, recounted in a letter to the deputy chairman of the Council of Peoples' Commissars from an amateur designer of monuments to Gor'kii and party boss Sergo Ordzhonikidze, concluded dejectedly: "I have doubts that workers' opinions are being considered."[73] At points, the regime had trouble keeping up with the enthusiasm for monument building, which it itself encouraged by sponsoring public discussions and other forms of participation. In any case, as the regime had hoped, wide sections of the public evidently felt that they were being commemorated (or, at any rate, expressed the yearning to be commemorated) in collective monuments to the era.

But even if these expressions attested to a genuine desire to be remembered by posterity, was this sentiment limited to those who had internalized the regime's ideology and values in toto? Jochen Hellbeck's study of genuine, self-reflexive "true believers" revealed, for instance, that the diary writer Stepan Podlubyi "wrote because he saw himself as participating in a transformational process of epic dimensions. One day he wanted to tell his children about the '1930s', when the whole country had been built."[74] The evidence suggests, however, that support for the monument-building program was not confined to such true believers, but extended even to those who did not actively support the Stalinist political project. This is best exemplified in the case of grassroots monument building in the years of the Great Patriotic War. In these extraordinary conditions, the Committee for Arts Affairs' prerogative of approving the design and construction of all stand-alone monuments was largely ignored. In fact, servicemen and civilians constructed monuments to their fallen comrades on their own initiative, on a scale and of a character sufficiently divergent from the regime's approved archetypes to eventually provoke a hostile response. In 1950, the first systematic study of the phenomenon estimated tens to hundreds of thousands of only *registered* graveside monuments.[75] Incomplete military data counted at least 752 large, stand-alone monuments to the Great Patriotic War.[76] Built spontaneously and quickly, these unsanctioned tombstones, monuments, and memorials were, for the most part, of a haphazard character: of variable artistic quality, often utilizing temporary materials available close at hand.[77]

In early 1944, chairman of the Committee for Arts Affairs Mikhail Khrapchenko approached Stalin with a proposed decree to reaffirm his organization's authority. He complained that "local institutions, the public, and Red Army servicemen take the initiative, constructing many monuments and tombstones." The design and construction of these, Khrapchenko alleged, "is carried out without state and artistic control and very often brings unsatisfactory results."[78] Such concerns were mirrored in other discussions of the necessity of a designated institution to oversee the design and construction of war monuments. One such proposal, in early 1945, came from the Peoples' Commissariat of Defense, and was supported by leading military men, including Marshals Georgii Zhukov, Ivan Konev, Konstantin Rokossovskii, Lev Mekhlis, Rodion Malinovskii, and others.[79] A few months later, Army General Andrei Khrulev suggested instituting a similar Committee for the Construction and Protection of Monuments to the Great Patriotic War.[80] As it happened, these initiatives were successfully opposed by the Committee for Arts Affairs (which jealously guarded its remit), but the underlying concerns were not ignored.

Although opposition to grassroots monument construction was supposedly motivated by quality considerations, it hid underlying ideological worries. For instance, the regime was uncomfortable with unsanctioned memorialization of the Holocaust (the official narrative did not recognize the specificity of

Jewish victimhood); nearly all such monuments and memorial plaques were dismantled by the authorities in the postwar period.[81] Such concerns with the ideological liabilities of spontaneous, grassroots monument construction may partially explain the officially sponsored development of standardized, prefabricated graveside monuments for individual and mass graves throughout the second half of the war and into the postwar period.[82] These and other centrally commissioned war monuments attempted to coopt and channel popular commemoration into an officially approved mold, a dynamic recognized in existing literature.

Adrienne Harris' account of the commemoration of Soviet partisan Zoia Kosmodemianskaia, martyred in late 1941, presents one such case of rechannelling popular, grassroots commemoration for political advantage. As the site of Kosmodemianskaia's execution, "the village of Petrishchevo," she recounts, "initially developed comparatively organically into a site significant to Zoya's cult . . . As early as 1942, compelled by a need to mourn Zoya and countless other victims, Soviet citizens began travelling to Petrishchevo to honor Zoya, to retrace her barefoot steps and to speak with witnesses. Aware of the significance of this site and the nation's prerevolutionary mourning rituals, Communist Party officials quickly began discussions to transform Petrishchevo into a political site. While citizens continued to come to venerate and mourn Zoya individually, in 1944 the Komsomol began shaping Petrishchevo into a monument."[83] As Dmitrii Khmel'nitskii summarizes, the authorities "realized the propagandistic significance of memorial architecture . . . Military memorials were the only type of architectural structures which could arouse natural, human feelings in Soviet people."[84] Clearly, therefore, neither monument building as a practice nor the desire for perpetuating memory were limited to official culture and its true believers. Rather, the value of being remembered was shared, and this underlying cultural assumption structured the politics of monument building in key respects. It was a prerequisite for commemoration to act as a symbolic incentive for the Soviet public, or as tribute to regime leaders' vanity. The striving to be remembered also facilitated collective identification with Stalinist monuments, and generated enthusiasm for the monument-building program, even to the point of provoking a certain degree of hostility from the regime.

Ultimately, the shared value of being remembered enabled actors to strategically manipulate the monument-building program in pursuit of alternate goals, a dynamic vividly exemplified in negotiations between the regime and its art professionals. Artists and architects appeared to revel in their preeminent position in fashioning definitive and lasting representations of their times. In the early 1930s, Ivan Zholtovskii confessed: "with the passage of time I feel more deeply and sharply the greatness and responsibility of the social role of the architect, [for] the history of our epoch may be read in the future from our architectural monuments."[85] Vera Mukhina characterized the memorialization of war heroes as a "soul-deep need," which would be carried out with "enthusiasm . . . great zeal and love."[86] Sculptor Ivan Shadr's explanatory note accompanying his model of the Chkalov monument bombastically proclaimed: "The sculptor INJECTS LIFE INTO STONE! To him ETERNITY is subject! He has the power to brand his enemy with shame for all time, and to passionately glorify his hero-friend in a Bronze legend."[87]

If the public felt collectively immortalized in monuments by participating in their creation, this mode of identification was undoubtedly more pronounced for artists and architects. After all, monuments immortalized not only their *subjects*, but also acted as "artistic monuments" (*pamiatniki iskusstva*), durable testaments to their designers. Thus, for instance, the sculptor Boris Korolev proclaimed that while "the Palace of the Soviets is the greatest monument to the Stalin epoch . . . we do not doubt that it will also become the greatest monument of our art."[88] The artist Evgenii Lansere's earliest diary entries exemplify artists' ambitions of going down in history through their monumental creations. "I want to serve humanity, to be great and to be preserved in history . . . Art is the only immortal history (at least it seems so), it is the voice of the People, it is the voice of God! I want to be an artist, and a great one, the greatest artist!" he recorded in 1893.[89] Later that year, he elaborated: "I must remain after my death for millennia. I do not desire . . . wealth, glamour, fame during my life. I'd rather starve to death in an attic, but then, to have my name thunder through the universe and remain forever great and unshakable."[90] Lansere's colleague Pavel Korin similarly confessed: "the thing I wish for above all else is for people to be able to say about me, many years hence: 'now *he* was an artist.'"[91] For his part, Aleksandr Deineka suggested more modestly that he "would like to show his biography through [his] works."[92] These aspirations encapsulated the Romantic ideal of creative genius: a Promethean artist staking their claim to immortality through enduring works, a nineteenth-century fantasy originating in the cults of individualism and youth, the realization of which was made possible through a (partially) democratized commemorative pantheon.[93] Intriguingly, the persistence of these ambitions demonstrates the enduring elements of Romanticism not only in Stalinist aesthetics, but also in the worldview of Soviet art professionals, and the perpetual, posthumous recognition that they aspired to.

Accordingly, artists and architects saw monuments primarily as a vehicle to immortalizing their own names. In 1951, the sculptor Sergei Konenkov had the audacity to state this explicitly in an argument with the Committee for Arts Affairs' council of experts, which was reviewing his monument to the gynecologist Vladimir Snegirev. "An artist must do as he wanted to originally, he notes all the criticism and does as he wishes, because this is not a monument to Snegirev, this is a moment to Konenkov. They don't say the Medici monument; they say Michelangelo's monument."[94] In a similar vein, at Shadr's funeral in 1941, Mukhina publicly pledged to finish the Gor'kii monument, on which he had been working, "in *his* [Shadr's] memory."[95] Indeed, five years later, Mukhina complained in a letter to Stalin that several of her own monumental projects were languishing without a decision to go ahead. Urging speedy decisions, she confessed: "I am already 57 years old and I want to succeed in leaving something behind for the country."[96]

Aside from their physical permanence, monuments could potentially join the emerging Soviet artistic canon, which promised to sustain an artist's legacy even more powerfully. After all, canons functioned not only as a censorship device but, as Hans Gunther notes, also created "barriers (if not a dam) against the flow of time and change[, having] a stabilizing function."[97] "The select body of canonical texts . . . was supposed to be sacral and eternal," concurs Plamper.[98] With socialist realism proclaimed early in this period, artists and architects were fascinated by the opportunity to consciously fashion a new, lasting template that would channel the development of all subsequent art. Stalin himself had called for the creation of "Soviet classics" in 1936 (in a conversation with the writer Mikhail Sholokhov and the directors of the opera *Quiet Flows the Don*), a slogan thereafter endlessly repeated. The excitement of art professionals in defining socialist realism can be felt clearly, and for many, pathbreaking was inseparable from trendsetting. This was particularly so given the formulaic, ritualized, iconic quality of socialist realist artistic production, which rested fundamentally on the mimicry of canonical "proper language . . . and syntax."[99] Deineka, for instance, felt that he and other Soviet artists were "pioneers and in this sense people will learn from us."[100] The sculptor Matvei Manizer was even more explicit: "We are standing at the doorstep of the new, remarkable art of a communist society. We cannot but feel satisfaction from the awareness that the foundations of this art are being laid by *us*."[101] Clearly, artists and architects were cognizant and flattered by the prospect that their creations would become the templates that would be copied subsequently. Accordingly, they referred to their monuments as "a classical model of socialist realism for centuries," representing a "sketch . . . of the great socialist style of the future," a definitive representation of contemporary events and individuals, with which "everyone will be aligning themselves" in the future.[102]

Large architectural monuments, to which Stalinist monumental practice gravitated, could achieve canonicity in an additional way: through the dictates of ensemble construction. Ensembles, as mentioned, demanded that the architecture of a given area be coherent and complementary. The form and style of contemporary constructions was in part limited by their historical antecedents. However, through superior dimensions, Soviet monuments were expected to dominate the ensemble for the foreseeable future (at least in the medium term), setting the tone, in turn, for subsequent construction. Thus, monumental buildings were said to "determine the composition of the city for decades and centuries to come."[103] As Boris Iofan explained, "it is our monumental structures that will influence decisively the crystallization of the new Soviet architectural style, the character [obraz] of our new and reconstructed cities."[104] For instance, the Palace of the Soviets was expected to "determine the style of Moscow."[105] Its sheer size demanded "boulevards, parterres, sculpture, fountains, and pools," as well as a string of large, monumental public buildings (of which the postwar high-rises were an example).[106] These high-rises, in turn, were expected to determine the character of their future surrounding neighborhoods. "The high-rises initiate, rather than conclude, a most important period in Moscow's reconstruction, they become a powerful point of departure for the radical reconstruction of large adjacent neighborhoods," proclaimed the head of the Moscow branch of the Union of Architects Nikolai Kolli.[107] "These buildings ... open entirely new prospects for the further development of the city as a huge holistic ensemble," agreed his colleague Grigorii Zakharov.[108] Thus, architects expected that their monumental constructions would become in some sense canonical, remaining the reference point for generations of builders to come.

Recognizing the desire of artists and architects to be immortalized through their work, the regime used this prospect to interest professionals in monument construction and to incentivize high-quality work. The very opportunity to participate in the monument-building program (and by extension, to enter history along with the memorialized subjects) was framed as a gift from the state.[109] As the vice president of the Academy of Architecture summarized: "the Party and government create all the conditions for fruitful work for Moscow architects, for implementing great creative ideas, which will immortalize the great feats of the Lenin-Stalin epoch."[110] Editorials in professional periodicals referred to the "honorable and important" role, the "historically unprecedented task of exceptional influence in the future" that artists and architects had been given through their commission to build for the centuries.[111] Lansere's diary testifies to the admonitions of the artistic director of the Palace of the Soviets construction, who confronted Lansere's indifference: "How can you be so petty! The Bolshoi theater [the reconstruction of which Lansere was also working on]—that is, perhaps, for 100 years, but the Palace of the Soviets—that is for 1,000 years. The [Lenin] library will disappear [with time], the Bolshoi Theater will disappear, but the Palace of the Soviets will stand!" Lansere remained unconvinced about the artistic value of the palace, but, importantly, only insofar as it was a poor means to building his own legacy. "The subjects of the Palace of the Soviets are boring and false, how is one to be inspired by them," he recorded. Its composition is "scholastic, which with the passage of time will perhaps become as abstract [as] anything."[112]

At points, the regime directly facilitated its architects' ambitions for personal immortalization. Following the deaths of Aleksei Shchusev and Viktor Vesnin, the Council of Ministers decreed that memorial plaques be affixed to the architects' most important constructions.[113] As mentioned, the Committee for Architectural Affairs even discussed widening and regularizing the procedure. Not only did it suggest that memorial plaques be affixed to major Soviet buildings immediately at their unveiling, architects were to compose their own text for the plaque (this initiative eventually stalled).[114]

Importantly, however, the authorities made the prospect of going down in history conditional on high-quality work. After all, monuments were permanent; because of sunk expenses, any imperfections would be conserved for centuries. A 1946 resolution of the Union of Soviet Architects exhorted: "the Soviet architect should remember that each of his works is not only a part of his personal artistic portfolio, but is above all a part of the Soviet construction project, into which are invested the resources and efforts of the whole people, and that every architectural mistake, executed in concrete and stone, is almost impossible to fix."[115] Similarly, as one representative of the Committee for Arts Affairs explained, sculptural "monuments are made of durable materials and are intended to last many decades and centuries." A monument cannot be simply "replaced by a better one" if it turns out to be poor, and "that is why . . . we are so careful and so highly critical toward each entry."[116] Evidently, such logic even extended to easel art. Lansere, for instance, lamented that despite "its tastelessness and provincialism," even something as seemingly ephemeral as Vasilii Iakovlev's painting *General Zhukov on Horseback* would be preserved as a "typical [work] of our time [because . . .] its durable execution [*dobrotnost'*] ensures that it will not be thrown into the trash."[117] Such admonitions remained a constant feature of interactions between the regime and art professionals. An early 1947 report of the Ministry of State Audits, which criticized the state of artistic production, reaffirmed that monument construction "requires of artists a deep appreciation and understanding of their responsibility before the people, before history."[118]

Furthermore, because of their profound effects on canon formation and on future ensembles, monuments could also jeopardize future developments. Thus, an opponent of Iofan's Palace of the Soviets design, the artist Boris Chernyshev, warned in 1934 that "in the case of [the design's] implementation, it will leave a heavy mark on all architecture and art in the coming years."[119] To be sure, the approval of monumental constructions was heavily curated by the regime, and the Stalinist artistic canon was malleable enough to accommodate retroactive exclusions (once again, at the behest of the political authorities). In this context, exhortations to higher quality acted as a subtle reminder that the regime had the ultimate power to decide whether given monuments (and their creators' names) would go down in history.

Nevertheless, the idea that permanent monuments demanded higher quality was itself coopted by artists and architects and was used to criticize the works of their colleagues in the competitive environment of Stalinist art production. At a meeting discussing Moscow's wartime exhibition *Heroic Front and Rearguard*, Merkurov decried the majority of works as mediocre and able to "serve history only as auxiliary material for major works in the future."[120] Merkurov applied the same logic in explaining why Iofan should not take offence at criticism of his postwar plans for the reconstruction of the Vakhtangov Theater. It is important to ensure that people a century later would stop at the sight of the building and praise the work of the architect, Merkurov explained, "and that they may pause and say—what a fine fellow—that is why we must criticize [Iofan]."[121] At an early 1949 meeting of Moscow's Architectural Council discussing V. Duvidzon's design of a residential building, the chairman and chief architect of Moscow was merciless: "We are not allowed to make architectural and planning mistakes . . . The building should stand for centuries, for no one gave us the right to construct buildings which, by their architecture, become outdated . . . We would like to leave this meeting having endorsed your design [but] I would have to present [it] to the Executive Committee of the Moscow City Soviet, to defend it as a project of high Soviet architectural quality, as a building that will stand for centuries. I'm sure that if I do that, they'll turn their backs on me."[122]

Artists and architects also appealed to posterity in their strategic negotiations with political patrons for commissions, superior resources, and additional time. Thus, for instance, the artist Evgenii Katsman, petitioning Voroshilov to paint Stalin from life, argued that he "[is waiting] for those hours when we can do the kind of work that our contemporaries and descendants will be grateful for." Similarly, members of the Moscow Union of Soviet Sculptors and Artists lobbied Voroshilov for permission to take sketches of Kirov at his funeral, arguing that the "immortalization in the fine arts of S. M. Kirov's memory is indispensable."[123] Monument builders also presented their enduring works as a more economical use of limited resources. Deineka recommended that the funds spent on ephemeral outdoor decorations for mass festivities could instead "be used more rationally and seriously if they were directed toward creation of outdoor frescoes executed in durable materials"—of which he, uncoincidentally, was the foremost practitioner.[124] At other points, in lobbying for extra resources, artists could benefit from reframing their work as a monument. Worrying about her languishing Worker and Kolkhoz Woman statue (which was hastily reassembled after its return from the 1937 Paris World Fair), Mukhina considered suggesting that a new, suitably large pedestal be built for it as a monument to the constitution of 1936, its text engraved in steel lettering.[125] Finally, when pressed for timely fulfillment of production plans, artists could counter by appealing to the importance of "getting it right" in compositions built for the centuries. This was precisely the argument that architect Iakov Kornfel'd advanced when questioning the authorities' demands to complete the interior decoration of the Palace of Soviets by the end of the Third Five-Year Plan.[126]

Thus, artists and architects understood the importance of monument building to regime leaders, and this informed the ways in which they criticized the work of their competitors and demanded commissions. But the authorities knew that art professionals were also hardly immune to the desire for fame everlasting. Perdurable monuments could immortalize their creators, influence the formation of the Soviet artistic canon, and determine the development of future ensembles. The regime presented the opportunity to participate in the monument-construction program as a gift, but one contingent on high-quality artistic output.

Clearly, then, the Stalinist monument building cannot be reduced to the political aims of the regime. To be sure, the politics of immortalization were inseparable from the regime's goals and vision, although it was also negotiated and instrumentalized by other actors, which neo-totalitarian approaches largely sideline. Crucially, the cultural value of being remembered, shared by regime leaders, the public, and art professionals, was the fundamental precondition to these political dynamics—and it remained fundamentally uncontested. The striving to be remembered informed authorities' use of monuments as symbolic incentives and as tribute to their superiors, it generated public support for official monuments and drove grassroots monument construction, and it structured art professionals' negotiations with the regime. The drive to be remembered was therefore not specific to official Stalinist ideology (nor, indeed, directly related to regime support), but was a broadly based and more universal cultural value.

CHAPTER 5

The Cultural Foundations of Stalinist Monument Building

What conditions made self-commemoration a central cultural value of the era, and what does this reveal about the temporal culture of Stalinism? Throughout the period, the regime ascribed the striving to immortalize the epoch to the confidence of the Soviet people, allegedly unshakeable after the successes of the "Great Break" and the passing of the so-called Constitution of Victorious Socialism (*Konstitutsiia pobedivshego sotsializma*) in 1936. Implicitly invoking Stalin's famous proclamation that "life has become better; life has become more joyous," Vera Mukhina set out the official position. Soviet art was "the art of popular happiness": "the people has triumphed and wants to immortalize its deeds."[1] But more specifically, the regime and its representatives framed the vast monument-building program as the popular celebration of newfound national power. As the wartime head of the Committee for Architectural Affairs Arkadii Mordvinov proclaimed, monumental architecture "was always expressive of the dignity, strength and greatness of the state." "In the most progressive historic periods, the need of great individuals to express in the eternal forms of architecture their deeds, the dignity of the people and the state ... was especially strong," he explained.[2] The unspoken argument was that rapidly expanding Soviet power could not but fashion great monuments to itself.

Such posturing is still taken at face value by some scholars, who claim that confidence in "the uncontested importance of their times [was] understood as the right to project their present values into [the] future," that Stalinist monuments expressed "such positive feelings as pride in one's country, people, and its great achievements," and revealed "mass culture's unshakable optimism, exploited by Stalinist propaganda, but not born of it."[3] To be sure, treating the yearning to be remembered as an expression of confidence and belief in one's uniqueness is not without precedent. Over a century ago, sociologist Charles Horton Cooley interpreted the desire for the "appreciation of posterity [. . . as] simply a larger form of personal ambition [. . . reflecting] the need to associate ourselves with some enduring reality, raised above the accidents of time." As he explained, "all of us would regard it as the mark of a superior mind to wish to *be* something of imperishable worth, but social beings as we are, we can hardly separate this wish from that for social recognition of the worth."[4] Yet the confidence of Stalinist culture cannot be inferred merely from the bombastic character of its monuments and the political slogans through which the regime framed their interpretation. If anything, genuine joyousness and triumphalism appear improbable against the actual record of the Stalin period, which buffeted society from one crisis to the next.

Rather, the culture of self-commemoration was compensatory, and masked widespread disillusion in the possibilities of tomorrow. Underlying anxieties lurked behind the enormous efforts to submit idealized self-representations to the judgment of posterity. In fact, it was in this imaginary audience that the meaning and significance of the culture of immortalization was to be found. The yearning to be remembered was a constitutive part of a larger fantasy of an enduring *national collective*, the stability and identity of which would be anchored in intergenerational memory. As sociologist Anthony Smith observes, the idea of "persisting [national] communities" is in large part dependent on the supposedly "indissoluble links [formed by] a chain of [generational] memories," which "stretch back into the mists of obscure generations of ancestors and forward into the equally unknowable generations of descendants."[5] In the context of declining utopian hopes, the fantasy of enduring nationhood responded to unresolved anxieties surrounding the future, including those stemming from the social dislocations of forced-pace modernization and the trauma of the devastating Great Patriotic War.

To be sure, the Stalinist regime never endorsed nationalism as such, being constrained by enduring elements of Bolshevik political culture, which had long attacked the former as "false consciousness." Nonetheless, just as official discourse deftly referred to the people (*narod*) rather than the nation (*natsiia*) (even as the two became semantically indistinguishable), vaguely defined notions of posterity and future generations acted as euphemisms for referring to the national future. While in theory, these terms could have referred to other forms of biosocial collectives, they acquired a definite national character in this period: posterity was never described as a supranational, liberated proletariat living under communism. Rather, as demonstrated in chapter 2, monument builders envisioned a distinctly *national* posterity (and drew upon the respective aesthetic vocabularies of Soviet ethnicities, which were expected to endure). In so doing, these artists displayed a keen sense of the political winds: throughout the period, Stalinist ideologues pushed traditional Marxist expectations of the inevitable "fusion of nations" to an increasingly distant timeframe.[6] Furthermore, the opacity with which posterity was conceptualized was likely intentional. Stalinist culture never adequately resolved the tensions in cultivating pan-Soviet, Russian, and minority identities all at once. By its very ambiguity, the concept of posterity allowed these multiple national visions to work in parallel, resonating with whichever meaning a given subject wished to see in it.

Posterity was not the only component of the rising national imagination, which, in fact, was supported by *both* retrospective and prospective memorialization, structured in a mutually reinforcing way. To date, theorists of nationalism—including Smith—and historians of Stalinism alike have focused almost exclusively on the uses of the imagined *past* in constructing national consciousness. Accordingly, these scholars documented a remarkable "return of the past" throughout the Stalin period—an upsurge in commemorative discourses, activities, and practices—that undergirded the progressive revival of Great Russian and pan-Soviet nationalism. Indeed, from the mid-1930s, the regime committed significant resources to mass celebrations of national histories (such as the 1937 centenary of Aleksandr Pushkin's death), patriotic historical films (for instance, Sergei Eisenstein's *Aleksandr Nevskii*), hagiographic novels (such as Aleksei Tolstoi's *Peter the Great*), and other initiatives.[7] However, in neglecting the role of prospective memory (the immortalization of the present for a future audience), such accounts are not only incomplete, but risk misinterpreting key aspects of retrospective commemoration. Given the pronounced futural dimensions of self-commemoration, the Stalinist fascination with history hardly constituted a genuine, reactionary "retreat," as Nicholas Timasheff originally argued.[8] Neither were the expanded horizons of the usable past merely employed in the service of the Bolshevik project of building communism (as the neo-traditionalist school suggests). In fact, commemoration of the past *joined* with immortalizing the Stalin era to sustain a new, nationalized vision of the future, which revolved around the hope of national survival. Only through self-commemoration could the Stalinist memory regime complete the intergenerational chain of memory, assuring individuals that their community possessed not only an ancient past, but also a limitless future: a future in which collective identity would live on through perpetual remembrance.

Commemoration of the past, in turn, was critical for reinforcing the hope of immortalization: that the Stalin era would not be forgotten, that future generations would continue to look back to it with reverence and adulation. Retrospective commemoration acted as the concrete demonstration and assurance that hopes of continuity and endurance were not unfounded, that canonized histories do remain stable and survive the centuries. As the sociologist Zygmunt Bauman observes, the "hope of transcending the present and stretching it into the future can be rooted only in making the past last. That hope lies behind the constant temptation to retrieve the past, never to let it out of living memory—as if to demonstrate in such a roundabout way the non-transience of things."[9] Thus, it is no accident that Stalinist immortalization decrees, which institutionally guaranteed perpetual remembrance, covered both contemporary and historical subjects. Yet particularly evocative of this mutually reinforcing relationship was the progressive insertion of Stalinist monuments into the heritage preservation regime (itself strengthened throughout the period), which gave assurance that contemporary prospective monuments would be preserved, just as those of bygone days.

Soviet preservation efforts can be traced to 1918, but understandings of heritage did not originally encompass recently constructed monuments. Plagued by underfunding and disorganization, responsible organizations were hardly able to manage protecting the heritage of the past. However, true to the general turn to self-commemoration, with the creation of the intergovernmental Committee on the Protection of Revolutionary, Cultural, and Artistic Heritage in 1932, "monuments of the revolution" also became eligible for protection. Significantly, this open-ended category expanded preservationists' potential remit to certain newly built objects, such as memorial plaques commemorating revolutionary events, and the sculptural and graveside monuments of Bolshevik cultural and political notables (including those currently alive and active).[10] Nonetheless, care for these heritage objects remained sporadic: one 1936 memo estimated that the committee was able to monitor only 10 percent of the 1,200 objects within its purview, these being located mainly in Moscow and Leningrad.[11] In consequence to its poor performance, the Committee on the Protection of Revolutionary, Cultural, and Artistic Heritage was disbanded in 1938, its functions transferred to the republican-level subsidiaries of the Committee for Arts Affairs.

With the onset of the Great Patriotic War, however, the preservation of both historical and contemporary monuments became a concerted policy. This growing attention to heritage—doubtless prompted by the unparalleled and often irreversible destruction—was also supplemented by its conceptual broadening. Early 1942 saw the establishment of a Group for the Protection of Revolutionary, Historical, and Artistic Heritage, under the auspices of the Museum and Local-Historical Section of the Commissariat of Enlightenment. Among other initiatives, this organization ordered local offices of the commissariat to register and protect newly constructed graveside monuments, as well as to place memorial plaques on battlefields and significant buildings in the rearguard.[12]

Stalinist monuments became fully integrated into the national heritage preservation regime through the October 14, 1948 decree of the Council of Ministers "On measures ameliorating the protection of cultural heritage." This decree established clear lines of responsibility, and affirmed that contemporary monuments were to come under the revamped protection regime. This included "buildings and places connected with the most important historical events in the life of the peoples of the USSR, the revolutionary movement, civil and Great Patriotic wars, and socialist construction; monuments of memorial significance related to the life and work of outstanding state and political figures, popular heroes and famous figures in science, art and technology, their graveside monuments; monuments of the history of technology, military affairs, economy, and everyday life." Also eligible for protection were public buildings, parks, triumphal arches, and bridges.[13] The decree ordered the registration of all protected heritage by the end of 1949, set up restoration workshops and a special council on preservation and restoration at the USSR Academy of Science, and legally required republican governments to spend money on heritage.[14] Individuals and organizations threatening heritage would be liable to criminal prosecution and fines.[15] According to the follow-up January 13, 1949 decree of the Committee for Arts Affairs, only organizations and persons approved by the committee would be allowed to restore heritage, thereby preventing unqualified personnel from making "improvements."[16]

These developments touched off a wave of activity. In mid-1951, the RSFSR draft heritage protection list numbered 152 monuments of republic-level importance, which included all "monuments constructed by decree of the Council of Ministers of the USSR, busts of two-time recipients of the "Hero of the Soviet Union" award, as well as other highly artistic monuments."[17] While the RSFSR and Union-wide lists of protected heritage were not approved until the post-Stalin period (possibly due to their incessant updating), the regime already began to function at the local level. By the end of 1949, for example, local officials in Moscow had registered sixty-three sculptural monuments. Some of these they assigned directly to parent organizations that would be responsible for their upkeep: for instance, the Triumph of Victory bridge-side monument was entrusted to the Gormostekspluatatsiia enterprise (which was in charge of all municipal bridge maintenance).[18] After all, due to their less-than-perfect construction, some contemporary monuments required restoration already in the postwar period. For instance, the bronze Maksim Gor'kii monument, which in 1951 crowned the fifteen-year-long architectural reconstruction of Moscow's Belorusskaia train station square, underwent cleaning, crack-filling, and rewelding of seams from 1953 to 1954.[19] Altogether, by the early 1950s, twenty-two restoration workshops had been created Union-wide, restoring more than 1,500 objects at the cost of around 600 million rubles.[20]

Stalinist restorative work often involved rebuilding impermanent monuments anew, in durable materials. Many wartime monuments, hastily completed in wood, plaster, cement, and other temporary materials, were demolished in the postwar period and immediately rebuilt to last indefinitely; these included the above-mentioned Triumph of Victory bridge-side monument in Moscow, obelisks in Kerch and Chernovtsy, the triumphal Victory Arch in Baku, and others.[21] Concomitantly, wooden graveside markers were replaced with those made of stone.[22] In some sense, this was a fulfillment of original wartime aspirations, which were frustrated by the lack of resources. But this process eventually widened to encompass prewar monuments as well: for instance, Sergei Merkurov's ferroconcrete Stalin monument at the *All-Union Agricultural Exhibition* was slated for replacement with a bronze one, as was the Monument to the Defenders of the Perekop in Crimea.[23] Monuments of the more distant past were also candidates for such radical approaches to ensuring preservation. For instance, in 1948, head of the Moscow party committee and chairman of the city Soviet's executive committee Georgii Popov lobbied for the Kremlin's brick walls to be rebuilt in red granite, which would be "capable of standing for centuries."[24]

Care for monuments of the past thereby played a vital role in supporting fantasies of posterity's perpetual remembrance of the Stalin era. The strengthened and expanded heritage regime provided assurance that contemporary monuments would indeed outlast the ages. The inscription of Soviet monuments into the heritage protection regime also altered the character of historical preservation, giving it a decidedly future-oriented vector. Heritage—historical and contemporary—was to be stewarded and preserved for future generations as a key guarantor of the intergenerational chain of memory. This memory chain encompassed both past and present, and undergirded the fantasy of an enduring national collective. In the Stalinist period, this fantasy became increasingly important for alleviating acute anxieties about the future, a dynamic particularly evident in relation to the extreme social dislocations induced by forced-pace modernization, and the trauma of the Great Patriotic War. Extant theoretical and historical scholarship connects the rise of nationalism—and national commemoration—to these contexts, but neglects the vital role played by prospective memorialization. But as in the case of heritage preservation dynamics, retrospective and prospective memorialization were complementary, and together upheld the vision of enduring nationhood, at a time when utopian expectations of social progress appeared increasingly untenable.

Russia had suffered the cultural stresses of rapid modernization from the late nineteenth century, but Stalinist social engineering increased their severity to the breaking point. Breakneck industrialization, Cultural Revolution, forced collectivization, and mass purges induced social dislocations on an unprecedented scale. These involved colossal demographic shifts. Reeling from the collectivization disaster, and drawn by the precipitous expansion of heavy industry, tens of millions of peasants left the countryside to labor in the rapidly expanding cities. Between 1928 and 1932 alone, the number of urbanites increased by 44 percent (a situation even more pronounced in Moscow and other major cities). This produced what Richard Stites calls "a giant urban trauma," characterized by overcrowding, unsanitary conditions, and a lack of basic social services.[25] The authorities responded frantically with radical reconstruction programs, which saw entire neighborhoods raised to make way for new factories, domiciles, and infrastructure. Yet the need to convert traditional peasants into disciplined workers demanded an equally far-reaching program of cultural transformation. Empowered by a ballooning ideological and repressive apparatus, the regime launched a frontal assault on traditional cultural patterns, institutions, and values. Family, religion, language, and "personal" habits (no longer viewed as personal) all became targets of a fundamental and violent reconstitution, in line with regime policies.

Those embracing change were buoyed upward by rapid social mobility, yet new, "solid" cultural coordinates were slow in the making. Because the regime demanded constant readjustments to its latest visions, Stalinist ideology could not integrate society effectively.[26] Mass repression—which targeted categories of those deemed resistant to the regime's social engineering projects—further exacerbated feelings of uncertainty and insecurity. This period is captured well in Moshe Lewin's concept of "quicksand society": one in which "social, administrative, industrial, and political structures were all in flux."[27] Not only were individuals unmoored from their traditional social milieu, the future promised an unabating whirlwind of change: even if detached from their original utopian impulse after 1931, the pace of the regime's modernization projects did not slow significantly.

Many experienced these changes pathologically; anomie, disorientation, and social alienation were widespread. In this context, individuals sought out assurances of constancy and stability. Even Stalin's *vydvizhentsy*, the "upwardly mobile segments of the population, wanted . . . structure [and] permanence."[28] These dynamics largely reproduced the situation which accompanied modernizing processes in the nineteenth-century West, in the course of which, as Aleida

Assmann explains, change "produce[d] a state of crisis, because longer-term security [became] lost when expectation [was] cut off from experience."[29] However, as elsewhere, the identities and social relationships of the ancien régime, whose breakdown was precipitated by Stalinist industrialization, were replaced by a rising national imaginary. As Ernest Gellner argues, "the alienated victims of early industrialism," those "illiterate, half-starved populations sucked from their erstwhile rural cultural ghettoes into the melting pots of shanty-towns[,] yearn[ed] for incorporation into [a] cultural [pool]" in which they might acquire "full cultural citizenship."[30] This cultural pool was almost always the imagined national community, and the Stalinist Soviet Union was no exception.

Amid the breakdown of traditional identities and relationships, and the ever-accelerating pace of change, the national imagination provided a way of anchoring identity and fostering a stable community among atomized individuals.[31] But this dynamic was predicated on the impression that this new collective was indeed stable and solid (indeed, the only truly solid one) in the face of pervasive change and liquefaction (to borrow Bauman's famous metaphor).[32] It is largely for this reason that the nation, as Karl Deutsch posits, "offer[ed] to most of its members a stronger sense of security, belonging, or affiliation, and even personal identity, than [did] any alternative large group. The greater the need of the people for such affiliation and identity under the strains and shocks of social mobilization and alienation from earlier familiar environments, the greater [became] the potential power of the nation-state to channel both their longings and resentments."[33] Thus, in late 1937, against the backdrop of further dislocations induced by the "Great Terror," Stalin personally affirmed the transcendental character of the nation, asserting that "only the people are eternal[,] all else is transient."[34]

The nation's ancient pedigree provided assurance of its stability even in the face of modernization. It is no accident, therefore, that in the West, elaborate national histories and "invented traditions" rose to prominence in the wake of the social transformations induced by industrialization in the nineteenth century.[35] Although scholarship on Stalinist nation building and commemoration almost always assumes a top-down perspective (focusing on the mobilizing and legitimating qualities of nationalism, in the service of regime goals), this social function—which made the national imagination attractive to Soviet citizens—comes through in some accounts. David Brandenberger demonstrates that already in the early to mid-1930s, mass culture was overtaken by a wave of populist Soviet patriotism, which saw an increasing identification based on collective belonging rather than class. In this context, he suggests, the "celebration of patriotism and its official pantheon of heroes provid[ed] a higher goal, an ideological code of honor, and a sense of belonging to offset the hardship and discontent" of industrialization and collectivization.[36] Likewise, James von Geldern notes the public's enthusiasm for prerevolutionary cultural figures as "bearer[s] of their own culture and language," allowing individuals to "[find] comfort in continuities and ignor[e] the discontinuities that were quite striking after two decades of Soviet rule."[37]

The national past helped foster a sense of continuity and stability, yet it did so only indirectly: glorious histories could only *imply* the survival of the nation in the increasingly uncertain future. The hope of prospective memory, by contrast, assured that the national collective would always retain its character and identity. Even though the world would change, perhaps unrecognizably, generations would remain linked by a chain of memory stretching out for centuries (*veka*), as the very term *uvekovechenie* ("immortalization") implied. Through immortalization, Soviet individuals could thereby communicate and commune with an imagined posterity, joining an enduring, stable national collective—a solid bulwark in a world of violent flux, and one which rendered the future safer and more familiar. This fantasy required materialization, and durable-looking monuments became the principal anchor for such yearnings. Aside from their purported ability to speak to future generations, monuments' structural solidity contrasted markedly with ephemeral, mass-produced consumables, temporary constructions, and other transitory artefacts of the newly industrialized society.[38] As philosopher Henri Lefebvre points out, durability made monuments appear "to have escaped time [...] transmuting] the fear of the passage of time [...into] splendor."[39] In the context of accelerating social transformations and the breakdown of tradition, monuments imbued a "sense of continuity" "[buttressing] identity" in an effort to "stop time, inhibit forgetting, [and] fix a state of things."[40]

Unsurprisingly, while the Stalinist regime demanded that its monuments be genuinely permanent, it also insisted that this quality be showcased aesthetically. Anatolii Lunacharskii signaled this requirement from the outset in his commentary on the Palace of the Soviets' design, which, he argued, "should express the idea of solidity and stability . . . it should proclaim 'I exist', 'I stand.'"[41] Later, the art historian Aleksandr Gabrichevskii elaborated that all monuments must "*express* the idea of permanence, above all in the choice of material, which must not only be actually durable . . . but must '*show*', must *symbolize* this durability."[42] Permanent monuments thereby acted as zones of exception in a rapidly changing built environment. It was precisely the flux of the Stalinist social order—not any pretentions to timelessness, as some scholars hold—that rendered monuments so culturally important, as anchors of a limited sense of continuity that the fantasy of an enduring national collective offered.

Previously, utopianism had presented an alternative way of addressing the anxieties associated with the social dislocations of modernization. In fact, powerful Russian utopian currents had grown out of an *opposition* to the changes induced by industrialization in the late nineteenth century. In some sense, important elements of Bolshevik culture were party to this antimodern disposition. After all, the utopia to which Bolshevik strivings were directed was fundamentally conceived of as static and unchanging, an everlasting reign of peace and plenty. At their most extreme, the revolutionaries expected an immediate, millenarian "end-time" rupture.[43] As Joan Platt writes, this outlook "reject[ed] transience fundamentally, either as a flaw in the architecture of creation or in our perception of it," instead yearning "for time to halt in a single, violent rupture, restoring or revealing an eternal order of pure forms."[44]

As the revolution failed to deliver on these expectations, Soviet utopianism turned to embrace the ever-increasing tempo of socialist modernization, in the hopes that the promised land would be reached by evolutionary progress. The counterintuitive, paradoxical character of this strategy should not obscure its ultimate aims. In this vein, for instance, the early avant-garde "aspired to resurrect by technological means the wholeness of God's world that had been disrupted by technology; to halt technological progress and the march of history in general by placing it under complete technological control; to conquer time and enter into eternity."[45] If Bolshevik utopian currents embraced social and technological modernization, it was only in the hope of foreshortening the path to the final resolution of these pathologies, including the ever-accelerating pace of change. Utopia would forge the cultural "solids" that would overcome anomie once and for all. Yet by the early 1930s, these long-frustrated hopes gave way to the culture of self-commemoration.

The fantasy of enduring nationhood, embodied in an intergenerational chain of memory, not only grounded unstable identities in a transcendental community. It also alleviated anxieties about the future in the context of the trauma and devastation of the Great Patriotic War. In a narrow sense, immortalization assured that fallen servicemen would live on in collective memory, embodying the hope of "symbolic immortality."[46] Yet individual immortalization was only the microcosm of a greater fantasy: that of national survival, which was rendered increasingly tenuous by the trauma of war. It was the resonance of this hope that gave impetus to massive and spontaneous public involvement in wartime monument building—the most vivid instance of widespread support for the culture of self-commemoration. In this context, monuments not only secured individuals' posthumous life in posterity's memory. Immortalization implied that there would be a posterity to do the remembering as such, thereby acting as an assurance of national endurance. As Lisa Kirschenbaum observes, "commemoration, after all, usually assumes an 'after.'"[47]

This dynamic explains why popular monument designs were often dreamed up in the harshest, most anxiety-ridden stages of the war. One unsolicited victory monument proposal, which reached Stalin in early 1947, recounted: "the idea of creating this monument came to us back in 1942, during the winter blockade of Leningrad, when we wore military uniform, and ... on the verge of death by starvation and enemy bombardments, dreamed of bright, happy days of victory."[48] The regime immediately recognized the benefit of such fantasies for morale, and attempted to harness popular enthusiasm for monument building. In the most difficult years of the war, and even as actual monument construction lagged, the regime insisted that its art professionals continue to reflect on the theory of monumentalism and develop designs for memorials. As early as 1942, the resolution of the X Plenum of the Union of Soviet Architects called for the "development of theoretical questions [including those concerning] the reflection of images of the Great Patriotic War in monumental art," and encouraged local authorities to sponsor monument competitions.[49] The 1943 Committee for Arts Affairs and Union of Soviet Architects joint circular (*tsirkuliarnoe pis'mo*) called for "the design of monuments to the Heroes of the Patriotic War, the organization of comradely and open competitions on this topic, a broad discussion of the draft designs, the study of compositional issues associated with the construction of monuments, and the organization of cooperation between architects and sculptors in this matter."[50] Concomitantly, the Academy of Architecture assigned the development of war monuments to its research institutes, design workshops, and graduate students.[51]

Ultimately, these institutions organized a series of morale-boosting monument design competitions. The first of these was held in 1942, the most difficult year of the war, in the course of which the Moscow and Leningrad branches of the Union of Soviet Architects, as well as the Academy of Architecture, independently launched competitions for monuments to the Great Patriotic War.[52] Late that year, the Committee for Arts Affairs and Union of Soviet Architects opened another Union-wide design competition. Many of these were extensively covered in the press and profiled at exhibitions.[53] Clearly, submitted designs were never meant to be realized (revealingly, competitions placed no restrictions on the resources that designers could commandeer).[54] Yet it was not the case, as Alexei Tarkhanov and Sergei Kavtaradze suggest, that because "the designs were never intended to be built ... their creators were victims of a cynical deception."[55] Undoubtedly, these competitions performed an important instrumental function: imagining posterity's remembrance shored up the fantasy of national survival. But such fantasies were spontaneous; by supporting research into monumentalism and hosting design competitions, the regime merely encouraged and institutionalized them.

This conclusion furthers existing accounts of the sources and expressions of wartime nationalism. Historians have long noted the veritable explosion of patriotic themes in Soviet wartime propaganda, and the revival of prerevolutionary national symbols (especially those derived from the Russian military tradition). Indeed, within only a few months of the German invasion, Stalin's speech on the anniversary of the October Revolution authoritatively signaled the official rehabilitation of Russian national history. "May the courageous example of our great ancestors—Aleksandr Nevskii, Dimitri Donskoi, Kuz'ma Minin, Dmitrii Pozharskii, Aleksandr Suvorov, Mikhail Kutuzov—inspire you in this war!" he proclaimed.[56] Henceforth, the celebration of these and other heroes of the national past (many of whom Bolsheviks had once condemned as reactionaries and imperialists) became a staple of wartime propaganda. Eventually, the pantheon of past heroes came to include representatives of other Soviet nations.[57]

Typically, scholars such as David Brandenberger ascribe the cultivation of national past(s) to the regime's pragmatic realization that the Soviet public was more receptive to nationalist propaganda, in contrast to the limited mobilizational capacities of far-removed Bolshevik abstractions.[58] This argument is convincing, but neglects the question of *why* the war critically boosted the attractiveness of the national imagination. To be sure, comparative studies note the unifying effects of external military threats, and the mass mobilization required to counter them, as conducive to the development of national consciousness.[59] But appreciating the temporal culture of nationalism (not only its relationship to the past, but also to the future) reveals an additional way in which it commanded a special appeal in wartime conditions. The chain of memory that linked generations past, present, and future promised that the nation was truly an enduring collective. The national imagination thereby offered a future-oriented, hope-filled fantasy of collective survival and victory. It was on this facet, in part, that the superior mobilizing potential of wartime nationalism rested, in the Soviet context and, as the next chapter reveals, elsewhere.

The appeal of this fantasy did not abate immediately with victory. Despite the regime's posturing, wartime traumas were not easily forgotten, and the gathering storm clouds of a new Cold War (which threatened to turn nuclear) provided fertile ground for the persisting resonance of self-commemorative practices. However, the regime increasingly recognized that monuments also drew attention to the very anxieties for which they compensated. Ubiquitous war memorials demonstrated the true scale of wartime destruction, undercutting the regime's triumphalist war myth. Graves and graveyards especially threatened to overawe viewers with the spectacular loss of life, belying the official count that pegged wartime losses at a mere seven million (at least four times fewer than contemporary estimates).[60] These considerations probably contributed to the low priority accorded to the preservation and care for military monuments, attested to in various internal memos.[61] For instance, according to an early 1949 report prepared by the Main Political Directorate of the Soviet army, in the Leningrad military district alone, 277 of 394 monuments required urgent repairs and restoration.[62]

These drawbacks did not, on the whole, dampen the monument-building drive. However, they did affect the character of postwar Stalinist monumentalism. Officials increasingly demanded that monuments exude an unequivocally optimistic and triumphant character.[63] At a 1944 meeting of Moscow's Architectural-Planning Commission, the city's chief architect Dmitrii Chechulin opposed the "Egyptian" motifs of Pavel Abrosimov and Boris Iofan's design for a reconstructed Vakhtangov Theater, which he took to be excessively sepulchral and gloomy. Exclaiming in exasperation: "Enough graves! They are always shooting, killing. Graves are everywhere," Chechulin clarified that the Soviet people "want to achieve a brilliant, happy life."[64] At a later meeting, members of the commission maligned the draft design of the Academy of Sciences building for recalling the Mausoleum at Halicarnassus, and Kaluzhskaia metro station's surface vestibule for resembling a "graveside monument."[65] Yet despite this attempted concealment of underlying insecurities, Stalinist monuments' stage-managed, triumphal character only underscores their fundamentally compensatory function: alleviating anxieties surrounding collective endurance in the face of a war of national survival.

In their own way, Bolshevik utopian hopes had also responded to the unprecedented carnage of the First World War and the civil war, which were not extensively commemorated but nonetheless affected public culture in important ways. Against the backdrop of mass death, the 1920s and early 1930s saw a massive research program into life prolongation and rejuvenation, including cryogenics, suspended animation, and hormone therapy.[66] Some of the more colorful experiments involved attempts at hybridizing humans and apes, and using pregnant women's urine (*Gravidan*) for rejuvenation (notable patients included Maksim Gor'kii and Politburo member Valerian Kuibyshev).[67] Importantly, individual physical immortality was not the sole objective of this utopian project. Key cultural and political elites of the 1920s (including Lunacharskii and People's Commissar for Foreign Trade Leonid Krasin, the poet Vladimir Maiakovskii, the writers Gor'kii and Andrei Platonov, the leader of the *Proletkult* cultural movement Aleksandr Bogdanov, the architect Konstantin Mel'nikov, and the Marxist historian Mikhail Pokrovskii), were strongly influenced by the mystical philosophy of Nikolai Fedorov (1829–1903). For Fedorov, attaining individual immortality (and, eventually, bodily resurrection) through scientific means was ultimately significant in asserting humanity's domination of nature and guaranteeing its indefinite collective survival.[68] The postrevolutionary decade also saw Taylorist activists of the "League of Time" working toward a mechanized, robotic, supra-individual collective, whose eternal self-propagation would render individual death meaningless.[69] A similar ethos was expressed in the oeuvre of avant-garde painters like Aleksandr Deineka. According to cultural historian Boris Groys, Deineka's recurring depictions of immaculate athletic bodies illustrated the "promise of . . . serialization in the communist future . . . a blueprint for future transhistorical, eternal life" by means of a succession of standardized individuals.[70]

Nevertheless, by the early 1930s, hopes for both collective immortality and an atemporal, static utopia rapidly collapsed. Recognizing the gap between such millenarian strivings and disappointing everyday realities, and wary of being held accountable to its promises, the regime did its best to quietly retire Bolshevik utopianism from public view. To be sure, official culture and its socialist realist aesthetic incarnation continued to exude a positive outlook on the future, and to nominally promise the eventual achievement of communism. But this optimism was increasingly affected and half-hearted. As demonstrated at the outset of the book, references to communism declined in political rhetoric. Descriptions of the utopian future in literature and film became increasingly hollow and ultimately disappeared entirely. After all, while attempting to buoy up confidence in the bright tomorrow, socialist realism at once reigned in "hare-brained utopianism." Effectively, rather than speculate on the shape of the world come, socialist realism demanded concreteness—a focus on immediate struggles, typically bounded by the temporal horizon of a production plan. Interpreted contextually, against the backdrop of preceding utopian archetypes, the true significance of depicting "reality in its revolutionary development" was its fundamental pivot away from the vistas of tomorrow to the embellished reality of today.

The collapse of Bolshevik utopianism stemmed not only from its official disavowal, but also from popular disillusionment. To an extent, this can be attributed to a natural fatigue in sustaining utopian energies for over a decade.[71] It is, furthermore, impossible to ignore the series of particularly severe disappointments in the wake of the First Five-Year Plan. These were triggered by the mass famine that accompanied the forced collectivization of agriculture, the mixed record of industrial achievements (which depressed the standard of living), mounting fears of war accompanying the rise of European fascism, and the gathering momentum of the regime's campaigns of terror. Even if public performances of optimism and jubilation were not entirely simulated, they were, without a doubt, fundamentally ritualistic. The composer Dmitrii Shostakovich later characterized the spirit of the times as "someone . . . beating you with a stick and saying, 'your business is rejoicing, your business is rejoicing,' and you rise, shaky and go marching off, muttering 'our business is rejoicing, our business is rejoicing.'"[72]

In a context in which this frozen rictus effectively replaced spontaneous popular utopianism, an alternate imagining of the future emerged, one primarily defined by the endurance of the nation, anchored in perpetual practices of collective remembrance. The inverse relationship between the two outlooks on the future can explain, to some degree, why the commissioning of key monumental projects often accompanied particularly severe crises, which sapped confidence in a better tomorrow. As mentioned in the book's introduction, the competitions for the Palace of the Soviets were conducted against the backdrop of the unfolding debacle of collectivization. The third, ever-more-sumptuous group of Moscow metro stations were completed throughout the early, disastrous years of the Great Patriotic War. The decision to build the eight Stalinist high-rises in Moscow was made at the height of the postwar famine (1947). As demonstrated, the construction of the intergenerational chain of memory addressed these anxieties in its own peculiar fashion. The building of prospective monuments was therefore born of fundamental fears and insecurities about the future, not a triumphant self-assurance—as both contemporaneous accounts and more recent scholarship have claimed.

This fantasy of national survival depended not only on retrospective, but also (and crucially) on prospective commemoration. Not only did this unity fashion the image of collective endurance, the two vectors were mutually reinforcing: hope in posterity's perpetual remembrance was grounded in the present generation's dutiful commemoration of the past. This alternative vision of the future was constitutive of the broader turn toward nationalism under Stalinism—and reinforces the conclusion that nationalism was not a backward-oriented retreat. This was so not only because nationalism, as neo-traditionalist scholars observe, was harnessed toward Stalinism's futural political project. As demonstrated, even on its own terms, the emerging national imaginary was inherently forward looking, despite its narrow and compensatory character.

Appreciating the cultural factors that gave rise to this nationalized outlook on the future also revises the dominant causal model accounting for Stalinism's nationalist turn. This shift was not (or, at least, not entirely) the result of top-down decision making. It cannot be reduced to Stalin's personal neo-traditional or quasi-imperialist proclivities, nor to a pragmatic wager on a mobilizing strategy "naturally" superior to Bolshevik sloganeering. Rather, the national imagination—and its vision of the future—was favored by the specific cultural context of the Stalin years: the social dislocations and trauma induced by rapid modernization and a devastating war. These circumstances, and the failure of the utopian response to them, favored an alternate culture of time, in which imaginings of the future revolved around the fantasy of an enduring nation. As the next chapter will demonstrate, this fantasy acted as a vital support at moments when progressive hopes were particularly under strain, a dynamic which helps explain similar impulses to self-commemoration beyond the borders of the Soviet Union in the wider interwar conjuncture.

CHAPTER 6

Self-Commemoration and the Interwar Culture of Time

Somewhat unexpectedly, the shift from Bolshevik utopianism to the Stalinist obsession with self-commemoration helps to illuminate broader trends in the interwar culture of time. Indeed, the striving to immortalize their times was not the sole preserve of interwar dictatorships, as neo-totalitarian accounts suggest.[1] Rather, in a darkening world beset by a systemic economic crisis, the trauma of the First World War, and the threat of its repetition, the fantasy of national endurance resonated across borders and ideological divides. By shifting the emphasis to an alternate (but fundamentally compatible) vision of the future, immortalization stabilized the temporal order of modernity at a time of widespread disillusionment with the progress narrative.

Neo-totalitarian accounts foreground the fundamental democratic deficit that underlay the vast monument-building programs in both the Stalinist Soviet Union and Nazi Germany, to which I alluded in the introduction. In both states, the narrative goes, real public necessities (such as acute housing shortages) were ignored without consequence, in favor of costly prestige projects. As Igor Golomstock summarizes, "the need of ordinary people for elementary comforts was considered by totalitarianism to be one of 'the small changing needs of everyday life' that were so insignificant before the face of eternity."[2] This position is not so much incorrect as it is heuristically limited, for it ignores the underlying *cultural* character of monument building, which responded to the *shared* striving to be remembered. Accordingly, neo-totalitarianism cannot explain why these regimes—if they built monuments *against* the popular will and in defiance of public needs—in fact took pains to *advertise* these projects.

As an example, I would like to return to the mosaics for Moscow's Novokuznetskaia metro station, which were airlifted from blockaded Leningrad in 1943, a case which Golomstock specifically refers to.[3] On first glance, the resources expended on this operation appear to convey the leadership's criminal heedlessness for the lives of civilians, starving to death in the besieged city. Indeed, the journalist and writer Il'ia Erenburg later attested to a train car full of vintage 1891 Bordeaux being "rescued" from the blockaded city.[4] What is remarkable is that unlike the case of the rescued wine (which came as a Khrushchev-era revelation), the Stalinist regime did not believe that publicizing the story of the Novokuznetskaia mosaics would generate public resentment. The feat was proudly recounted in *Pravda*, and one postwar commentary reflected: "it would seem that the difficult war that our country was waging with [fascism] would halt the construction of the metro [. . . but] the Soviet government approached this question in a different way [. . . demanding] the creation of elevated artistic ensembles that would serve as architectural monuments to the heroic era of the Great Patriotic War."[5] Indeed,

FIGURE 12. "Constructed in the days of the Great Patriotic War." This inscription graces Moscow's Paveletskaia metro station, unveiled 1943. Photograph by Mikhail Trakhman, late 1940s. "Moscow Metro underground railway" folder. Soviet Information Bureau Photograph Collection. Davis Center for Russian and Eurasian Studies Collection at H.C. Fung Library, Harvard University.

in order that this unique approach to wartime expenditure remained unforgotten, metro stations were outfitted with granite plaques proudly bearing the words "Constructed in the Days of the Great Patriotic War." Evidently, the leadership was confident that the construction of prospective monuments was sufficiently popular, and that immortalization on a grandiose scale, even among everyday deprivation, would be received favorably. Indeed, as I suggested in the previous chapter, prospective monuments appealed precisely because of popular anxieties, deprivation, and trauma. Thus, the juxtaposition of real needs to the supposed frivolity of monument building cannot be supported.

Furthermore, ignoring the sociocultural underpinnings of the drive to self-commemoration, and reducing it to high politics, allows neo-totalitarian approaches to seal off monument-building dynamics in dictatorships from similar processes in the interwar liberal democracies. In view of newer research, this analytical divide is increasingly untenable. While recognition of monuments' common prospective orientation remains fragmentary, scholars increasingly note significant transnational convergence in interwar monument construction. Edwin Heathcote, for one, goes so far as to claim that while "grand neoclassicism was almost universal during this period . . . its ultimate achievement was not to be seen in Berlin, Rome or Moscow but in Washington DC, the only major capital city which is conceived as a huge monument to a man and an ideal."[6] Of course, the question of which regime accorded greater priority to the creation of prospective monuments is difficult, if not impossible, to answer unequivocally. There is simply no metric for such comparisons: assessing the absolute volume of monument building is not productive, as each regime had its unique constraints (of both resources and time in power), limiting the realization of its aspirations. Even so, it is apparent that the mass construction of prospective monuments was a global phenomenon. As in the Stalinist Soviet Union, it largely reflected the period's changing culture of time.

As cultural historian Francois Hartog demonstrates, in the aftermath of the First World War, acute challenges faced the progressive outlook on the future. Confidence in the triumphant march of civilization was critically imperiled by the barbarity of technologized (and for this reason unprecedented) destruction and loss of life. Compounding this shock, in Western Europe and America, postwar austerity soon gave way to a full-blown, systemic economic depression. These specific problems, of course, differed from the Soviet context. There, anxieties stemmed from the social dislocations induced by forced-pace modernization, not by economic reversals. Furthermore, while the memory of the "imperialist" First World War was repressed (official discourse attempted to neutralize it as a relic of a bygone era), the Soviet public experienced the trauma of the Great Patriotic War much more painfully. Yet the underlying dynamic was the same. Faith in progress, which, as Zygmunt Bauman observes, boiled down to the "self-confidence of the present," was everywhere on the defensive.[7] In the context of "ruins, devastation, the millions of dead, the vanished, the broken generations," the "modern time regime [could not] escape unharmed," Hartog concludes.[8]

Even so, new narratives emerged, responding to these setbacks and stabilizing the progress-centered, modern order of time. Hartog identifies the notion of "revolution" as one such innovation that "rendered [the modern temporal regime] more capable of surviving through the years to come."[9] Thus, Bolsheviks, for instance, viewed crisis phenomena as a harbinger of capitalist collapse and its immanent revolutionary supersession. Even so, hope in the transformative possibilities of a Bolshevik-style revolution had declined markedly by the 1930s—and in any case had only a limited following beyond Soviet borders. I propose that the vision of national endurance, anchored in prospective commemoration, also helped stabilize the modern temporal order by (temporarily) shifting attention away from progress onto an alternative future. In this way, the turn to memory, which attempted to restore the "thread[s] of continuity," did more than *symptomatize* declining confidence in progress, as Hartog contends.[10] Rather, on account of its future-oriented character, self-commemoration *sustained* the beleaguered temporal regime of modernity at a moment of crisis.

Indeed, it is only superficially that the distance between the two visions of the future—those contained in the hopes of progress and prospective memory—appears vast. Despite their formal incongruence, both operated within the assumptions of a modern temporal culture and the linear historical model. As the case of Stalinism demonstrates, despite its frequent invocation of the past, the culture of self-commemoration preserved a fundamental orientation on the future, continuing to "danc[e] to [its] tune," the defining feature of modern temporality, in Hartog's conceptualization.[11] It was not the case, as Vladimir Paperny suggests, that "the future, having become eternity, was so homogeneous and unchanging that it was pointless even to look there."[12] To the contrary, Stalinist culture not only continued to peer into the future, in which it hoped to find a grateful posterity, but consciously manipulated the built environment to this effect. Although these interventions were directed at ensuring posterity's remembrance, not the construction of an earthly utopia, the future remained open-ended and subject to human action—another key feature of the modern temporal order, according to cultural historian Reinhardt Koselleck.[13] Even while substituting disappointed progressive expectations with the fantasy of enduring nationhood, the future remained the "locus of expectation and hope."[14]

In fact, the fantasy of enduring nationhood at no point contradicted progressivist claims, sidestepping only the promise of uninterrupted social betterment. The culture of self-commemoration did not attempt to "freeze time" or even to slow down the pace of change. It was precisely because constant, accelerating change was believed to be inevitable that limited islets of continuity assumed such pressing importance. The Stalinist regime, for one, had never let up on its ever more ambitious projects of social engineering, through to the postwar unveiling of the Stalin Plan for the Transformation of Nature (a land development megaproject). In Koselleckian terms, the culture of self-commemoration accepted "the difference which was torn open between one's own time and that of the future."[15] It was merely the normative valuation of this "difference" that had shifted fundamentally. Promises of a *better* tomorrow had less traction; the future was now viewed with suspicion, as a source of anxiety rather than succor. In response, prospective commemoration offered the fantasy of a single, limited, but enduring continuity: the perpetual national collective, whose identity would be grounded in an intergenerational "chain of memory." Thus, despite disillusionment in Bolshevik utopian promises, the culture of self-commemoration under Stalinism manifested the survival of the basic structures of the modern temporal order. This alternative imagining of the future was woven into the modern order of time, thereby sustaining it at a moment of severe strain.[16]

Dynamics in interwar liberal democracies followed a similar pattern. To be sure, the shift was not as dramatic as in the Bolshevik case: from utopian hopes to a nationalized future. Here, by contrast, the progressive outlook was embedded in the national project from the beginning. As sociologist Craig Calhoun observes, nations "provided the idea of progress with one of its primary subjects. Along with classes and individuals, nations figured as both the agents and the beneficiaries of potential progress. Progress was assessed by measuring the strength, freedom, or material well-being of nations."[17] But at the same time, the national imagination also included the belief in a nation's timelessness—"loom[ing] out of an immemorial past, and, still more important, glid[ing] into a limitless future."[18] The relationship between these two visions (progressive and ahistorical) is rarely theorized; typically, they figure as parallel or mutually supporting facets of the temporality of nationalism. For Bauman, for instance, the hope of national immortality depends upon the nation's apparent progress toward perfection.[19] Conversely, Anthony Smith treats claims of a nation's timelessness as foundational to its promises of future glories.[20] Nevertheless, the dynamics of the interwar period reveal that these two outlooks on the future did not always command equal emphasis. Rather, challenges to the progress narrative muted this aspect of the national imagination, and accordingly reinvigorated the fantasy of enduring nationhood. As in the Soviet case, the future-oriented dimensions of this latter vision were embodied in prospective memorialization and materialized in the construction of monuments for posterity.

As mentioned, the greatest shock to the progress narrative was the experience of the First World War, a cultural trauma that reverberated throughout the entire interwar period and produced an incitement to monument building. Unlike in past wars, all identifiable fallen received individual graveside markers in expansive military cemeteries, and nearly all Western European villages raised monuments to the dead. The process took the better part of two decades, and many of the largest and most famous monuments were completed only in the 1930s: Britain's Thiepval Memorial (1928–1932), France's Ossuary at Douaumont (1923–1932), Canada's National Vimy Memorial (1925–1936), and others. The three large American monuments at Château-Thierry (1926–1930), Montsec (1926–1932), and Montfaucon (1926–1934), were dedicated as late as 1937.[21] Local memorials were still being unveiled well into the second half of the decade.[22]

Such monuments expressed the hope for, and were believed to serve as the guarantee of, national endurance. As Stephen Goebel demonstrated, affirming the perpetuity of the nation, for which soldiers had ostensibly sacrificed their lives, promoted collective healing.[23] The fallen were also described as ideal citizens, whose example, inscribed in memorials for posterity's edification, "was seen as essential to solving whatever problems the future might hold for the nation."[24] As such, these monuments had a distinctly prospective character. Winston Churchill, in his capacity as War Secretary, called for monuments to be executed for "periods as remote from our own as we ourselves are from the Tudors"; General John Pershing, head of the American Battle Monuments Commission, hoped that they would "outlast time itself."[25] These aspirations were earnest, supported by extensive research and reflected in monument design. Just like their Soviet counterparts, architects and preservationists developed technical innovations including silicone-based varnishes for stonework, pluvex damp-proofing, aluminous and bituminized cement blocks (capable of withstanding corrosive soils), and selected the hardiest stone for respective geographic locales.[26] In the face of a progressive future shattered by wartime devastation, the hope of national endurance, anchored in memory, still found favor.

The trauma of a war was compounded by flagging postwar economic recovery, which finally devolved into the worldwide Great Depression. In the ensuing chaos, poverty and unemployed swelled, industries scaled back, and tensions mounted domestically and internationally. In this context, monumental constructions spoke of a stability and continuity. Art historian Barbara Miller Lane expresses a now-common view in arguing that the "resemblances among public buildings in almost every Western country during the 1930s and 1940s were . . . spurred by similar underlying political and social needs. These were depression years in every Western country. Each government felt the need to assure its citizens of its strength and durability, and each wanted a building style which was both modern and somehow old."[27] The "strength and durability" of these monuments were expressed not only in their formal qualities, but also by their widely publicized prospective mission. Importantly, however, this prospective character supported the fantasy of national endurance, rather than the stability of any given government or political order, as Miller Lane and others contend. After all, the discourse framing interwar monument-building projects gravitated to biosocial terms like "future generations" and "posterity," whether in the Stalinist Soviet Union, the fascist dictatorships, or the interwar liberal democracies. In the last instance, it was the survival of the nation, rather than the endurance of failing political systems, that was counterposed to the unravelling of progressive hopes.

As such, self-commemoration was no less culturally central in interwar liberal democracies than in the Stalinist Soviet Union, and their monument-building programs were by no means inferior in either scope or ambition. In Depression-era America, for instance, over a thousand new federal structures were constructed, doubling the building stock of the Treasury Department which formally owned them.[28] The architectural brief for many of these articulated both utilitarian and commemorative functions. Competition guidelines for Washington's Federal Reserve building, for example, explicitly called for an "architectural concept of dignity and *permanence.*"[29] Indeed, even buildings as humble as post offices were adorned with murals, which, as Marlene Park and Gerald Markowitz demonstrate, were to "record American beliefs for future generations or civilizations, just as the pyramids had done for the ancient Egyptians . . . murals [being] the most public and permanent form of paintings."[30] Neither were American monument builders strangers to gargantuan dimensions. The National Gallery of Art (1937–1941) was unveiled as the largest marble-faced edifice in the world; the Pentagon (1941–1943), slated to eventually house the national archives, as the largest office building. Supported by federal funding, the granite Mount Rushmore in South Dakota (1927–1941) was carved into a national monument of colossal size.[31]

Mass media presented New Deal infrastructure projects as monuments of near-apocalyptic significance. The Hoover (Boulder) Dam (1931–1936), then the tallest and most powerful in the world, was consciously fashioned as a synthetic monument, adorned with numerous sculptures and reliefs. These included an enormous star map which indicated the *precise* astronomical date and time of the dam's unveiling (along with the dates of the Biblical exodus and the birth of Jesus Christ), for the edification of "visitors from century to century," in the words of its sculptor Oskar J. W. Hansen.[32] Newspapers feted the dam in rhetorical flourishes that could easily have been lifted from Stalinist official pronouncements: "a monument to the will of the people," and "a gigantic monument to American energy." Articles mused over what "countless thousands of years [later . . .] a strange race of men [would] glean from the mighty dam."[33] Racked by the trauma of war and in the throes of economic crisis, ebbing progressive hopes gave way to a greater emphasis on national endurance, materialized in the extensive construction of prospective monuments.

The situation in Nazi Germany (and other fascist states) was more complex, but in certain respects also conformed to this pattern. From the late nineteenth century, the experience of rapid and extensive industrialization fomented extreme nationalist tendencies in German political culture.[34] These were further radicalized by the devastating experience of war, political uncertainty, and economic austerity, culminating in a full-blown economic crisis that catapulted the Nazis to power. Generally, fascist ideology foregrounded deep national continuities at the expense of progressive visions. Even so, in its rejection of the "degenerate" past, its fetishism of technology, its drive to create a "new man," and its faith in the radical possibilities of social engineering, fascism bore more than a passive resemblance to early Bolshevik utopianism. It is due to such revolutionary impulses that scholars increasingly characterize fascism as a fundamentally modernist movement, even if "reactionary," "rooted," or "organic." Fundamentally, the fascist "third way" vision of the future revolved around national regeneration (in Roger Griffin's influential conceptualization, "palingenesis").[35] This goal welded a radical progressive vision to the "ontological security and 'roots' afforded by the narratives of organic nationalism."[36]

At points, this ideological context imbued prospective monuments with a different function. National continuity depended on the endurance of the race, not on a common identity sustained by an intergenerational chain of memory. As such, Nazi ideologues saw the chief business of prospective monuments as edifying and inspiring future generations of Aryans, rather than preserving the memory of the present era as such. Monuments expressing the "eternal genius" of the *Volksgemeinschaft* (racial community) were charged with "awakening" future generations to their inherent superiority and grand destiny.[37] This is how court architect Albert Speer summarized Hitler's views of the matter: "Periods of weakness are bound to occur in the history of nations, [Hitler] argued; but at their lowest ebb, their architecture will speak to them of former power. Naturally, a new national consciousness could not be awakened by architecture alone. But when after a long spell of inertia a sense of national grandeur was born anew, the monuments of men's ancestors were the most impressive exhortations. Our architectural works should also speak to the conscience of a future Germany centuries from now."[38]

The drive to capture the "eternal" German character sometimes conflicted with commemorative functions. After all, instead of marking out historical difference—the uniqueness of the present moment, slated for immortalization—"the history of the Volk could only be a chronicle of its identity with itself, of its immalleability."[39] This can explain why, in contrast to their Stalinist (and, to some extent, liberal democratic) analogues, the few synthetic adornments of German monuments largely eschewed contemporary attributes and props. For instance, Nazi sculpture, charged as it was with illustrating primordial racial continuities, typically embraced nudity for its ability to "[lift] the image of the community out of any concrete historical temporality that would inevitably be conferred upon it by clothing."[40] Revealingly, Nazi discourse consistently referred to "building for eternity" much more than to immortalizing the present.

Even so, this model, in which monuments were expected to reinvigorate future generations, in fact coexisted with a more universal, noninstrumental impulse to self-commemoration. In practice, after all, sculptural monuments dedicated to contemporary subjects, and architecture expressing its era, remained equally prominent. In *Mein Kampf*, Hitler lamented that Germany possessed "no monuments dominating the city picture, which might somehow be regarded as the symbols of the whole epoch."[41] Speer promised to rectify this situation, assuring the public that "the buildings of [the] Führer will speak of the greatness of *our age* to future millennia."[42] Indeed, Hitler could hardly separate monument construction from fashioning his own undying legacy, and Speer too relished the thought that his new commissions would "place [him] among the most famous architects of history."[43] Yet the cultural salience of self-commemoration is best revealed in the regime's extensive efforts to publicize its building program, which assumed that the creation of prospective monuments would appeal to Germans *here and now*.

As in the Soviet and liberal-democratic contexts, this appeal was closely related to unresolved anxieties about the future. For one thing, the utopian elements of the Nazi vision of the future were markedly underdeveloped. Fernando Esposito and Sven Reichardt argue that while fascism promised a brighter tomorrow, its "orientation towards an alternative future remained oddly abstract [... lacking] concrete ideas of how, and to what end, the future was actually being shaped." Rather, the true contribution of "palingenetic chronopolitics were ... to bestow roots and a foothold upon a society desperately longing for orientation and hence deceleration."[44] Thus, irrespective of its *attempts* to "revolutionize time" and build a racial utopia, the chief draw of Nazism may well have been its insistence on deep continuities and, specifically, its promise of national endurance.

The Nazi regime implicitly recognized the gap between its promises of national greatness and the deep scars left by the economic and political instability of the preceding period. Indeed, it was only by the end of the 1930s that German economic recovery appeared assured, and even then this hardly engendered an atmosphere of optimism; anxieties lingered. It was in this context that Hitler expounded at Nuremberg in 1935 that "when the poor human soul . . . has no longer a clear and definite belief in the greatness and the future of the nation to which it belongs, that is the time to stimulate its regard for the indisputable evidences of those eternal racial values which cannot be affected in their essence by a temporary phase of political or economic distress."[45] Monuments comprised precisely such "indisputable evidence"; their prospective character provided assurance that "racial values" were, indeed, "eternal"—regardless of momentary fortunes. Similarly, when Hitler reassured his listeners at a 1937 Nuremberg rally that "the great cultural documents of humanity, built of granite and marble [are the only] truly stable element in the rush of all other phenomena," he appealed to the fantasy of national endurance, not to expectations of progress and national greatness, which remained uncertain.[46] To be sure, as in the Stalinist USSR, and (to a lesser extent) in the liberal democracies, the Nazi regime continued to promise a brighter tomorrow; but these slogans were tired and abstract, and prompted a countervailing emphasis on the more limited hope of collective survival.

German commemoration of the First World War was especially evocative of this theme. As Hitler promised in *Mein Kampf*, "thousands of years may pass, but . . . the iron front of the gray steel helmet will emerge, unwavering and unflinching, an immortal monument . . . As long as there are Germans alive, they will remember that these men were sons of the nation."[47] Memorials to the First World War, of which by 1939 Germany had the most amongst all combatant nations, made up a significant proportion of the total number of stand-alone, sculptural monuments built in the Nazi period.[48] War memorials were also synthetically integrated with monumental architecture. Berlin's Olympic complex (1936), for example, incorporated an expansive Langemarck Hall commemorating the eponymous 1914 battle.[49] Illustrative of the centrality of war commemoration, the regime commissioned a massive, record-breaking triumphal arch (on which would be recorded the names of Germany's 1,800,000 fallen soldiers) as the main monument of the redeveloped Berlin, second only to the aforementioned *Volkshalle*. Other Nazi monuments—such as those dedicated to "martyred" *Friekorps* paramilitaries and party activists—

implicitly (and deviously) presented their subjects as part of the dead of the First World War.[50]

While Nazi war memory was singularly militarist, revanchist, and chauvinist, the importance of prospective war commemoration for imagining and securing the identity (and hence vitality) of the nation echoed practices outside Germany. Even memorial forms perceived as quintessentially Nazi—such as the so-called *Totenburgen* (fortresses of the dead), gloomy and massive mausoleums—were not specific to the regime. Developed in the late 1920s by the German War Graves Commission, the last of these were, in fact, constructed in the 1950s in North Africa.[51] Thus, as Roger Griffin summarizes, even though it was "more pronounced in the case of fascism," the commemorative model connecting the remembrance of the fallen to the survival of the nation was universal. "When death occurs for the sake of the nation it becomes a portal to a fully temporalized eternity, the supra-individual, suprahistorical, but not supratemporal metaphysical eternity of the organic nation ... a concept or conceit which recurs not just in Fascist and Nazi ceremonies of the fallen soldier, but in all modern patriotic celebrations."[52] Across borders and political divides, the trauma of war, which undercut progressive expectations, was transmuted into the hope of national survival.

By the late 1930s, German war monuments shifted from processing past losses to assuaging present anxieties, as the regime prophesied (and eventually unleashed) a new war. Plans for a reconstructed Berlin envisioned an expansive *Soldatenhalle* (Soldier's Hall) pantheon and a world war museum—both to perpetually commemorate a conflict not yet begun.[53] These planned constructions implied a victorious war, but in so doing expressed uncertainty rather than optimism. As Adam Tooze demonstrates, long before the tide of war turned decisively against Germany, both the Nazi leadership and the German public assessed the country's strategic situation as bleak (and this pessimism, in fact, drove Hitler's policy of brinkmanship).[54] Indeed, Nazi leaders gloomily warned that Germany's new monuments might outlast their creators, remaining as the people's last testament. In 1933, in Nuremberg, Hitler assured that "even if a people fades away and its men fall silent, the stones will speak."[55] Two years later, at the laying of the cornerstone of the Nuremberg Congress Hall, he declared that "if the [Nazi] movement should ever be silent then this witness will still speak after thousands of years."[56] As late as 1941, SS head Heinrich Himmler was still paraphrasing this refrain.[57] The aforementioned theory of "ruin value" expressed similar anxieties. As Julia Hell argues, fears of Germany's defeat and devastation, in retaliation for its own barbarity, prompted an obsession with perdurable monuments.[58]

As in the Stalinist Soviet Union, imagining posterity's perpetual remembrance was constitutive of the fantasy of national survival, if not of victory. It is therefore not coincidental that Nazi self-commemorative projects ballooned in step with military setbacks. This perspective provides an alternate interpretation to another vignette that Golomstock presents as a demonstration of the "totalitarian" neglect for real public needs. "In December 1941," he recounts, "when [General Heinz] Guderian's tanks had exhausted their supplies of fuel and come to a stop on the outskirts of Moscow, when tens of thousands of hungry and poorly clothed German soldiers were dying in the frosts, a German train arrived at a local station. Instead of fuel, winter clothing or provisions for the dying army, it was loaded with slabs of red marble with which to construct a monument to Hitler in Moscow."[59] In fact, such projects testified to the Nazi leadership's sensitivity to widespread demoralization, rather than to its delusional optimism, as Golomstock implies. Like the Stalinist regime, its German counterpart attempted to minimize military setbacks by appealing to the fantasy of a war already won. "Military battles are eventually forgotten. Our buildings, however, will stand," expostulated Hitler at the height of the Russian campaign.[60] In 1942, Hitler commissioned a series of designs for *Totenburgen*, to be positioned on the frontiers of the enlarged Reich. Even at that point, the execution of these plans was highly unlikely, but they were utterly unrealizable by early 1944—the moment when the designs were published for a mass audience.[61] As German defeats turned to unavertable disaster, Hitler devoted ever more time to his architectural plans.[62] As late as February 1945, confined to his Berlin bunker, the dictator spent hours consulting with architects and pouring over models of a reconstructed Linz, his hometown. This project, which envisioned prominent mausoleums for the Führer and his parents, had increasingly attracted Hitler's attention since the Wehrmacht's debacle at Stalingrad.[63]

This image of Hitler planning Linz's monuments to the reverberations of exploding shells in his capital encapsulates a general pattern in interwar temporal culture. In a world reeling from economic crisis, the trauma of the First World War, and the eventual relapse into further devastation, visions of progress commanded little traction. Rather, a more limited hope, centering on the fantasy of enduring nationhood (and anchored in prospective monuments) helped assuage anxieties about the future in an alternative fashion. Even though the specific problems facing the Soviet Union differed (its social dislocations were the result of breakneck modernization rather than economic depression, and its wartime trauma related primarily to the Great Patriotic, not to the First World War), self-commemoration represented a shared response. To be sure, Stalinist temporal culture shifted more dramatically: from a Bolshevik, utopian vision of the future to a nationalized outlook. In the interwar liberal democracies, by contrast, notions of both progressive change and collective endurance were already firmly embedded in the national imagination. Under the weight of wartime trauma, and the economic difficulties of the Great Depression, it was the relative significance of these elements that shifted; nationhood itself remained a constant. In the case of Nazi Germany, the devastating First World War ended in a humiliating defeat, and economic crisis reached unprecedented dimensions, easing the way for an ideology which foregrounded the nation in its vision of the future. Despite its revolutionary-utopian elements, the Nazi leadership was also drawn to the culture of self-commemoration, especially as its wartime fortunes ebbed.

In all three iterations, self-commemoration stabilized the modern temporal order, upholding its fundamental orientation on the future (which remained subject to human control and the locus of hope, in however limited a sense), at a moment of collective disillusionment with the progress narrative. It did so by offering a fantasy of an undying nation, whose identity would be anchored in a chain of remembering generations. The materialization of this hope resulted in extraordinary resources committed to the building of prospective monuments, in the Stalinist Soviet Union, the fascist dictatorships, and interwar liberal democracies alike. True, monuments bore the imprint of the political ideologies of the respective regimes that commissioned them. But in the last instance, they evoked the endurance of the biosocial collective—the nation and its remembering posterity—rather than the strength and stability of the given political order. In some sense, this dynamic reflected the apogee of the nation-state in the interwar period, whereby divergent systems—dictatorships and democracies—all derived their legitimacy by claiming to serve "the people," the wellspring of sovereignty and historical agency. This conclusion nuances our understanding of the temporalities of modern nationalism. Rather than being universal and codependent qualities, visions of national progress and claims to the permanence of the nation were, to some extent, inversely proportionate. In crisis conditions, when promises of a better tomorrow seemed increasingly improbable, the more limited hope of national survival assumed greater public salience.

If the self-commemorative impulse under Stalinism dovetailed with broader processes, so too did its decline. Following Stalin's death, the party leadership hoped that a renewed emphasis on the construction of communism would mobilize society and help resolve the legitimation crisis induced by partial de-Stalinization.[64] These attempts to rekindle utopianism sidelined prospective commemoration (although retrospective commemoration, now encompassing the increasingly distant October Revolution and Great Patriotic War, continued unabated). Even so, by the late 1960s, the brief utopian renaissance quietly wound down as the regime claimed that Soviet society had reached "developed socialism," a new (and, to all appearances, indefinite) stage. This time, however, the striving to immortalize the present did not reemerge. In this as well, Soviet culture was broadly in step with global developments: the unraveling of the modern temporal order, in which the antinomy of progress and national survival no longer applied. In this new "presentist," post-historical context, the fantasy of an enduring nation became increasingly marginal—and, arguably, this marginality itself contributed to the collapse of the modern temporal regime.

One would have expected that the relapse into world war (and more importantly, the experience of the Holocaust) would undermine faith in progress in the postwar West. Nonetheless, while pessimism and anxiety were felt keenly by many cultural figures, popular hopes were given a second lease on life by a speedy economic recovery and political stabilization: American "prosperity," the "German miracle," France's "thirty glorious years."[65] This rendered prospective commemoration increasingly irrelevant. Initial plans for extensive monuments to the fallen were stillborn; instead, so-called living memorials came to dominate the memorialization of the Second World War. Art professionals and commissioning bodies explicitly counterposed such practical memorials—roads, community halls, recreation centers, libraries, and gardens—to the "uselessness" of traditional monuments.[66] Fundamentally, postwar living memorials channeled the commemorative impulse into utilitarian modernization projects, a vivid illustration of the revived cultural hegemony of the progressive vision of the future. Obligations to the memory of the fallen were otherwise quickly dispensed with by inscribing new names onto existing First World War monuments.[67]

By the late 1970s, however, the mounting problems of the welfare state sowed doubt in progressivist promises; rising inequality and precarity again rendered the future increasingly uncertain. These disappointments were compounded by a sense of powerlessness (epitomized in voluntary deregulation) and the lack of viable political alternatives (in the form of Marxist programs or a new "third way"). Postcolonial critiques laid bare the injustices of the modernization project, while environmentalism pointed to the looming ecological debts yet to be settled. At the same time, ever-accelerating technological change increasingly frustrated attempts to model and predict developments.[68] The future was thereby transformed from a locus of hope to one of an unspecific but unavertable menace, fatally undermining modernity's underlying future-oriented order of time.

In its stead arose a new, "presentist" temporal regime. As Hartog's term suggests, this new temporal culture is characterized by an emphasis on the immediate present and the blurring of its boundaries with the past and the future. Today's contingent needs filter the recollection of the past. The future, in turn, disappears from view: "stretches of time labelled 'future' get shorter . . . sliced into episodes dealt with 'one at a time.'"[69] It was this posthistorical, "presentist" temporal culture that the Soviet Union joined after its final burst of utopianism dissipated in the late 1960s. As Boris Groys recounts, Soviet society discovered that "history no longer existed . . . in the West that was to be 'overtaken,' no one was hurrying anywhere anymore; all hopes of change had vanished, because the historical perspective or orientation to the future had itself disappeared."[70] In this new context, neither utopian dreams, nor the fantasy of future remembrance, have much traction, for both placed their hopes in a future that no longer meaningfully exists.

This cultural shift is reflected in the almost complete disappearance of prospective monuments. Contemporary monument design favors abstraction over figuration, interaction over inertness, open-endedness over didacticism. All of these developments impede the intergenerational transfer of memory, but none more than the conscious eschewal of durability in favor of evanescence and ephemerality, exemplified by "vanishing" countermonuments, "memory sculpture" installations, "invisible" monuments composed of empty space, temporary shrines, and digital memorials. Similarly, the lifespan of iconic public buildings and infrastructure, objects that are no longer vested with commemorative functions, is calculated in accordance with the (ever-shrinking) timelines of their projected use-value.[71] Some contemporary monuments may cling to a traditional aesthetic (and, by extension, may sometimes employ durable materials), but not to the prospective mission that informed it. Monuments for posterity are no longer built, for society has little interest in immortalizing the present.[72]

This development may seem at odds with the recent epidemic of commemoration and heritage conservation that has been termed the "memory boom." Pierre Nora speaks of this as "an age . . . in which we attempt to preserve not only all of the past but all of the present as well, [in] museums, libraries, depositories, documentation centers, and databases."[73] This trend, however, has little to do with prospective memorialization. For one, ever-accelerating social transformations rapidly render the present into an alien and exotic past—and it is this recent *past* which is, more precisely, the subject of commemoration.[74] Equally importantly, beneath the obsessive accumulation of records and artefacts lie no underlying, stable narratives that could be passed on to future generations. By itself, this "archive" is largely latent.[75] When drawn upon, it facilitates representations of the past shamelessly tailored to today's ever-shifting needs.[76] All too often, these needs are rooted in the logic of the nostalgia industry, which markets contextless historical simulacra: vintage look-alikes, retro fashion, Disneyesque architecture, and pastiche historical drama. These stylizations have only the most superficial and tendentious relation to the past, privileging emotional engagement over distanced, critical reflection.[77] Thus, because the memories that "we consume are 'imagined memories' to begin with, [they are] more easily forgotten than lived memories," notes literary scholar Andreas Huyssen.[78] Even lived memories of the past have little temporal duration: drowned in a tide of "accelerated informational overload," they surface only briefly.[79] This constant flux underscores the lack of a reliable "supra-generational mechanism of self-reproduction" for memory, a priori rendering attempts at immortalization futile.[80] As Nora concludes, "the past can now be constructed out of virtually anything, and no one knows what tomorrow's past will hold."[81]

The 1970s were not the first time that modernity's progress narrative appeared increasingly tenuous. So why did the interwar, alternative vision of the future, encapsulated in the hope of national continuity and endurance, not revive? Effectively, this stems from the parallel collapse of the national imagination. In its wake, individual identities now coalesce in multiple, deterritorialized, and intersectional communities. These collective identifications (and their associated particularistic commemorative practices) are contingent and flexible, with "emergent and mutable temporal and spatial coordinates."[82] Precisely because they depend upon individuals' voluntary identification, these "'communities [are] as fragile and short-lived as scattered and wandering emotions, shifting erratically from one target to another and drifting in the forever inconclusive search for a secure haven: communities of shared worries, shared anxieties or shared hatreds—but in each case 'peg' communities, a momentary gathering around a nail on which many solitary individuals hang their solitary individual fears," as Bauman, somewhat pessimistically, puts it.[83]

These elective identity communities construct a shared past (refracted through the lens of the present), but envision no stable future. Provisional communities cannot, by definition, be "solid" in a way in which the national collective claimed to be, and which allowed it to ground identities and assuage anxieties about tomorrow. Accordingly, there is no meaningful posterity to which prospective memory could be addressed. To be sure, some identities claim a greater degree of permanence—those, for instance, stabilized through continued structural injustice and enduring trauma. But even these communities struggle for recognition and redress to ultimately transcend their "historical wounds." Once these injustices are commemorated, as Aleida Assmann argues, "a symbolic self-distancing [occurs] making it possible both to recognize the crimes and, at the same time, to break from them;" a mnemonic strategy premised on the promise of "rupture and change."[84]

This situation can explain the paradox that even while the desire to be remembered remains, it has no corresponding public embodiment. Philanthropists continue to make legacy endowments, diary and memoir writing remain popular, and digital technologies have seemingly multiplied the means available for self-commemoration. Photographs and home videos are taken incessantly, and not only does the internet archive all content by default, it empowers individuals to intentionally "lifelog" for posterity, curating their digital afterlives. Yet these initiatives stand out for their markedly private character, both in their subject (the individual self) and their means. Immortalization practices in the final decades of the Soviet Union evidenced this very shift from public culture (connected to a collective vision of the future) to a private way of overcoming death anxiety. For instance, elderly communists and fellow travelers often donated their personal papers to the archives as a way of coming to terms with their death and "achieving immortality."[85]

Thus, owing to the instability of both historical narratives and the loss of a national imagination, collective immortalization projects are now effectively blocked. If the culture of self-commemoration previously sustained the modern temporal order at a time of declining hopes in social betterment, this is no longer the case. We are not only "no longer able to bequeath anything to posterity" because the future has disappeared, as philosopher Hans Gumbrecht argues.[86] Perhaps, it is also the disappearance of (a national) posterity that has facilitated the rapid demise of the future, and the dawning of a postmodern, "presentist" order of time.

Epilogue
Posterity's Monuments

The Stalinist culture of self-commemoration—and its associated temporality—have long since dissipated, but the material legacies remain. While more concerned with the act of memorialization as such, the Stalinist regime nonetheless had every intention of passing down specific narratives and values to posterity, through a warped retelling of the era's history. Its monument builders made careful preparations to this end, and these efforts appear not to have been entirely in vain. To be sure, they could hardly have envisioned the radically different context in which future generations would be viewing their creations. And yet in Moscow, Stalinism's symbolic heartland, grand synthetic monuments still stand prominently, having weathered iconoclastic campaigns and preserved their associations with Stalinism. Troublingly, they retain a fundamental productivity, continuing to influence the ways in which the Stalin era is remembered in Russia—and supporting the political ends to which this memory is harnessed. True to their original mission, Stalinist monuments persist in immortalizing their "glorious" era, even as new discourses partially reframe their meaning and significance.

Heretofore, discussions of how to relate to this difficult heritage have largely discounted the possibility that Stalinist monuments may play an active role in contemporary commemorative dynamics. Implicitly, scholarship dismisses these objects as either "invisible" or as fundamentally resignified through a far-reaching process of commercialization. After all, the Stalinist ideology that gave these monuments meaning has been repudiated, while the monuments themselves have been physically modified through a combination of iconoclasm and redevelopment. Yet the extent of these processes should not be overstated. True, the de-Stalinizing Twentieth Party Congress of 1956 inaugurated an extensive program of iconoclasm that targeted most of the existing representations of the dictator. Having lost its focal point, the regime began a rapid transition from the "cult of personality" to alternative forms of legitimation. Throughout the Soviet Union (as well as its satellites), nearly all depictions of Stalin's likeness were destroyed. In Moscow, over one hundred statues and panels were removed from the metro alone, and even war memorials were not spared such interventions.[1] Concomitantly, authorities excised nearly all toponyms honoring Stalin and his closest surviving associates, whose so-called Anti-Party Group was conclusively defeated in 1957. This campaign of urban cleansing culminated on the night of October 31, 1961, when Stalin's body itself was unceremoniously removed from the mausoleum on Red Square.

However, the de-Stalinization of public space remained incomplete. After all, the Stalinist regime had focused the bulk of its efforts on the construction of synthetic monuments—sumptuously adorned architectural constructions—as the ultimate testament to the times. While shorn of references to the dictator, these impressive edifices continued to showcase the full arsenal of Soviet symbols and to exult the era's achievements (collectivization, industrialization, national "unification," wartime victory). This compromise reflected the general character of the de-Stalinization campaign, which deftly blamed Stalin for violent "excesses" and policy errors, all the while affirming the legitimacy of Stalinist institutions that had by then become intrinsic to Soviet state socialism. Furthermore, wary of social discord and upheaval, as well as of guilt-by-association, the authorities conducted their iconoclastic program with great discretion. As a result, art professionals confined themselves to minimal alterations of monuments, and carefully camouflaged even these (Stalin's likeness, for instance, was often unobtrusively replaced with Lenin's). Wholesale demolition, even of dedicated Stalin monuments, was a last resort. For instance, the world's largest Stalin monument, on Prague's Letna Hill, was destroyed only after experts had concluded that preserving his sculptural entourage of workers, peasants, and soldiers would be unfeasible from a technical point of view.[2]

The fall of the Soviet Union catalyzed a second, more thorough wave of iconoclasm, in Russia as elsewhere. Bowing to grassroots pressures, local governments moved to relocate or demolish many of the remaining sculptural incarnations of the Stalinist pantheon, to restore pre-Revolutionary toponyms, and to strip certain Stalinist edifices, which now housed new public institutions, of their decorative adornments. But once again, the most important Stalinist monuments survived, not least due to the immortalizing intentions of their creators. At the end of the day, demolishing imposing public buildings, luxurious apartment complexes, and outstanding infrastructural projects such as metro systems, was clearly impracticable. Indeed, given that the "cults of eternity and of vastness went together," as Igor Golomstock observes, the sheer financial obstacles of merely removing sculptural and other decorations often proved too difficult for cash-strapped local authorities.[3] By the late 1990s, as democratic reforms foundered and the public increasingly reassessed the Soviet experience as positive, the momentum had dissipated. As such, the current situation appears to vindicate the Stalinist regime's policy of constructing vast synthetic monuments, which through sheer size and utility have largely weathered iconoclastic campaigns. As Aleksei Shchusev put it in 1935, "once read, a book can easily languish in the library, whereas *architectural monuments* stand in the middle of the city and cannot be removed, remaining always a clear reflection of their epoch."[4]

Shchusev's prediction can be productively juxtaposed to the writer Robert Musil's well-known quip that "there is nothing in this world as invisible as a monument." Although this observation, which he made in 1927, referred primarily to public sculpture rather than to architecture, Musil brought attention to the visual irrelevance of all static landmarks "in an age of noise and movement."[5] This suggests that surviving Stalinist monuments may be mute, simply forming the visual backdrop to contemporary urban life. As Muscovites commute through the extravagant metro system, or bustle down stately boulevards, they might not so much as think of the Stalinist origins of their built environment. But Musil's observation is typically taken out of context: he specifically noted that inherently "forceful monuments do exist," although they require "very particular preparations."[6] Chapters 2 and 3 have demonstrated that Stalinist art professionals did just that, carefully considering how to make their creations understandable, meaningful, and relevant to future viewers.

In some sense, these efforts appear to have paid off. Stalinist constructions are certainly eye-catching, and the superior dimensions of these landmarks secure their dominance in the city's ensemble. As Graham Gill states, "the faded grandeur of the [former *All-Union Agricultural Exhibition*], the evocative aura of the Lenin Mausoleum and its immediate surrounds, and the still-soaring gigantism of Stalin's skyscrapers give [Moscow] a tangible sense of Sovietness which cannot be eliminated," an observation equally applicable to the Stalinist core of other post-Soviet cities.[7] Furthermore, this visually forceful urban landscape inadvertently "demands the unconditional subordination of new objects to the established order," as Galina Pitchnikova argues.[8] Indeed, Moscow's 2020 Municipal Development Plan lauded the ensemble effects of

Stalinist high-rises and further accentuated their role by means of an extensive lighting program.⁹

Not only has superlative size guaranteed Stalinist monuments enduring visibility, the gamble on grand, historicist aesthetics (analyzed in chapter 2) has also seemingly paid off. The Stalinist style remains understandable and appealing to contemporary Russian audiences.¹⁰ One 2009 poll, for example, reflected Muscovites' distinct preference for Stalin-era metro stations, over later, modernist designs.¹¹ In any case, Stalinist monuments undoubtedly exude a strong magnetism: witness the gratuitous descriptions of derelict metro stations in Dmitrii Glukhovskii's postapocalyptic *Metro 2033* bestseller (2005), or the hyper-Stalinist cityscape visualizations in Aleksei Andrianov's blockbuster *Spy* (2012). Indeed, Andrianov's thriller, set on eve of the Great Patriotic War, positively reveled in Stalinist monumental aesthetics. The set design anachronistically included the bombastic architecture of the postwar period and, capitalizing on the possibilities of computer-assisted graphics, not only brought to life unrealized projects such as the Palace of the Soviets, but also other purely fictitious "Stalin-esque" behemoths.

On a more practical level, the public still views Stalinist residential buildings as comfortable and durably built, and they remain highly sought-after.¹² This is especially true of the high-rises—not least for their being perceived as German made (POWs having been involved in their construction). Property developers have capitalized on such associations with durability, quality, and status by commissioning new constructions explicitly evoking the Stalinist style. In Moscow, such edifices include metro stations (Park Pobedy (2003)), high-rises (Triumph-Palace (2006), Oruzheinyi (2016)), and major residential developments (Dostoianie (2019), Nasledie (2020)). Furthermore, despite occasional attempts to

FIGURE 13. Still from Aleksei Andrianov's *Spy* (2012), featuring a super-monumentalized Lenin Library and a completed Palace of the Soviets.

skirt their historical origin by euphemistic references to "Soviet art deco" or "the heritage of the 1930s–1950s," Stalinist aesthetics retain strong associations with their era. In common parlance, look-alike residential complexes and high-rises are matter-of-factly referred to as "Stalinist." Indeed, as Ol'ga Zinov'eva notes, developers "not only turn to the style of [Stalinist] classicism, but also advertise it, marketing their buildings in the terminology of Stalin era [such as] the 'Eighth high-rise,' the 'Near Dacha' and many others."[13]

For example, the developers of Moscow's Alcon Tower (projected for completion in 2022) promote their multifunctional complex in the following way: "A vertical composition, expressive facades, bright and laconic details, monumental architecture—all these features emphasize the similarity of the Alcon Tower with legendary Moscow and New York high-rises. The Alcon Tower will harmoniously fit into the current development of the city and emphasize the high taste and status of future residents."[14] Alongside attempts to link the development to American art deco, Stalinist archetypes dominate both the marketing strategy and the building's aesthetic composition. According to one journalist, Muscovites already refer to it as "the Eighth Sister" (the seven being the original Stalinist high-rises). The city's architectural council awarded Alcon Tower the title of the best public-use project of 2015 (when the design was approved), with the capital's chief architect proclaiming that "we must not shy away from continuing Moscow's [building] traditions."[15]

FIGURE 14. Perspective drawing of the Alcon Tower multifunctional center (detail), Evgeny Gerasimov and Partners, 2015.

Admittedly, the mere fact that Stalinist monuments remain visible, retaining aesthetic appeal and associations with the regime that created them, does not necessarily mean that Russians experience them as "memorials" to the Stalin era. After all, scholars typically question whether monuments can truly outlast the narratives that give them meaning. Even as interwar governments busied themselves with cultivating an adoring posterity, important voices already decried the feebleness of such endeavors. In 1938, urban theorist Lewis Mumford warned that "stone gives a false sense of continuity, and a deceptive assurance of life: the shell seems to pledge continuity by the fact that it continues to exist, outwardly unaffected by the passage of events. But the fact is that exterior form can only confirm an inner life: it is not a substitute. All living beliefs, all living desires and ideas, must be perpetually renewed, from generation to generation: re-thought, re-considered, re-willed, re-built, if they are to endure."[16] These ideas are now widely accepted; social theorist Anthony Giddens effectively summarizes prevailing opinion in stating that "monuments turn into relics once formulaic truths are disputed or discarded."[17]

In this view, monuments retain their commemorative capacity only in contexts where their perceived message is considered relevant to contemporary life. This is vividly demonstrated in the recent wave of monument defacements and removals, galvanized by the Black Lives Matter movement. From America to the United Kingdom to Australia, mass protests have targeted monuments whose political ideologies (and related structural injustices) are perceived to have endured—specifically, those promoting imperial projects and ideas of racial supremacy. Similarly, it is seemingly only *beyond* Russia's borders that Stalinist monuments have avoided becoming inconsequential "relics." There, these monuments were and often continue to be seen primarily as tools legitimating Russian imperial domination (rather than the political ideology of Stalinism). By evoking anxieties over Russian irredentism, these monuments draw attention to their historical narratives. This is particularly evident in the public controversies surrounding the removal of Soviet monuments in the wake of the so-called decommunization laws adopted in Lithuania (2008), Georgia (2011), Latvia (2013), and in the post-Crimean context—in Ukraine (2015).

In Russia, by contrast, the public significance of Stalinist monuments was always more closely tied to Stalinist political ideology. This interpretative prism no longer meaningfully exists, even among fringe circles of self-proclaimed neo-Stalinists. On first glance, this situation appears to confirm James Young's pronouncement that ultimately "neither the monument nor its meaning are truly everlasting," because "time drags old meanings into new contexts."[18] This perspective foregrounds the fact that ordinary Russians often relate to Stalinist monuments in the apolitical, quasi-consumerist ways discussed above: as beautiful domiciles, efficient means of transportation, and spacious recreation venues. These sites also offer unique opportunities for the tourism industry.[19] Physical alteration and functional repurposing further resignify these objects. For example, for over a decade, a giant rooftop Mercedes-Benz logo graced the House on the Embankment, Boris Iofan's famous residence for the Stalinist elite. Two of Moscow's high-rises have been acquired and modernized by international luxury hotel chains. Hotel Moscow, another of Iofan's early creations (now owned by Four Seasons), was demolished and rebuilt with a copy of its "historical" façade, a notorious case of "mock-up" (*muliazh*) construction common under Iurii Luzhkov's mayoralty (1992–2010). In this view, despite their inescapable visual prominence and aesthetic reputation, Stalinist monuments in Russia remain ineffective and irrelevant from a commemorative standpoint.

However, this approach significantly overstates the symbolic plasticity of these objects, and ignores alternative modes of identification. Some of these remain rooted in older and more stable interpretative frameworks, which like the built environment, are palimpsestic and path-dependent.[20] After all, the Russian regime has condemned only select aspects of the Stalinist experience, and continues to uphold important elements of latter's mnemopolitical culture. Most notably, many of the tropes of the Stalinist myth of the Great Patriotic War manifest great continuity. Specifically, the Russian state supports a triumphalist narrative (*paradnaia istoriia*), which emphasizes stalwart national unity, widespread heroism, and military prowess, while sidelining such themes as collaborationism, war crimes, political incompetence, and corruption.[21] Accordingly, Stalinist war monuments blend seamlessly into the official commemorative landscape; they are carefully restored and continue to act as focal sites of memory. Their symbolism resonates in today's context in much the same way as over the previous decades.

Further, the status of the Great Patriotic War as the foundational myth of contemporary Russian national identity has required a partial (if at times begrudging) sanitization of the wider history of Stalinism. Apologetic narratives—which justify, minimize, and even occasionally deny Stalinist crimes—have enjoyed some official support, and are affirmed by significant sections of the public.[22] This context insulates other Stalinist monuments from critical gazes and implicitly affirms the authority of their idealized self-representations. Indeed, the entire built heritage of the period can be (and sometimes is) interpreted as the legacy of a regime which saved the nation from destruction and led it to glorious victory. Some educators even suggest integrating the study of postwar Stalinist architecture into the school curriculum, for the "spiritual-ethical and patriotic edification" of Russian youth.[23] The state-supported Russian Military-Historical Society has gone further yet: recouping the "losses" of de-Stalinization, it has unveiled a spate of new, stand-alone sculptural monuments to Stalin, in his capacity as the wartime leader of the Soviet state and its army.

Aside from immortalizing the Great Patriotic War (in a fashion not substantially different from how they were intended to do), Stalinist monuments also figure as testaments to national and imperial greatness, both stylistically (being beautiful, imposing, and unique), and through the achievements that they memorialize. True, the neo-Stalinist aesthetic is only one among several stylistic revivals in evidence today, contributing to the pastiche cityscape of postmodernity, which encompasses everything from the neo-Byzantine to the hypermodern. But while private developers cater to all tastes, the regime distinctly favors Stalinist monumentalism. In cultural diplomacy, the latter increasingly serves as the country's architectural calling card. For instance, Russia's grand historical narrative, choreographed for the televised opening ceremonies of the 2014 Winter Olympics in Sochi, profiled the Stalinist highrises, Vera Mukhina's Worker and Kolkhoz Woman sculpture, and Shchusev's Komsomol'skaia-kol'tsevaia metro station (Shchusev himself was feted as "the foremost representative of our architecture"). The Olympic Gorod gorki ski resort was constructed in an unabashedly neo-Stalinist architectural style.[24]

At another international venue—the 2016 Venice Biennale of Architecture—the Russian pavilion was devoted to the restoration and reconstruction of the *All-Union Agricultural Exhibition* (now the *Exhibition of Economic Achievements*).[25] In large part, this state-supported project aims at recreating the fairgrounds' Stalinist appearance (of the 1939 and 1954 iterations), by demolishing the pavilions and facades of later periods. This reflects a wider pattern: Stalinist monuments benefit from extensive state-funded preservation efforts, while heritage of other Soviet periods is more likely to suffer from "abandonment, rejection and [only] fragmentary restoration," as Julie Deschepper notes.[26] This policy, she argues, aims "to remind [people of] the aspirations to greatness represented by the most famous Stalinist buildings."[27] As with the war narrative, this framing at least partially adheres to the original objectives of Stalinist monument builders: to memorialize the period as a time of national rebirth and imperial greatness. After all, Stalinist monuments showcased the revival of national styles (interpreted and hierarchically arranged through Russocentric lenses), demonstrated newfound power through their gargantuan size, and commemorated important national achievements. Currently, the exhibition's bronze statue to the biologist Ivan Michurin (1954) continues to stand as an inspiring reminder of Russia's history of scientific leadership, as do monuments to other Stalin-era notables elsewhere. The famous gold-leaf sculptures of the

Friendship of the Peoples fountain (1954), recently restored to former glory, may continue to conjure up fantasies of a post-Soviet space unified under Russian leadership.

Andreas Schönle, in turn, sees the reconstruction of the exhibition as a testament to enduring statism: the regime's "power vertical" and its paternalistic social engineering projects (in this case, the promotion of "enlightened" recreation). The revitalized exhibition grounds demonstrate "what the state does, in its munificence, for its grateful, bedazzled and supine citizens," just as they did in the Stalin period.[28] Following a strong scholarly tradition linking the revival of Soviet symbolism to the endurance of Russian statist ideology, Marina Dmitrieva also sees the Stalinist aesthetic revival as an "attempt to legitimize the new state" and display "the continuity of political power."[29] Thus, both in their subject matter and execution, surviving Stalinist monuments play an important role in supporting the triumphalist memory of the Great Patriotic War and in extolling the achievements a strong, imperial state. Troublingly, these narratives have become cornerstones in the Russian regime's legitimation of both domestic repression and foreign aggression, most recently in the ongoing, brutal invasion of Ukraine. In smearing the Kyiv government with accusations of fascism, and in refusing to recognize Ukrainian nationhood, the Russian regime invokes both the Manichean war narrative and the thinly veiled cultural chauvinism characteristic of Stalinist ideology and its monumental incarnations.

Importantly, the affinity between the mnemonic narratives embodied in Stalinist monuments and contemporary official discourses not only gives these objects positive meaning, but also conditions their contestation. In August 2009, for instance, lyrics from the Soviet anthem "Stalin reared us on loyalty to the people and inspired us to labor and heroism," were reinscribed in the surface vestibule of Kurskaia metro station, then under renovation. These lyrics had been erased in the first wave of de-Stalinization, and their reappearance ignited a public controversy. One may speculate that opposition stemmed not only from revulsion at the dictator's perceived rehabilitation, but also from discomfort with the mythology of a paternalistic state and its benevolent leader(ship). Similarly, in a 2014 protest against Russian meddling in Ukraine, activists painted the star adorning the Stalinist high-rise on the Kotel'nicheskaia embankment to resemble the Ukrainian flag (which was also hoisted onto the spire). A year later, following Russia's illegal annexation of Crimea and ongoing military involvement in the Donbas, another group of protestors again unfurled the Ukrainian flag, this time from scaffolding covering the building. Presumably, the iconic Stalinist high-rise was chosen as the site of these actions to highlight continuities in Russian imperialism.

FIGURE 15. "Stalin reared us on loyalty to the people and inspired us to labor and heroism." These words from the Stalin-era Soviet national anthem were reinscribed inside the surface vestibule of Moscow's Kurskaia-kol'tsevaia metro station, restored in 2009. Photograph by Anton Dolin, 2021.

Thus, as testaments to the triumphant victory in the Great Patriotic War, and more broadly—to national and imperial rebirth under the guidance of a strong state—Stalinist monuments continue to evoke narratives at least partially aligned with their original commemorative mission. Of course, by itself this says more about the continuities in Russian mnemopolitical culture than about the ability of Stalinist monuments to truly weather the years and continue to immortalize their era. However, I believe that these monuments' prospective design significantly bolsters their *active* role in influencing current understandings of the Stalin period. For one, as Henri Lefebvre points out, "a monumental work, like a musical one, does not have a 'signified' (or 'signifieds'); rather, it has a horizon of meaning."[30] Although Lefebvre invokes this metaphor to underscore the *multiplicity* of interpretations inherent in a given monument, the notion of "horizon" also implies a certain semantic *boundedness*. As demonstrated in chapter 3, Stalinist art professionals took care to ensure that their creations remained semantically stable with the passage of time. Synthesis, for instance, was a key technique, and indeed, surviving epigraphy, as well as visual symbols encoded in decorative art and sculpture, continue to suggest particular avenues of interpretation. They not only specify the era to which Stalinist architectural monuments belong, and render memorialized subjects comprehensible, they also reduce complex narratives into the simplified, "rigid schema of 'good'-'bad,'" as Elena Bykova observes.[31] As their creators had intended, this property discourages nuanced interpretations and resists resignification. Experience has shown that only the most allegorical Stalinist monuments (which were a small minority in the artistic practice of the time) have proven adept to fundamental reinterpretations.[32] Indeed, this semantic inflexibility has conditioned critical responses to Stalinist monuments outside of Russia: predisposing posttransitional iconoclasts to wholesale destruction (of statuary and synthetic adornments) rather than resignification. Therefore, in large part due to their original design, these monuments are naturally inclined to promote positive, triumphal representations of their era. Even if ultimately requiring mediation by contemporary discourses, Stalinist monuments are not empty signifiers, but have a degree of memorial agency, if only through favoring certain interpretations and inhibiting others.

Further, aside from immortalizing their proper subjects, Stalinist monuments operate as instruments of *amnesia*. After all, as Paul Connerton suggests, monuments "conceal the past as much as they cause us to remember it," an observation particularly germane to prospective monuments.[33] As demonstrated in chapter 4, the Stalinist hierarchy of commemorability ensured that only a narrow spectrum of subjects qualified for immortalization. Yet the amnestic quality of these monuments is not simply a case of certain objects monopolizing the memorial landscape and thereby not reflecting the sordid aspects of the Stalinist experience. Stalinist monuments also obscure the very context of their own creation. Thus, for instance, the decorative artwork of the Moscow metro portrays Komsomol *metrostroevtsy*, but, unsurprisingly, representations of convict laborers involved in its construction are nowhere to be found. Neither are the atrocious labor conditions, the terror that enforced the servility of art professionals, and the diversion of key resources from other priorities. More saliently, in a material and spatial sense, the destruction of other monuments was a *precondition* for the construction of Stalinist ones: entire neighborhoods were razed (and their residents unceremoniously displaced) to make room for these developments, and other architectural landmarks were cannibalized for building materials. Most notoriously, marble from the dynamited Cathedral of Christ the Savior was used for the Okhotnyi Riad and Dvorets Sovetov metro stations (as well as for the Lenin Library), but in fact a full fifty churches were dismantled for construction inputs during the building of the Moscow metro alone.[34] Finally, and perhaps most importantly, the fact that Stalinist monuments were selected to outlast the centuries, whereas others were condemned to transience, created a fundamental disbalance in the built environment, with far-reaching effects on contemporary memory. As Valery Lazarev observes, for example, "it is easy to misjudge the Gulag's contribution because its more lasting monuments—the Moscow metro, the Moscow University . . . are what remain. Forgotten are the 'roads to nowhere,' long fallen into . . . decay."[35] Thus, the consciously prospective orientation of Stalinist monuments fundamentally obscures the wider ecosystem of violence that was inseparable from the Stalinist project.

Unfortunately, this dynamic is especially powerful given the rising salience of physical artefacts in contemporary collective memory, as younger generations lack personal experience of Soviet state socialism. As Serguei Oushakine observes, "the decreasing prominence of the firsthand knowledge of socialist lifestyle is compensated by the increasing visibility and importance of socialist things."[36] Curiously, the latter often induce sympathetic attitudes among today's youth. This "second-hand nostalgia," as Oushakine terms it, "foregrounds objects instead of memory, offering a particular form of affective experience."[37] This affective property is crucial, as the immediacy and tactility of material objects may trump the abstract, narrative-based "history" of Stalinist crimes. This is especially true of monumental works of art and architecture, which were intentionally designed to play on posterity's emotions. As Mukhina prophesied, "the contemporary life of our people, its suffering and great victories, will be transmitted to posterity primarily through works of art. No scientific or official documents will transmit the spirit of our times as colorfully as artwork."[38] Experience seems to bear this out, as odd juxtapositions surface in contemporary youth attitudes toward the Soviet past. One study of such perspectives noted that while Russian youth recognize the tragedy of Stalinist repressions, they nonetheless hold that at least Moscow has the best metro system in the world.[39] Thus, Stalinist monuments retain a fundamental productivity in contemporary Russia, actively shaping the memory (and amnesia) of their era, and resisting resignification—much as their creators had hoped.

Counteracting these significant mnemonic effects requires a concerted effort at exposing these monuments' fundamentally mendacious and amnestic character. There are, of course, various strategies for dealing with the monumental heritage of authoritarian regimes, ranging from intentional neglect to artistic mutilation, from fundamental repurposing to desacralization.[40] Needless to say, recommending specific strategies for reframing Stalinist monuments would require a separate study. Not only are these monuments diverse, but they also inhabit perennially shifting political contexts. Given their potentially high "discord value" (to use Gabi Dolff-Bonekämper's term), the fate of these monuments, and the way they are to be reframed, should in the last instance be decided by Russian citizens themselves, through a democratic and reflective process that appears improbable in the near future.[41]

What can be firmly established at this point, however, is the marked inadequacy of leaving Stalinist monuments "to their own devices," to stand prominently in their status as protected heritage. Among other places, this situation largely appears to be the case in Moscow, the focal point of the regime's monument-building program. As mentioned, under the Soviet de-Stalinization campaign and during the post-Soviet transition, the synthetic adornments of important edifices suffered partial attrition. But these demolitions simultaneously obliterated opportunities to critically reflect on the wider practice of monument building under Stalinism, and its effects on the post-Soviet memory landscape. Only a handful of sculptures were relocated to Moscow's Muzeon statue park, opened in early 1992. In theory, by creating a special, demarcated place for these objects, they were to have been symbolically separated from public life and robbed of their political salience.[42] Yet Muzeon's displays provide only minimal information about these monuments (listing little beyond their date of creation, authors, and subject).[43] Besides, scores of Stalinist statues, monumental artworks, and architectural monuments remain intact—and the work of contextualizing them, as objects with a conscious and mendacious commemorative mission, has not yet begun in earnest.

Museums can be effective in contextualizing the Stalinist monument-building program—its execution and aims—but here there is a notable dearth of exhibits and displays. The chronological coverage of the Museum of Moscow's permanent exhibition ends in the Petrine era. Despite its namesake, neither does the Shchusev State Museum of Architecture have a permanent exhibition on the Stalinist period. Until mid-2019, the former *All-Union Agricultural Exhibition* complex lacked even the smallest display devoted to its own history. Indeed, the massive pedestal of its Worker and Kolkhoz Woman monument, which in the years 2010–2017 hosted a small display devoted to the story of this famous sculpture, is now an open exhibition space. Mukhina's former workshop, for its part, now functions as a museum of Orthodox icons. True, the history of the Moscow metro is covered in a small permanent exhibition at the metro workers' recruitment center. However, the display manifests a rather superficial approach to the metro's Stalinist origins, lacking in critical distance. For instance, the ruthless secret police chief Feliks Dzerzhinskii, whose Lubianka station bust had been "saved for posterity" (sic) amid the iconoclastic wave of the early 1990s, is described as "a notable political, state, and economic functionary." Elsewhere, the exhibit capitalizes on the "retro appeal" of Soviet propaganda posters and photographs, which are reproduced in a vast collage, running along the perimeter of its exhibit hall. Taken together, the displays leave one entirely ignorant of any "peculiarities" of Stalinist metro construction, and how this might affect its legacy.

Explanatory plaques and information may also be affixed to monuments to frame them historically. The *Uznai Moskvu* initiative goes some way toward this. A collaborative project between the municipality's departments of education, culture, heritage, and IT, this interactive mobile app enables the public to get detailed information about the city's architectural and sculptural monuments by scanning QR codes. However, these information blurbs are typically limited to describing the technical and formal features of the monuments, usually in a neutral but sometimes exultant tone (the latter, presumably, due to the touristic mission of the *Uznai Moskvu* project). Thus, for instance, the text accompanying the Stalinist Ukraina Hotel high-rise explains that "for Russia, 'Stalinist classicism' and 'Stalinist architecture' have now become art, objects of national pride."[44] To be fair, some texts do refer to the use of prisoner labor,[45] to the political repression of architects,[46] and to the destruction of other heritage to make space for Stalinist constructions,[47] if only in passing.

By contrast, only a handful of physical counter-monuments dot Moscow's memorial landscape. One of the earliest examples of these was a memorial stone from the Solovki archipelago (the birthplace of the Gulag), placed in front of the former secret police headquarters on the Lubianka Square in 1991. Similarly, at the end of the decade, another countermonument dedicated to the victims of Stalinism was unveiled directly in front of a Stalin monument relocated to the Muzeon sculpture park. Such countermonuments may be particularly suitable as a critical backdrop to Stalinist infrastructural monuments, in which prisoner labor was often used. As Cynthia Ruder suggests, the Stalinist construction program "in spite of itself created fertile ground for planting . . . memorials to those who suffered and died in the quest to build that which had not been built before."[48] In addition to the Moscow-Volga Canal, which Ruder profiles, the metro, the high-rises, and other spaces may be especially effective for countermonuments prompting public discussion and reflection. After all, these were often sites of victimhood as much as of monumental achievements. Since 1989, for example, Iofan's House on the Embankment has hosted a permanent exhibition devoted to the repression of its residents—the Soviet cultural and political elite, hit particularly hard in the years of the Great Terror. A few other Stalinist constructions are overlayed by more unobtrusive countermonuments, such as the memorial plaques installed by the "Last Address" initiative (which are affixed to victims' last known residence), or inscriptions in "The Topography of Terror" online database (which maps Moscow sites connected to political repressions). However promising, these newer initiatives are unfortunately still fledgling and remain largely confined to Russia's major cities. Furthermore, in the increasingly repressive climate in the lead-up and wake of the invasion of Ukraine, their future is uncertain. Troublingly, Memorial, the main human rights group advocating for the memory of Stalinist crimes, was disbanded by court order in December 2021. Regardless of its specific (and fluctuating) assessment of the Stalin period, the regime's intolerance for grassroots activism will likely impede the process of reframing Stalinist monuments for the foreseeable future.

This is highly concerning. Stalinist monuments were built in order that posterity would remember the era favorably. Thanks in part to their design, these objects remain visually prominent and aesthetically pleasing. Often defying reinterpretation, they continue to support contemporary nationalist, imperialist, and statist commemorative discourses in Russia. Obscuring more than they reveal about the period, these monuments constitute powerful, affective representations that shape the collective memory of Stalinism in significant ways. Accordingly, they demand concerted efforts at contextualization, which would recover their problematic histories, counteract their immortalizing effects, and make manifest their intentional attempts to seduce us, the posterity for whom they were built.

NOTES

Introduction

1. Aleksandr Solzhenitsyn, *The Gulag Archipelago, 1918–1956. An Experiment in Literary Investigation. III-IV*, trans. Thomas Whitney (New York: Harper & Row, 1975, 86.

2. Richard Stites, "Stalinism and the Restructuring of Revolutionary Utopianism," in *The Culture of the Stalin Period*, ed. Hans Gunther (London: Macmillan, 1990), 83–85.

3. Sheila Fitzpatrick, *The Russian Revolution* (Oxford: Oxford University Press, [1982] 2017, 144.

4. Theodore Denno, *The Communist Millennium: The Soviet View* (The Hague: Martinus Nijhoff, 1964), 67–73.

5. Richard Stites, *Revolutionary Dreams: Utopian Vision and Experimental Life in the Russian Revolution* (Oxford: Oxford University Press, 1989), 236.

6. Nikolai Atarov, *Dvorets Sovetov* (Moscow: Moskovskii rabochii, 1940), 15.

7. Boris Iofan, "Stroitel'stvo Dvortsa Sovetov i sodruzhestvo iskusstv. Doklad akademika arkhitektury B. M. Iofana," in *Arkhitektura Dvortsa Sovetov. Materialy V plenuma Pravleniia SSA SSSR*, ed. I. Sushkevich (Moscow: Izdatel'stvo Akademii arkhitektury, 1939), 20; Evgenii Lansere, "Monumental'naia zhivopis'," *Izvestiia*, June 30, 1939, 3.

8. Vladimir Kholodkovskii, *Moskovskie vstrechi* (Moscow: Moskovskii rabochii, 1948), 97.

9. Nicholas Timasheff, *The Great Retreat: The Growth and Decline of Communism in Russia* (New York: Dutton, 1946), 278.

10. For a classic formulation of this argument, see Eric Hobsbawm and Terence Ranger, eds., *The Invention of Tradition* (Cambridge: Cambridge University Press, 1983).

11. Katerina Clark, *Petersburg, Crucible of Cultural Revolution* (Cambridge, MA: Harvard University Press, 1995), 25–27; David Hoffmann, "Was There a 'Great Retreat' from Soviet Socialism? Stalinist Culture Reconsidered," *Kritika: Explorations in Russian and Eurasian History* 5, no. 4 (2004).

12. This Foucauldian concept is applied to Stalinist monuments by Monica Ruthers, "Sovetskaia rodina kak prostranstvo gorodskoi arkhitektury," *Ab Imperio* 2 (2006): 205–208.

13. This doctrine was officially introduced—and duly endorsed—at the First Congress of Soviet Writers (1934) by the party's Central Committee secretary Andrei Zhdanov, "Soviet Literature—The Richest in Ideas, the Most Advanced Literature," in *Soviet Writers' Congress 1934: The Debate on Socialist Realism and Modernism in the Soviet Union*, ed. Maksim Gorkii (London: Lawrence & Wishart, 1977), 21.

14. Lars Blomqvist, "Some Utopian Elements in Stalinist Art," *Russian History* 11, no. 2–3 (1984): 298–299.

15. Evgenii Dobrenko, *Stalinist Cinema and the Production of History: Museum of the Revolution* (Edinburgh: Edinburgh University Press, 2008), 6; Evgenii Dobrenko, "Socialist Realism and Stasis," in *Utopian Reality: Reconstructing Culture in Revolutionary Russia and Beyond*, ed. Christina Lodder, Maria Kokkori, and Maria Mileeva (Leiden: Brill, 2013), 194.

16. In this respect, I build on recent social histories of Stalinist urbanism, including Heather DeHaan, *Stalinist City Planning: Professionals, Performance, and Power* (Toronto: University of Toronto Press, 2012); Michal Murawski, *The Palace Complex: A Stalinist Skyscraper, Capitalist Warsaw, and a City Transfixed* (Bloomington: Indiana University Press, 2019); Katherine Zubovich, *Moscow Monumental: Soviet Skyscrapers and Urban Life in Stalin's Capital* (Princeton, NJ: Princeton University Press, 2021).

17. Anatolii Lunacharskii, "Sotsialisticheskii arkhitekturnyi monument," *Stroitel'stvo Moskvy*, no. 5–6 (1933): 3.

18. Anatolii Lunacharskii, "Ob arkhitekturno-khudozhestvennom oformlenii Moskvy," *Stroitel'stvo Moskvy*, no. 6 (1934): 33.

19. Vlas Chubar', "Rech' zamestitelia Predsedatelia Soveta Narodnykh Komissarov SSSR tov. V. Ia. Chubaria," in *Postanovleniia i materialy. Pervyi vsesoiuznyi s"ezd sovetskikh arkhitektorov*, ed. A. Barkhudarian and N. Kirsanova (Moscow: Izdatel'stvo Akademii arkhitektury, 1937), 26.

20. Alois Riegl, "The Modern Cult of Monuments: Its Character and Its Origin," in *Oppositions Reader: Selected Readings from a Journal for Ideas and Criticism in Architecture, 1973–1984*, ed. Kenneth Michael Hays (Princeton, NJ: Princeton Architectural Press, 1998), 621. Riegl did not use the term "prospective monument," but this later concept is evocative of future-oriented memorialization that he brought attention to, see Jan Assmann, *Cultural Memory and Early Civilization: Writing, Remembrance, and Political Imagination* (Cambridge: Cambridge University Press, 2011), 45–48, 54.

21. David Arkin, "Monumenty geroiam Velikoi Otechestvennoi voiny. Zametki o konkurse," *Arkhitektura SSSR*, no. 5 (1944): 3.

22. I have been unable to locate an exhaustive list of all stand-alone sculptural monuments constructed or commissioned in the Stalin period. However, according to an interim report, only half of the sculptural monuments commissioned by the central government in the years 1932–1945 memorialized individuals who had been active since 1932, GARF f. R5446, op. 50, d. 2826, ll. 107–122.

23. This included such themes as Stalin's [sic] struggle for industrialization (250–300 m^2), Stalin's struggle for collectivization (250–300 m^2), Stalin's struggle for completing the construction of a socialist society, and Stalin's drafting of the new Soviet constitution of 1936 (750 m^2), TsGAM f. 694, op. 1, d. 136, ll. 3–7, 36–37.

24. See, for instance, I. Sushkevich, ed., *Arkhitektura Dvortsa Sovetov. Materialy V plenuma Pravleniia SSA SSSR* (Moscow: Izdatel'stvo Akademii arkhitektury, 1939), 23, 62.

25. Isaak Eigel', *Boris Iofan* (Moscow: Stroiizdat, 1978), 108–116.

26. Hermann Lübbe, *V nogu so vremenem. Sokrashchennoe prebyvanie v nastoiashchem*, trans. Aleksei Grigor'ev and Vitalii Kurennoi (Moscow: Izdatel'skii dom Vysshei shkoly ekonomiki, 2016), 185–203.

27. Aaron Cohen, *War Monuments, Public Patriotism, and Bereavement in Russia, 1905–2015* (Lanham, MD: Lexington Books, 2020), 7–9.

28. Matthew Bown, *Art under Stalin* (New York: Holmes & Meier, 1991), 87.

29. This was no exception: in 1935, the jury panel of even such a minor project as the (ultimately uncompleted) "Monument to the Cheliuskin Expedition" included such notables as Politburo members Valerian Kuibyshev and Andrei Andreev, as well as Ivan Akulov, Nikita Khrushchev, and Nikolai Bulganin, RGASPI/17/120/163/6-7, GARF/R3316/65/132/1-2.

30. Robert Davies et al., eds., *The Stalin-Kaganovich Correspondence, 1931–36* (New Haven, CT: Yale University Press, 2008), 177–178.

31. RGALI f. 619, op. 1, ed. khr. 1077, ll. 9, 17–18.

32. For instance, sculptors Nina Zelenskaia, Vera Mukhina, and Zinaida Ivanova were forced to rework their design of Moscow's Maksim Gor'kii monument in response to Stalin's remarks, RGASPI f. 17, op. 132, d. 424, l. 55; RGALI f. 3024, op. 1, ed. khr. 20, l. 2.

33. Igor Golomstock, *Totalitarian Art: In the Soviet Union, the Third Reich, Fascist Italy, and the People's Republic of China*, trans. Robert Chandler (London: Collins Harvill, [1990] 2011, 267.

34. For a discussion of the term, see Anna Neimark, "The Infrastructural Monument: Stalin's Water Works under Construction and in Representation," *Future Anterior* 9, no. 2 (2013).

35. Quoted in Eric Michaud, *The Cult of Art in Nazi Germany* (Stanford, CA: Stanford University Press, 2004), 208.

36. Quoted in Peter Adam, *Art of the Third Reich* (New York: Harry N. Abrams, 1992), 225.

37. Albert Speer, *Inside the Third Reich: Memoirs*, trans. Richard Winston and Clara Winston (New York: Macmillan, 1970), 56.

1. Stalinist Monuments in Context

1. Quoted in Anatolii Lunacharskii, "Lenin o monumental'noi propagande," *Literaturnaia gazeta*, January 29, 1933, 1.

2. Quoted in Lunacharskii, "Lenin o monumental'noi propagande," 1.

3. Anatolii Lunacharskii, "Monumental'naia agitatsiia," in *A. V. Lunacharkii ob iskusstve. Tom 2*, ed. Igor' Sats and A. Ermakov (Moscow: Iskusstvo, [1918] 1982), 51.

4. "Spisok lits koim predlozheno postavit' monumenty v g. Moskve i v drugikh gorodakh RSFSR, predstavlennyi v Sovet Narodnykh Komissarov Otdelom izobrazitel'nykh iskusstv Narodnogo komissariata po prosveshcheniiu," *Izvestiia*, August 2, 1918.

5. "O pamiatnikakh respubliki," *Izvestiia*, April 14, 1918, 3.

6. Christina Lodder, "Lenin's Plan for Monumental Propaganda," in *Art of the Soviets: Painting, Sculpture and Architecture in a One-Party State*, ed. Matthew Bown and Brandon Taylor (Manchester: Manchester University Press, 1993), 18, 27–30.

7. Respectively, Katerina Clark, *Petersburg, Crucible of Cultural Revolution* (Cambridge: Harvard University Press, 1995), 141; Susan Buck-Morss, *Dreamworld and Catastrophe: The Passing of Mass Utopia in East and West* (Cambridge, MA: MIT Press, 2000), 139.

8. GARF f. R8300, op. 26, d. 587, l. 101.

9. Catherine Merridale, *Night of Stone: Death and Memory in Russia* (London: Granta, 2000), 105–108.

10. Aaron Cohen, *War Monuments, Public Patriotism, and Bereavement in Russia, 1905–2015* (Lanham, MD: Lexington Books, 2020), 62.

11. Quoted in Marie Lampard, "Larger Than Life: Soviet Monumental Sculpture in the Stalin Period," *Experiment* 18, no. 1 (2012): 210.

12. Quoted in Jonathan Brooks Platt, "Snow White and the Enchanted Palace: A Reading of Lenin's Architectural Cult," *Representations* 129, no. 1 (2015): 93.

13. Merridale, *Night of Stone*, 189.

14. Benno Ennker, *Formirovanie kul'ta Lenina v Sovetskom Soiuze*, trans. Aslan Gadzhikurbanov (Moscow: ROSSPEN, 2011), 277–279.

15. Quoted in Nina Tumarkin, *Lenin Lives!: The Lenin Cult in Soviet Russia* (Cambridge, MA: Harvard University Press, 1983), 177.

16. Ennker, *Formirovanie kul'ta Lenina*, 315–320, 341–343.

17. "Ne torguite Leninym!," *LEF*, no. 5 (1924): 4.

18. Vladimir Paperny, *Architecture in the Age of Stalin: Culture Two*, trans. John Hill and Roann Barris (Cambridge: Cambridge University Press, 2002), 70–104.

19. Vladimir Mayakovsky, *Poems*, trans. Dorian Rottenberg (Moscow: Progress, 1972), 176, 265–266.

20. "Postanovlenie tsentral'nogo Komiteta Kommunisticheskoi partii Sovetskogo Soiuza i Soveta Ministrov Soiuza SSSR o sooruzhenii Panteona - pamiatnika vechnoi slavy velikikh liudei Sovetskoi strany," *Pravda*, March 7, 1953, 2.

21. Lazar' Kaganovich, *Za sotsialisticheskuiu rekonstruktsiiu Moskvy i gorodov SSSR. Pererabotannaia stenogramma doklada na iun'skom plenume TsK VKP(b)* (Moscow: OGIZ "Moskovskii Rabochii," 1931).

22. Nikolai Chernyshev, "Problemy monumental'noi zhivopisi," *Iskusstvo*, no. 1–2 (1933): 44.

23. RGALI f. 2943, op. 1, ed. khr. 186, l. 4.

24. RGALI f. 674, op. 2, ed. khr. 185, ll. 10, 22.

25. "Monumental'noe iskusstvo," in *Bol'shaia sovetskaia entsikolopediia. Tom 28*, ed. B. Vvedenskii (Moscow: Gosudarstvennoe nauchnoe izdatel'stvo 'Bol'shaia sovetskaia entsiklopedia', 1954), 263.

26. Nikolai Kolli, "Arkhitektura metro," in *Kak my stroili metro*, ed. Aleksandr Kosarev (Moscow: Istoriia fabrik i zavodov, 1935), 185.

27. "Iz predstavlennoi v SNK SSSR i TsK VKP(b) dokladnoi zapiski Moskovskogo oblastnogo i gorodskogo komitetov VKP(b) i Moskovskogo soveta RK i KD o general'nom plane rekonstruktsii g. Moskvy," in *General'nyi plan rekonstruktsii goroda Moskvy. Postanovleniia i materialy*, ed. Ia. Tsvankin (Moscow: Moskovskii rabochii, 1936), 73.

28. Ennker, *Formirovanie kul'ta Lenina*, 305.

29. On charges of treason and "wrecking," scores of art professionals and their managing counterparts were executed, sentenced to labor camps, or rotated into new positions (the latter, presumably, to break the power of local cliques).

30. Katerina Clark, "The New Moscow and the New Happiness: Architecture as the Nodal Point in the Stalinist System of Value," in *Petrified Utopia: Happiness Soviet Style*, ed. Marina Balina and Evgeny Dobrenko (London: Anthem Press, 2009), 194.

31. Karo Alabian and Vasilii Simbirtsev, "Arkhitekturnyi pamiatnik Krasnoi Armii," *Planirovka i stroitel'stvo gorodov*, no. 10 (1934): 22.

32. Quoted in Katerina Clark, "Sotsrealizm i sakralizatsiia prostranstva," in *Sotsrealisticheskii kanon*, ed. Evgenii Dobrenko and Hans Gunther (St. Petersburg: Akademicheskii proekt, 2000), 123.

33. RGALI f. 2075, op. 7, ed. khr. 51, ll. 124–125. Officially, the ban was lifted in 1944, GARF f. A259, op. 6 d. 1351, l. 8.

34. Aleksei Dushkin, "Stantsiia metro 'Zavod imeni Stalina'. 1939–1943. Stantsiia metro 'Paveletskaia-radial'naia'. 1941–1943," in *Aleksei Nikolaevich Dushkin. Arkhitektura 1930–1950-kh godov. Katalog vystavki*, ed. Natal'ia Dushkina (Moscow: A-Fond, 2004), 196.

35. Vladimir Tolstoi, "Leninskii plan monumental'noi propagandy v deistvii," *Iskusstvo*, no. 1 (1952): 64.

36. GARF f. A259, op. 4, d. 1522, l. 3. In fact, in 1949, the chairman of the municipal executive council, Aleksandr Shurpin, was fired, expelled from the party, and arrested for the project's massive cost overruns.

37. Mikhail Kalinin, "Bol'shaia obshenarodnaia zadacha," *Izvestiia*, December 10, 1943, 2.

38. RGALI f. 962, op. 3, d. 1367, ll. 30, 145.

39. Iuliia Kosenkova, *Sovetskii gorod 1940-kh—pervoi poloviny 1950-kh godov: ot tvorcheskikh poiskov k praktike stroitel'stva* (Moscow: Editorial URSS, 2000), 46.

40. Tat'iana Malinina and Elena Ogarkova, *Pamiat' i vremia: iz khudozhestvennogo arkhiva Velikoi Otechestvennoi voiny 1941–1945 gg.* (Moscow: Galart, 2011), 277.

41. See Dmitrii Chechulin, *Zhizn' i zodchestvo* (Moscow: Molodaia gvardiia, 1978), 97; Mikhail Posokhin, *Arkhitektura okruzhaiushchei sredy* (Moscow: Stroiizdat, 1989), 198–199, 202.

42. Iu. Shaposhnikov, "Dostoinstva i nedostatki arkhitektury novykh stantsii metropolitena," *Arkhitektura SSSR*, no. 4 (1952): 3.

43. Vera Mukhina, *Literaturno-kriticheskoe nasledie* (Moscow: Iskusstvo, 1960), 137, 145, 158.

44. Quoted in Aleksei Zotov, *Mukhina, Vera Ignat'evna, narodnyi khudozhnik SSSR* (Moscow: Iskusstvo, 1944), 12–13.

45. Quoted in Margarita Nekhezina, *Russkii Mikelandzhelo: o tvorchestve Evgeniia Vucheticha* (Volgograd: Izdatel', 2011), 19; Evgenii Vuchetich and Iakov Belopol'skii, "Pamiatnik general-leitenantu Efremovu," *Iskusstvo*, no. 3 (1947): 29.

46. Though not explicitly in response to Gundorov's memo, RGASPI f. 17, op. 125, d. 368, ll. 6–11.

47. Anders Aman, *Architecture and Ideology in Eastern Europe during the Stalin Era: An Aspect of Cold War History*, trans. Roger Tanner and Kerstin Tanner (Cambridge, MA: MIT Press, 1992), 37.

48. RGALI f. 674 op. 3 ed. khr. 1945 l. 1; RGAE f. 339, op. 1, d. 1132, l. 121.

49. Quoted in Iurii Gerchuk, "The Aesthetics of Everyday Life in the Khrushchev Thaw in the USSR (1954–1964)," in *Style and Socialism: Modernity and Material Culture in Post-War Eastern Europe*, ed. Susan Reid and David Crowley (Oxford: Berg, 2000), 82–83.

50. Lev Rudnev, "O formalizme i klassike," *Arkhitektura SSSR*, no. 11 (1954): 31.

51. Catherine Cooke, "Beauty as a Route to 'the Radiant Future': Responses of Soviet Architecture," *Journal of Design History* 10, no. 2 (1997): 139.

52. Graeme Gill, "Building the Communist Future: Legitimation and the Soviet City," in *Russian Politics from Lenin to Putin*, ed. Stephen Fortescue (Basingstoke, UK: Palgrave Macmillan, 2010), 91.

53. Steven Harris, *Communism on Tomorrow Street: Mass Housing and Everyday Life after Stalin* (Washington, DC: Woodrow Wilson Center Press, 2013), 191–192.

54. Dmitrii Khmel'nitskii, *Arkhitektura Stalina. Psikhologiia i stil'* (Moscow: Progress-Traditsiia, 2007), 335–345.
55. Nikita Voronov, *Monumental'noe iskusstvo vchera i segodnia* (Moscow: Znanie, 1988), 14.
56. A. Khalturin, *Monumenty SSSR* (Moscow: Sovetskii khudozhnik, 1969), 16.

2. Historicist Aesthetics

1. See Victor Buchli, "Moisei Ginzburg's Narkomfin Communal House in Moscow: Contesting the Social and Material World," *The Journal of the Society of Architectural Historians* 57, no. 2 (1998).
2. Sovet stroitel'stva Dvortsa Sovetov, "Ob organizatsii rabot po okonchatel'nomu sostavleniiu proekta Dvortsa sovetov SSSR v gor. Moskve," *Stroitel'stvo Moskvy*, no. 3 (1932): 16.
3. Richard Anderson, "The Future of History: The Cultural Politics of Soviet Architecture, 1928–41" (PhD dissertation, Columbia University, 2010), 77.
4. Anatole Kopp, *Town and Revolution: Soviet Architecture and City Planning, 1917–1935*, trans. Thomas Burton (New York: Braziller, 1970), 227.
5. "Uroki maiskoi arkhitekturnoi vystavki: tvorcheskaia diskussiia v Soiuze sovetskikh arkhitektorov," *Arkhitektura SSSR*, no. 6 (1934): 5.
6. I. Cherkasskii, "Zhilye doma, a ne korpusa-kazarmy. Tsentralizovannyi fond Mossoveta v 1932 g.," *Stroitel'stvo Moskvy*, no. 7 (1932): 8. Italics mine.
7. See Aleksandra Selivanova, *Postkonstruktivizm. Vlast' i arkhitektura v 1930-e gody v SSSR* (Moscow: BuksMArt, 2020).
8. Frank Lloyd Wright, "Architecture and Life in the USSR," *Architectural Record* 82, no. 4 (1937): 59.
9. Respectively, Pamela Davidson, *Cultural Memory and Survival: The Russian Renaissance of Classical Antiquity in the Twentieth Century* (London: School of Slavonic and East European Studies, UCL, 2009), 17; Alexei Tarkhanov and Sergei Kavtaradze, *Architecture of the Stalin Era* (New York: Rizzoli, 1992), 110.
10. Vladimir Paperny, *Architecture in the Age of Stalin: Culture Two*, trans. John Hill and Roann Barris (Cambridge: Cambridge University Press, 2002), 19.
11. Boris Groys, *The Total Art of Stalinism: Avant-Garde, Aesthetic Dictatorship, and Beyond*, trans. Charles Rougle (Princeton, NJ: Princeton University Press, 1992), 47–48, 73.
12. Monica Ruthers, "Sovetskaia rodina kak prostranstvo gorodskoi arkhitektury," *Ab Imperio* 2 (2006): 229.
13. Katerina Clark, *Moscow as Fourth Rome: Stalinism, Cosmopolitanism, and the Evolution of Soviet Culture, 1931–1941* (Cambridge, MA: Harvard University Press, 2011), 117–119.
14. Dmitrii Khmel'nitskii, *Zodchii Stalin* (Moscow: Novoe literaturnoe obozrenie, 2007), 309.
15. Ivan Fomin, "Tvorcheskie puti sovetskoi arkhitektury i problema arkhitekturnogo nasledstva. I. A. Fomin," *Arkhitektura SSSR*, no. 3–4 (1933): 15.
16. Il'ia Golosov, "O bol'shoi arkhitekturnoi forme," *Arkhitektura SSSR*, no. 5 (1933): 34.
17. Aleksei Shchusev, "Klassiki i my," *Izvestiia*, May 9, 1937, 3.

18. Andrei Bunin and Mariia Kruglova, *Arkhitekturnaia kompozitsiia gorodov* (Moscow: Izdatel'stvo Akademii arkhitektury SSSR, 1940), 1.

19. Bunin and Kruglova, *Arkhitekturnaia kompozitsiia gorodov*; Mariia Kruglova, *Monumenty v arkhitekture gorodov* (Moscow: Gosudarstvennoe izdatel'stvo literatury po stroitel'stvu i arkhitekture, 1952), 94–97. These postwar studies included samplings of both classical and national monuments.

20. Georgii Gol'ts, "Ob ideinosti v arkhitekture," *Stroitel'naia gazeta*, March 8, 1940, 3.

21. Moisei Ginzburg, "Organicheskoe v arkhitekture i prirode," *Arkhitektura SSSR*, no. 3 (1939): 76.

22. Georgii Borisovskii, "Narodnoe tvorchestvo, klassicheskii order i sovremennyi standart," *Arkhitektura SSSR*, no. 13 (1946): 30.

23. Viacheslav Shkvarikov, "Planirovka i stroitel'stvo russkikh gorodov," in *Russkaia arkhitektura: doklady, prochitannye v sviazi s dekadnikom po russkoi arkhitekture v Moskve v aprele 1939 g*, ed. Viacheslav Shkvarikov (Moscow: Gosudarstvennoe izdatel'stvo Akademii arkhitektury SSSR, 1940), 15.

24. Erik van Ree, *The Political Thought of Joseph Stalin: A Study in Twentieth Century Revolutionary Patriotism* (London: Routledge, 2003), 190–191.

25. Ginzburg, "Organicheskoe v arkhitekture i prirode," 77.

26. Nikolai Sokolov, "Klassika i sovremennost'," *Sovetskoe iskusstvo*, June 8, 1945, 2.

27. "Narodnoe tvorchestvo," *Arkhitektura SSSR*, no. 1 (1937): 13.

28. Mikhail Tsapenko, *O realisticheskikh osnovakh sovetskoi arkhitektury* (Moscow: Gosudarstvennoe izdatel'stvo literatury po stroitel'stvu i arkhitekture, 1952), 63–64. Italics mine.

29. RGALI f. 674, op. 2, ed. khr. 185, l. 36.

30. Aleksei Shchusev, "Natsional'naia forma v arkhitekture," *Arkhitektura SSSR*, no. 10 (1940): 57.

31. Greg Castillo, "Soviet Orientalism: Socialist Realism and Built Tradition," *Traditional Dwellings and Settlements Review* 8, no. 2 (1997): 40–41.

32. RGAE f. 339, op. 1, d. 1196, l. 168.

33. Terry Martin, *The Affirmative Action Empire: Nations and Nationalism in the Soviet Union, 1923–1939* (Ithaca, NY: Cornell University Press, 2001), 455–457.

34. Castillo, "Soviet Orientalism," 92.

35. In effect, the architectural style of high and late Stalinism manifested a "multiple personality disorder," Greg Castillo, "Peoples at an Exhibition: Soviet Architecture and the National Question," in *Socialist Realism without Shores*, ed. Thomas Lahusen and Evgeny Dobrenko (Durham, NC: Duke University Press, 1997), 112–113.

36. I am thankful to Jan Plamper for this formulation.

37. Andrew Jenks, "A Metro on the Mount: The Underground as a Church of Soviet Civilization," *Technology and Culture* 41, no. 4 (2000): 710.

38. Mikhail Yampolsky, "In the Shadow of Monuments: Notes on Iconoclasm and Time," in *Soviet Hieroglyphics: Visual Culture in Late Twentieth-Century Russia*, ed. Nancy Condee (Bloomington: Indiana University Press, 1995), 98–99.

39. Evgenii Dobrenko, *Politiekonomiia sotsrealizma* (Moscow: Novoe literaturnoe obozreniie, 2007), 439; Paperny, *Architecture in the Age of Stalin*, 18, 157, 161.

40. See Ihor Junyk, "'Not Months but Moments': Ephemerality, Monumentality, and the Pavilion in Ruins," *Open Arts Journal*, no. 2 (2013–2014).

41. RGAE f. 4372, op. 34, d. 110, l. 32, A. Vladimirskii, ed., *Otdelochnye materialy dlia Dvortsa Sovetov* (Moscow: Izdatel'stvo akademii arkhitektury SSSR, 1945), 16–17.

42. Sergei Merkurov, "Osnovnaia skul'ptura Dvortsa Sovetov - statuia V. I. Lenina," in *Arkhitektura Dvortsa Sovetov. Materialy V plenuma Pravleniia SSA SSSR*, ed. I. Sushkevich (Moscow: Izdatel'stvo Akademii arkhitektury, 1939), 35.

43. A. Peganov, "A. A. Peganov (Moskva)," in *Arkhitektura Dvortsa Sovetov. Materialy V plenuma Pravleniia SSA SSSR*, ed. I. Sushkevich (Moscow: Izdatel'stvo Akademii arkhitektury, 1939), 70.

44. Vladimirskii, *Otdelochnye materialy dlia Dvortsa Sovetov*, 124–130.

45. Quoted in in Nikolai Chernyshev, "O rabotakh nashikh monumentalistakh," *Iskusstvo*, no. 4 (1934): 33. RGALI f. 2932, op. 1, ed. khr. 99, ll. 21–22.

46. "Kamen' v arkhitekture," *Sovetskoe iskusstvo*, October 12, 1945, 4.

47. Anatolii Lunacharskii, "Dvorets Sovetov. Tov. A. V. Lunacharskii ob arkhitekturnykh proektakh," *Sovetskoe iskusstvo*, January 26, 1932, 1.

48. Soiuz Arkhitektorov SSSR, *Tvorcheskie voprosy sovetskoi arkhitektury i zadachi Soiuza sovetskikh arkhitektorov. Postanovlenie Prezidiuma Sovetskikh arkhitektorov SSSR 23 oktiabria 1946 goda* (Moscow: Izdatel'stvo Akademii arkhitektury SSSR, 1946), 6.

49. Aleksei Tolstoi, "Poiski monumental'nosti," *Izvestiia*, February 27, 1932, 2.

50. "Monumental'nost'," in *Bol'shaia sovetskaia entsikolopediia. Tom 40*, ed. O. Shmidt (Moscow: Gosudarstvennyi Institut 'Sovetskaia entsiklopedia', 1938), 132.

51. TsGAM f. 694, op. 1, d. 137, l. 17.

52. GARF f. R5325, op. 9, d. 2567, ll. 1, 5–6.

53. TsGAM f. 694, op. 1, d. 137, ll. 5–14.

54. B. Blokhin, "K voprosu o monumental'nom iskusstve," *Iskusstvo*, no. 4 (1934): 3; M. Sar'ian, "Narodnyi khudozhnik Armenii M. S. Sar'ian (Erevan)," in *Arkhitektura Dvortsa Sovetov. Materialy V plenuma Pravleniia SSA SSSR*, ed. I. Sushkevich (Moscow: Izdatel'stvo Akademii arkhitektury, 1939), 60.

55. Ivan Rakhmanov, "Skul'ptor I. F. Rakhmanov (Moskva)," in *Arkhitektura Dvortsa Sovetov. Materialy V plenuma Pravleniia SSA SSSR*, ed. I. Sushkevich (Moscow: Izdatel'stvo Akademii arkhitektury, 1939), 54. Relatedly, one visitor of a 1934 exhibition of Palace of the Soviets designs expressed skepticism over the long-term structural integrity of a monument soaring to over 300 meters, instead proposing a low-rise "palace composed in the old style," along with "a large sphinx of [Vladimir] Il'ich [Lenin] . . . for this would be a monument that would last several centuries," TsGAM f. 694, op. 1, d. 44, l. 22.

56. Nikolai Atarov, *Dvorets Sovetov* (Moscow: Moskovskii rabochii, 1940), 80.

57. RGALI f. 2943, op. 1, ed. khr. 352, l. 12.

58. Aleksandr Gerasimov, "A. M. Gerasimov," in *Voprosy razvitiia sovetskoi skul'ptury. Nauchnaia konferentsiia. 28–30 maia 1952 g*, ed. Matvei Manizer (Moscow: Izdatel'stvo Akademii khudozhestv SSSR, 1953), 154–155.

59. Vladimir Frolov, "Mozaika v arkhitekture," *Arkhitketurnaia gazeta*, February 8, 1935, 3.

60. Aleksei Dushkin, "Iz poiasnitel'noi zapiski k proektu stantsii 'Maiakovskaia'," in *Aleksei Nikolaevich Dushkin. Arkhitektura 1930–1950-kh godov. Katalog vystavki*, ed. Natal'ia Dushkina (Moscow: A-Fond, 2004), 173.

61. Aleksandr Deineka, "Khudozhniki v metro," *Iskusstvo*, no. 6 (1938): 80.

62. Vladimir Frolov, "Mozaika Dvortsa Sovetov," *Dvorets Sovetov*, January 11, 1940, 3.

63. Aleksandr Deineka, "K voprosu o monumental'nom iskusstve," *Iskusstvo*, no. 4 (1934): 4–5.

64. Robert Genin, "Nastennaia zhivopis' i ee tekhnika," *Arkhitektura SSSR*, no. 6 (1939): 26.

65. Chernyshev, "O rabotakh nashikh monumentalistakh," 33–34; Boris Iofan and Vladimir Gel'freikh, "Nekotorye problemy stroitel'stva Dvortsa Sovetov," *Stroitel'stvo Moskvy*, no. 5 (1939): 7. For encaustic painting, see RGALI f. 2943 op. 1, ed. khr. 1527, ll. 43–44. For tapestries, see Aleksandr Deineka, "Zhivopis' v inter'ere," *Arkhitektura SSSR*, no. 6 (1939): 25.

66. Respectively, Viacheslav Oltarzhevskii, *Stroitel'stvo vysotnykh zdanii v Moskve* (Moscow: Gosudarstvennoe izdatel'stvo literatury po stroitel'stvu i arkhitekture, 1953), 214; Sergei Balashov and Aleksei Voronkov, *Dvorets nauki* (Moscow: Moskovskii rabochii, 1954), 30.

67. Balashov and Voronkov, *Dvorets nauki*, 135.

68. Balashov and Voronkov, *Dvorets nauki*, 135, 167–169.

69. Nikolai Tomskii, "Khudozhestvennoe oformlenie dvortsa nauki," in *Dvorets nauki. Rasskazy stroitelei novogo zdaniia Moskovskogo gosudarstvennogo universiteta*, ed. V. Pospelov (Moscow: Izdatel'stvo VTsSPS Profizdat, 1952), 127.

70. RGALI f. 2943, op. 1, ed. khr. 2222, l. 48.

71. Balashov and Voronkov, *Dvorets nauki*, 162–163.

72. Andrew Day, "The Rise and Fall of Stalinist Architecture," in *Architectures of Russian Identity*, ed. James Cracraft and Daniel Rowland (Ithaca, NY: Cornell University Press, 2003), 188.

73. "Stripped classicism," as the dominant style of the global interwar period, was first conceptualized by Robert Stern, *Modern Classicism* (New York: Rizzoli, 1988).

74. William Rhoads, "Franklin D. Roosevelt and Washington Architecture," *Records of the Columbia Historical Society* 52 (1989): 162.

75. Quoted in Eric Michaud, *The Cult of Art in Nazi Germany* (Stanford, CA: Stanford University Press, 2004), 109.

76. Stern, *Modern Classicism*, 35.

77. Adolf Hitler, *Hitler's Table Talk, 1941–44: His Private Conversations*, trans. Norman Cameron and R. H. Stevens (London: Weidenfeld and Nicolson, 1973), 82.

78. Albert Speer, *Inside the Third Reich: Memoirs*, trans. Richard Winston and Clara Winston (New York: Macmillan, 1970), 181.

79. Quoted in Thomas Friedrich, *Hitler's Berlin: Abused City*, trans. Stewart Spencer (New Haven, CT: Yale University Press, 2012), 227.

80. Speer, *Inside the Third Reich*, 168.

81. Quoted in Aristotle Kallis, *The Third Rome, 1922–1943: The Making of the Fascist Capital* (Basingstoke, UK: Palgrave Macmillan, 2014), 135; Anna Vyazemtseva, "Soviet Fascination for Fascist Rome, or The International Style of Regimes," in *Blickwendungen: Architektenreisen nach Italien in Moderne und Gegenwart*, ed. Kai Kappel and Erik Wegerhoff (Munich: Hirmer, 2019), 125, 128.

82. Paperny, *Architecture in the Age of Stalin*, 31.

83. These included important exchanges linked to the Palace of the Soviets project, see Katherine Zubovich, *Moscow Monumental: Soviet Skyscrapers and Urban Life in Stalin's Capital* (Princeton, NJ: Princeton University Press, 2021), 40–54.

84. Irina Azizian, "Inobytie ar-deco v otechestvennoi arkhitekture," in *Arkhitektura Stalinskoi epokhi: opyt istoricheskogo osmysleniia*, ed. Iuliia Kosenkova (Moscow: KomKniga, 2010), 60.

3. Synthetic Composition

1. TsGAM f. 694, op. 1, d. 29, l. 58.
2. TsGAM f. 694, op. 1, d. 44, l. 81.
3. Viktor Vesnin, "Iazyk epokhi," *Sovetskoe iskusstvo*, March, 15 1932, 1.
4. David Arkin, "Monumenty geroiam Velikoi Otechestvennoi voiny. Zametki o konkurse," *Arkhitektura SSSR*, no. 5 (1944): 4.
5. RGALI f. 674, op. 2, ed. khr. 185, ll. 32–33, 66.
6. See Tat'iana Malinina and Elena Ogarkova, *Pamiat' i vremia: iz khudozhestvennogo arkhiva Velikoi Otechestvennoi voiny 1941–1945 gg.* (Moscow: Galart, 2011), 203–300.
7. Soiuz Arkhitektorov SSSR, *Tvorcheskie voprosy sovetskoi arkhitektury i zadachi Soiuza sovetskikh arkhitektorov. Postanovlenie Prezidiuma Sovetskikh arkhitektorov SSSR 23 oktiabria 1946 goda* (Moscow: Izdatel'stvo Akademii arkhitektury SSSR, 1946), 12–13.
8. "Zhiznennye zadachi arkhitekturnoi praktiki," *Arkhitektura SSSR*, no. 13 (1946): 1.
9. RGALI f. 2943, op. 1, ed. khr. 2222, l. 63.
10. TsGAM f. 534, op. 1, d. 110, l. 153.
11. Sergei Chernyshev, *General'nyi plan rekonstruktsii Moskvy i voprosy planirovki gorodov SSSR. Doklad prof. S. E. Chernysheva na Vsesoiuznom s"ezde sovetskikh arkhitektorov* (Moscow: Izdatel'stvo Vsesoiuznoi akademii arkhitektury, 1937), 11.
12. See Steven Maddox, *Saving Stalin's Imperial City: Historic Preservation in Leningrad, 1930–1950* (Bloomington: Indiana University Press, 2014).
13. TsGAM f. 150, op. 1, d. 1245, l. 341.
14. For a detailed discussion of ensembles in the theory of Stalinist urban planning, see Iuliia Starostenko, "Problema ansamblia v sovetskom gradostroitel'stve 1920-1930-kh gg," in *Sovetskoe gradostroitel'stvo, 1917–1941. Kniga pervaia*, ed. Iuliia Kosenkova (Moscow: Progress-Traditsiia, 2018).
15. Lev Il'in, "Ansambl' v arkhitekture goroda," *Arkhitektura SSSR*, no. 5 (1935): 50.
16. Serguei Oushakine, "Remembering in Public: On the Affective Management of History," *Ab Imperio* 2013, no. 1 (2013): 273.
17. Aleksei Shchusev and V. Lavrov, "General'nyi plan Novgoroda," *Arkhitektura i stroitel'stvo*, no. 5 (1946): 4–5.
18. Iulii Savitskii, "Ansambl' v sovetskom gradostroitel'stve," in *Problema ansamblia v sovetskoi arkhitekture. Sbornik statei*, ed. K. Trapeznikov (Moscow: Gosudarstvennoe izdatel'stvo literatury po stroitel'stvu i arkhitekture, 1952), 8.
19. See Dmitrii Chechulin, "Arkhitektura Moskvy," *Arkhitektura i stroitel'stvo*, no. 11 (1947): 12; Vladimir Gel'freikh and Mikhail Minkus, "Vystonye zdaniia v ansamble goroda," *Sovetskoe iskusstvo*, December 12, 1951, 2; Boris Iofan, "Novyi siluet stolitsy," *Sovetskoe iskusstvo*, July 18, 1947, 2.
20. Respectively, Vladislav Tukanov, "Monumenty v sovetskom gradostroitel'stve" (Kandidat dissertation, Moskovskii arkhitekturnyi institut, 1953), 75; Anna Opochinskaia, "Ansambl' vysotnykh zdanii Moskvy i natsional'nye traditsii russkikh zodchikh," *Sovetskaia arkhitektura*, no. 5 (1954): 60.

21. RGALI f. 962, op. 3, ed. khr. 560, l. 32.

22. Vlas Chubar', "Rech' zamestitelia Predsedatelia Soveta Narodnykh Komissarov SSSR tov. V. Ia. Chubaria," in *Postanovleniia i materialy. Pervyi vsesoiuznyi s"ezd sovetskikh arkhitektorov*, ed. A. Barkhudarian and N. Kirsanova (Moscow: Izdatel'stvo Akademii arkhitektury, 1937), 30. Likely, it was the rising Palace of the Soviets that was on Chubar's mind, but also, potentially, constructions of the more distant future.

23. Respectively, Boris Iofan, "O novatorstve v arkhitekture," *Stroitel'naia gazeta*, May 24, 1940, 2; Viktor Vesnin, "Dvorets Sovetov i sotrudnichestvo iskusstv. Vstupitel'noe slovo akademika arkhitektury V. A. Vesnina," in *Materialy V plenuma Pravleniia SSA SSSR*, ed. I. Sushkevich (Moscow: Izdatel'stvo Akademii arkhitektury, 1939), 5.

24. Vladimir Paperny, *Architecture in the Age of Stalin: Culture Two*, trans. John Hill and Roann Barris (Cambridge: Cambridge University Press, 2002), 180.

25. Il'ia Sosfenov, "Problema sinteza v metro. Sintez v oformlenii stantsii 'Ploshchad' revoliutsii' Moskovskogo metro," *Iskusstvo*, no. 2 (1938): 29–30.

26. David Arkin, "Arkhitektura i problema sinteza iskusstv," in *Voprosy sinteza iskusstv. Materialy pervogo tvorcheskogo soveshchania arkhitektorov, skul'ptorov i zhivopistsev (o kadrakh khudozhnikov-monumentalistov)*, ed. M. Zhitomirskii (Moscow: IZOGIZ, 1936), 10. Italics mine.

27. Mariia Silina, *Istoriia i ideologiia: monumental'no-dekorativnyi rel'ef 1920-1930-kh godov v SSSR* (Moscow: BuksMArt, 2014), 105.

28. Boris Korolev, "Skul'ptura Dvortsa Sovetov. Gruppy i barel'efy," *Arkhitektura SSSR*, no. 6 (1939): 18.

29. Iofan, "Stroitel'stvo Dvortsa Sovetov," 12.

30. Boris Ternovets, "Zadachi skul'ptury," *Arkhitektura SSSR*, no. 6 (1939): 21; also see Korolev, "Skul'ptura Dvortsa Dovetov," 19.

31. Evgenii Lansere, "Monumental'naia zhivopis'," *Izvestiia*, June 30, 1939, 3.

32. Aleksei Anagarov, "O nekotorykh voprosakh sovetskoi arkhitektury. Stennogramma vystupleniia tov. Angarova na obshchemoskovskom sobranii arkhitektorov 27 fevralia 1936 g," *Arkhitektura SSSR*, no. 4 (1936): 9. Italics mine.

33. Vladimir Tolstoi, *Monumental'noe iskusstvo SSSR* (Moscow: Sovetskii khudozhnik, 1978), 59.

34. "Tvorcheskie pobedy sovetskikh khudozhnikov," *Iskusstvo*, no. 3 (1947): 4.

35. Vera Mukhina, "Monumental'no dekorativnoe iskusstvo v ansamble goroda," in *Problema ansamblia v sovetskoi arkhitekture. Sbornik statei*, ed. K. Trapeznikov (Moscow: Gosudarstvennoe izdatel'stvo literatury po stroitel'stvu i arkhitekture, 1952), 89.

36. Evgenii Vuchetich and Iakov Belopol'skii, "Pamiatnik general-leitenantu Efremovu," *Iskusstvo*, no. 3 (1947): 29.

37. RGALI f. 2942, op. 1, ed. khr. 139, l. 29.

38. TsGAM f. 534, op. 1, d. 131, ll. 274–276.

39. RGALI f. 2458, op. 2, ed. khr. 1534, ll. 32, 34, RGALI f. 2458, op. 2, ed. khr. 1527, ll. 186–187.

40. RGALI f. 962, op. 6, ed. khr. 1402, l. 8.

41. Pat Simpson, "The Nude in Soviet Socialist Realism: Eugenics and Images of the New Person in the 1920s–1940s," *Australian and New Zealand Journal of Art* 5, no. 1 (2004): 118–119, 129.

42. Mikhail Zolotonosov, *Gliptokratos. Issledovanie nemogo diskursa: annotirovannyi katalog sadovo-parkovoi skul'ptury stalinskogo vremeni* (St. Petersburg: Inopress, 1999), 8.

43. Sergei Merkurov, *Vospominania. Pis'ma. Stat'i. Zametki. Suzhdeniia sovremennikov* (Moscow: Kremlin Multimedia, 2012), 340.

44. Respectively, Matvei Manizer, *Skul'ptor o svoei rabote. Tom 1* (Moscow: Iskusstvo, 1940), 36; Matvei Manizer, *Skul'ptor o svoei rabote. Tom 2* (Moscow: Iskusstvo, 1952), 38.

45. Vera Mukhina, "'Rabochii i kolkhoznitsa': Otryvok iz ustnykh vospominanii V. I. Mukhinoi, zapisannykh v 1939–1940 godakh, zapisannykh pisateliami L. Toom i A. Bekom," *Iskusstvo*, no. 8 (1957): 36.

46. TsGAM f. 694, op. 1, d. 697, l. 82; RGALI f. 2458, op. 1, ed. khr. 454, l. 26.

47. Quoted in Paperny, *Architecture in the Age of Stalin*, 178.

48. Liudmila Doronina, *Skul'ptura stalinskoi epokhi (1930–1950-e gody)* (Moscow: Moskovskii gorodskoi pedagogicheskii universitet, 2013), 45–46.

49. Sergei Zmeul, "Arkhitektura pamiatnikov Velikoi Otechestvennoi voiny" (Kandidat dissertation, Akademiia arkhitektury SSSR, 1950), 233, 178.

50. Il'ia Katsen and Konstantin Ryzhkov, *Moskovskii Metropoliten* (Moscow: Izdatel'stvo Akademii Arkhitektury SSSR, 1948), 15.

51. RGAE f. 552, op. 1, d. 164; N. Miliutin, "N. A. Miliutin (nachal'nik khudozhestvennoi chasti stroitel'stva Dvortsa Sovetov)," in *Arkhitektura Dvortsa Sovetov. Materialy V plenuma Pravleniia SSA SSSR*, ed. I. Sushkevich (Moscow: Izdatel'stvo Akademii arkhitektury, 1939), 43.

52. Alexei Tarkhanov and Sergei Kavtaradze, *Architecture of the Stalin Era* (New York: Rizzoli, 1992), 169.

53. GARF f. R5446, op. 86, d. 2441, l. 45.

54. GARF f. R5446, op. 86, d. 2441, l. 42.

55. RGALI f. 674, op. 2, ed. Khr. 185, ll. 22, 67.

56. Vera Mukhina, "Zametki khudozhnika," *Pravda*, September 19, 1951, 3.

57. RGALI f. 2932, op. 1, ed. khr. 777, l. 28; TsGAM f. 278, op. 1, d. 851, l. 31; TsGAM f. 278, op. 1, d. 854, l. 21.

58. TsGAM f. 534, op. 1, d. 110, ll. 153–156.

59. Tat'iana Astrakhantseva, "Stil' 'Pobeda' v dekorativno-ornamental'nom iskusstve 1940-1950-kh godov: k probleme definitsii v sovetskom iskusstve stalinskoi epokhi," in *Arkhitektura Stalinskoi epokhi: opyt istoricheskogo osmysleniia*, ed. Iuliia Kosenkova (Moscow: KomKniga, 2010), 145.

60. Nikita Voronov, *Sovetskaia monumental'naia skul'ptura* (Moscow: Znanie, 1976), 7.

61. See Mike O'Mahony, "Archaeological Fantasies: Constructing History on the Moscow Metro," *The Modern Language Review* 98, no. 1 (2003). In fact, the original plan was to commemorate the French Revolution, the Revolution of 1905, and the Revolution of 1917, but the design was revised to chronicle Soviet history up to the present moment, Aleksei Dushkin, "Stantsiia 'Ploshchad' Revoliutsii'. 1935–1938," in *Aleksei Nikolaevich Dushkin. Arkhitektura 1930–1950-kh godov. Katalog vystavki*, ed. Natal'ia Dushkina (Moscow: A-Fond, 2004), 156.

62. Annie Gerin, "Stories from Mayakovskaya Metro Station: The Production/Consumption of Stalinist Monumental Space, 1938" (PhD dissertation, University of Leeds, 2000).

63. RGALI f. 2943 op. 1, ed. khr. 1527, l. 20.

64. Here, I rely on the impressive reconstruction of the original appearance of Stalin-era metro stations found in Aleksandr Zinov'ev, *Stalinskoe metro. Istoricheskii putevoditel' po Moskovskomu metropolitenu* (Moscow: A. N. Zinov'ev, 2011).

65. Iakov Kornfel'd, *Laureaty Stalinskoi premii v arkhitekture. 1941–1950* (Moscow: GILSA, 1953), 83.

66. Margarita Tosunova, "Arkhitekturnyi obraz stantsii Moskovskogo metropolitena," *Sovetskaia arkhitektura*, no. 3 (1952): 10–11.

67. RGALI f. 2943, op. 1, ed. khr. 187, l. 21.

68. RGALI f. 674, op. 2, ed. khr. 185, l. 32.

69. TsGAM f. 534, op. 1, d. 108, l. 256.

70. Nikolai Chernyshev, "Mastera iskusstva o Moskovskom metro," *Iskusstvo*, no. 4 (1935): 27.

71. Vera Mukhina, "Tema i obraz v monumental'noi skul'pture," *Sovetskoe iskusstvo*, November 14, 1944, 2.

72. Quoted in RGALI f. 962, op. 6, ed. khr. 910, l. 37; RGALI f. 2942, op. 1, ed. khr. 132, l. 31.

73. Mukhina, "Tema i obraz v monumental'noi skul'pture," 2.

74. Mukhina, "Tema i obraz v monumental'noi skul'pture," 2.

75. Vera Mukhina, "Skul'ptor V. I. Mukhina (Moskva)," in *Arkhitektura Dvortsa Sovetov. Materialy V plenuma Pravleniia SSA SSSR*, ed. I. Sushkevich (Moscow: Izdatel'stvo Akademii arkhitektury, 1939), 45.

76. Evgenii Lansere, "O monumental'noi zhivopisi," *Sovetskoe iskusstvo*, April 19, 1945, 3.

77. Osip Beskin, "O monumental'nom iskusstve," *Iskusstvo*, no. 1 (1939): 74.

78. TsGAM f. 534, op. 1, d. 110, l. 186.

79. There was also little consensus among art professionals on which subjects would be more amenable to creating generalized representations. For instance, and by way of contrast, in discussions of mosaics for the Kievskaia-kol'tsevaia metro station, art historian Vladimir Tolstoi argued that industrial, labor themes were the short-lived ones, and instead supported depicting individuals, RGALI f. 2943, op. 1, ed. khr. 1527, l. 37.

80. Nikolai Mashkovtsev, "Proekty novykh pamiatnikov," *Iskusstvo*, no. 3 (1947): 34.

81. Vera Mukhina, *Literaturno-kriticheskoe nasledie* (Moscow: Iskusstvo, 1960), 136.

82. Mukhina, *Literaturno-kriticheskoe nasledie*, 136.

83. Quoted in Ivan Shevtsov, *Evgenii Viktorovich Vuchetich* (Leningrad: Khudozhnik RSFSR, 1960), 8. There is some trouble with dating the letter. Golikov held the rank of Army General from 1959, but it is possible that Shevtsov simply used his current title when transcribing the letter, so it could have been written earlier (very possibly during the Great Patriotic War, when Vuchetich was working on Golikov's sculptural portrait).

84. Merkurov, *Vospominania. Pis'ma. Stat'i*, 405.

85. Mukhina, "Tema i obraz v monumental'noi skul'pture," 2.

86. Mukhina, *Literaturno-kriticheskoe nasledie*, 136–137.

87. Lev Rudnev, "L. V. Rudnev," in *Voprosy razvitiia sovetskoi skul'ptury. Nauchnaia konferentsiia. 28–30 maia 1952 g.*, ed. Matvei Manizer (Moscow: Izdatel'stvo Akademii khudozhestv SSSR, 1953), 77.

88. Lansere, "O monumental'noi zhivopisi," 3.

89. Evgenii Lansere, *Dnevniki. Kniga tret'ia. Khudozhnik i gosudarstvo* (Moscow: Iskusstvo-XXI vek, 2009), 668; Pavel Pavlinov, "'Nu vot i voina . . .'. Evgenii Evgenievich Lansere. Tvorchstvo voennykh let," *Tret'iakovskaia gallereia* 47, no. 2 (2015): 74.

90. Quoted in Pavlinov, "Nu vot i voina," 74. The fear of such paranoid readings was not unfounded: the radically narrowed scope of appropriate symbols forced censors to look on a deeper level to find evidence of dissent and subversion, see Jan Plamper, "Abolishing Ambiguity: Soviet Censorship Practices in the 1930s," *Russian Review* 60, no. 4 (2001).

91. See Vladimir Gaposhkin, "Eshche o monumental'noi zhivopisi," *Sovetskoe iskusstvo*, June 8, 1945, 2; "Novye temy i starye atributy," *Sovetskoe iskusstvo*, June 29, 1945, 4; Nina Shantyko, *Evgenii Evgen'evich Lansere* (Moscow: Sovetskii khudozhnik, 1952), 31.

92. GARF f. R5446, op. 1, d. 365, ll. 326–327; RGALI f. 962, op. 3, ed. khr. 2228, l. 75.

93. RGASPI f. 17, op. 133, d. 375, ll. 145–146.

94. See RGALI f. 962, op. 6; RGALI f. 2329, op. 4; RGALI f. 2458, op. 2.

95. GARF f. A259, op. 6, d. 1351, ll. 9–10.

96. Nikolai Tomskii, "Problemy sovetskoi monumental'noi skul'ptury," in *Voprosy razvitiia sovetskoi skul'ptury. Nauchnaia konferentsiia. 28–30 maia 1952 g*, ed. Matvei Manizer (Moscow: Izdatel'stvo Akademii khudozhestv SSSR, 1953), 19.

97. Respectively, Sergei Merkurov, "Monumenty Lenina i Stalina," *Arkhitekturnaia gazeta*, 12 August 1937, 1; Sergei Merkurov, "Simvol epokhi," *Pravda*, January 20, 1939, 4.

98. Georgii Gol'ts, "O pamiatnikakh," in *Mastera sovetskoi arkhitektury ob arkhitekture. Tom 2*, ed. Mikhail Barkhin et al. (Moscow: Iskusstvo, 1975), 340.

99. RGALI f. 2943, op. 1, ed. khr. 2222, l. 19.

100. RGAE f. 339, op. 1, d. 1132, ll. 137–139.

101. Iofan, "Stroitel'stvo Dvortsa Sovetov," 11.

102. RGALI f. 674, op. 3, ed. khr. 1951, l. 1.

103. Respectively, Oksana Pavlenko, "Radost' tvorchestva," in *Voprosy sinteza iskusstv. Materialy pervogo tvorcheskogo soveshchania arkhitektorov, skul'ptorov i zhivopistsev (o kadrakh khudozhnikov-monumentalistov)*, ed. M. Zhitomirskii (Moscow: IZOGIZ, 1936), 115; Arkin, "Monumenty geroiam," 7.

104. Alan Borg, *War Memorials: From Antiquity to the Present* (London: Leo Cooper, 1991), 70, 134–135.

105. See Charlotte Benton, ed., *Figuration/Abstraction: Strategies for Public Sculpture in Europe 1945–1968* (Aldershot, UK: Ashgate, 2004).

106. Sabina Tanović, *Designing Memory: The Architecture of Commemoration in Europe, 1914 to the Present* (Cambridge: Cambridge University Press, 2019), 4.

4. The (Un)contested Politics of Stalinist Monument Building

1. Lars Blomqvist, "Some Utopian Elements in Stalinist Art," *Russian History* 11, no. 2–3 (1984): 298.

2. Anna Kutseleva, "Mesto moskovskogo metropolitena v sovetskom kul'turnom prostranstve," in *Arkhitektura Stalinskoi epokhi: opyt istoricheskogo osmysleniia*, ed. Iuliia Kosenkova (Moscow: KomKniga, 2010), 182.

3. To my knowledge, the first such decree of the Council of People's Commissars "immortalized the memory" of thermal engineer professor Karl Kirsh, in whose

honor an institute was renamed, see "Postanovlenie Soveta Narodnykh Komissarov ob uvekovechenii pamiati professora Kirsha," *Izvestiia*, August 3, 1920, 2.

4. See RGASPI f. 17, op. 3.

5. From early 1941, this practice was banned by a decree mandating a twenty-five-year moratorium on further immortalization measures following the death of "great individuals" (*velikikh liudei*), RGASPI f. 17, op. 132, d. 205, l. 48.

6. For the concept of "double murder," see Avishai Margalit, *The Ethics of Memory* (Cambridge, MA: Harvard University Press, 2002), 20–23.

7. Zygmunt Bauman, *Mortality, Immortality and Other Life Strategies* (Cambridge: Polity Press, 1992), 53.

8. I am thankful to Elena Rozhdestvenskaia for this formulation. On "commemorability," see Elizabeth Armstrong and Suzanna Crage, "Movements and Memory: The Making of the Stonewall Myth," *American Sociological Review* 71, no. 5 (2006).

9. Catriona Kelly, *Comrade Pavlik: The Rise and Fall of a Soviet Boy Hero* (London: Granta Books, 2014), 144–151, 188–189.

10. Katharina Kucher, *Park Gor'kogo. Kul'tura dosuga v stalinskuiu epokhu. 1928–1941* (Moscow: ROSSPEN, 2012), 236–237.

11. Ivan Rakhmanov, "Skul'ptura i gorod. Zadachi tresta skul'ptury," *Sovetskoe iskusstvo*, April 2, 1933, 1.

12. Boris Korolev, "Skul'ptury Dvotsa. Doklad skul'ptora B. D. Koroleva (Moskovskii Soiuz sovetskikh khudozhnikov-skul'ptorov)," in *Arkhitektura Dvortsa Sovetov. Materialy V plenuma Pravleniia SSA SSSR.*, ed. I. Sushkevich (Moscow: Izdatel'stvo Akademii arkhitektury, 1939), 41.

13. Igor' Rozhin, "Iz moego opyta raboty v metro," in *Arkhitektura moskovskogo metro: 1935-1980-e gody*, ed. Ol'ga Kostina (Moscow: BuksMArt, 2019), 173.

14. Although I have been unable to locate the decree instituting this policy, the initiative is mentioned in several documents, for instance, in the Committee for Arts Affairs' late-1950 memo to Central Committee secretary Mikhail Suslov, RGASPI f. 17, op. 132, d. 424, ll. 97–100.

15. GARF f. R7523, op. 4, d. 18, l. 25.

16. GARF f. R5446, op. 1, d. 278, l. 300.

17. RGALI f. 2943, op. 1, ed. khr. 2172, l. 5.

18. Nikolai Tomskii, "Problemy sovetskoi monumental'noi skul'ptury," in *Voprosy razvitiia sovetskoi skul'ptury. Nauchnaia konferentsiia. 28–30 maia 1952 g*, ed. Matvei Manizer (Moscow: Izdatel'stvo Akademii khudozhestv SSSR, 1953), 14.

19. GARF f. R7523, op. 4, d. 199, l. 44.

20. GARF f. R7523, op. 83, d. 3617, ll. 11–14.

21. Dzhodzh Morgan, "Luchshyi v mire," in *Rasskazy stroitelei metro*, ed. Aleksandr Kosarev (Moscow: Istoriia fabrik i zavodov, 1935), 496.

22. Sergei Dinamov, "O stile sovetskogo iskusstva," *Iskusstvo*, no. 4 (1935): 4.

23. Dmitrii Volkogonov, *Stalin: Triumph and Tragedy*, trans. Harold Shukman (New York: Grove Weidenfeld, 1991), xx.

24. Roy Medvedev and Zhores Medvedev, *The Unknown Stalin* (New York: IB Tauris, 2003), 78.

25. Sarah Davies and James Harris, *Stalin's World: Dictating the Soviet Order* (New Haven, CT: Yale University Press, 2014), 182.

26. Jan Plamper, *The Stalin Cult: A Study in the Alchemy of Power* (New Haven, CT: Yale University Press, 2012), 125–126; also see Oleg Khlevniuk, *Stalin. Zhizn' odnogo vozhdia* (Moscow: Corpus, 2005), 8–9. These documents have since been merged into the Stalin *fond* in RGASPI.

27. Karl Radek, "Zodchii sotsialisticheskogo obshchestva," *Pravda*, January 1, 1934; also see Robert Tucker, *Stalin in Power: The Revolution from Above, 1928–1941* (New York: WW Norton & Company, 1992), 244–247.

28. Lavrentii Beriia, "Velichaishii chelovek istorii," in *Stalin. K 60-letiiu so dnia rozhdeniia. Sbornik statei "Pravdy"* (Moscow: Pravda, 1940), 102.

29. Judith Devlin, "Soviet Power and Its Images: Celebrating Stalin's Seventieth Birthday," in *War of Words: Culture and the Mass Media in the Making of the Cold War in Europe*, ed. Judith Devlin and Christoph Muller (Dublin: University College Dublin Press, 2013), 34.

30. John Steinbeck, *A Russian Journal* (New York: The Viking Press, 1948), 19, 50–51.

31. TSGAM f. 694, op. 1, d. 44, l. 82.

32. Igor Golomstock, *Totalitarian Art: In the Soviet Union, the Third Reich, Fascist Italy, and the People's Republic of China*, trans. Robert Chandler (London: Collins Harvill, [1990] 2011), 235.

33. Mikhail Zolotonosov, *Gliptokratos. Issledovanie nemogo diskursa: annotirovannyi katalog sadovo-parkovoi skul'ptury stalinskogo vremeni* (St. Petersburg: Inopress, 1999), 137.

34. See, for instance, Ekaterina Krasil'nikova, "Memorializatsiia S. M. Kirova v zapadnoi sibiri (1934 g.—pervaia polovina 1941 g.)," *Vestnik Tomskogo gosudarstvennogo universiteta* 36, no. 4 (2015): 24.

35. TsGAM f. 278, op. 1, d. 853, l. 31.

36. Ernest Becker, *The Denial of Death* (New York: The Free Press, 1973), 5.

37. G. Kolokolov, "Metrostroevskaia moral'," in *Metro: Sbornik posviashchaetsia pusku moskovskogo metropolitena*, ed. Leonid Kovalev (Moscow: Rabochaia Moskva, 1935), 240–241.

38. Iu. Parshin, "Pod golubym kupolom," in *Dvorets nauki. Rasskazy stroitelei novogo zdaniia Moskovskogo gosudarstvennogo universiteta*, ed. V. Pospelov (Moscow: Izdatel'stvo VTsSPS Profizdat, 1952), 55.

39. Vladimir Paperny, *Architecture in the Age of Stalin: Culture Two*, trans. John Hill and Roann Barris (Cambridge: Cambridge University Press, 2002), 205–206.

40. Maksim Gor'kii, "Istoriia fabrik i zavodov," *Pravda*, September 7, 1931.

41. TsGAM f. 694, op. 1, d. 31, ll. 27–28.

42. RGALI f. 962, op. 3, ed. khr. 583, l. 38.

43. Mike O'Mahony, "Archaeological Fantasies: Constructing History on the Moscow Metro," *The Modern Language Review* 98, no. 1 (2003): 138.

44. Ultimately, Renfew argues, monument building can contribute to the formation of new ethnicities, Colin Renfrew, *Prehistory: The Making of the Human Mind* (New York: Random House, 2008), 133–134.

45. RGALI f. 962, op. 3, ed. khr. 442, l. 5.

46. RGALI f. 962, op. 6, ed. khr. 1402, l. 17.

47. RGALI f. 962, op. 6, ed. khr. 1118, l. 4.

48. Plamper, *The Stalin Cult*, 218.

49. RGALI f. 2458, op. 2, ed. khr. 210, l. 31.

50. Plamper, *The Stalin Cult*, 206.

51. As Karen Petrone observes, "even without alternative discourses, Soviet citizens could articulate unofficial points of view—they could express their anxieties and hopes within the officially sanctioned discourse," Karen Petrone, *Life Has Become More Joyous, Comrades: Celebrations in the Time of Stalin* (Bloomington: Indiana University Press, 2000), 203.

52. RGAE f. 9432, op. 1, d. 16, ll. 122–123.

53. Ivan Matsa, "Traditsii i sovremennost'," *Sovetskoe iskusstvo*, March 29, 1946, 2.

54. Susan Reid, "In the Name of the People: The Manège Affair Revisited," *Kritika: Explorations in Russian and Eurasian History* 6, no. 4 (2006): 680.

55. Sheila Fitzpatrick, "Supplicants and Citizens: Public Letter-Writing in Soviet Russia in the 1930s," *Slavic Review* 55, no. 1 (1996): 80.

56. As Judith Devlin notes, "*unsolicited* demonstrations of loyalty were reassuring confirmations that the oft-repeated public professions . . . were not wholly without substance," Devlin, "Soviet Power and Its Images," 34. Italics mine.

57. See Stephen Kotkin, *Magnetic Mountain: Stalinism as Civilization* (Berkeley: University of California Press, 1995), 198–237.

58. Tolstoi, "Poiski monumental'nosti," 3.

59. "Pamiatnik Pavliku Morozovu," *Pravda*, July 24, 1935.

60. For example, in 1936, several proposals called for a monument to the Stalin constitution, GARF f. R3316, op. 29, d. 821; B. Durov, "Obelisk konstitutsii," *Izvestiia*, December 18, 1936.

61. RGALI f. 2075, op. 7, ed. khr. 282, ll. 16–19.

62. RGAE f. 339, op. 1, d. 1132, l. 196. The next, "open" phase of the competition garnered a further 957 submissions from the general public, RGALI f. 674, op. 3, ed. khr. 1946, ll. 1–2.

63. GARF f. R3316, op. 30, d. 904, l. 2.

64. RGAE f. 9432, op. 1, d. 261a.

65. GARF f. R3316, op. 27, d. 262, ll. 32–33, 50–51, 55.

66. RGASPI f. 17, op. 125, d. 572, ll. 40–52.

67. GARF f. f. R7523, op. 14, d. 16, ll. 17–20.

68. Sergei Merkurov, *Vospominania. Pis'ma. Stat'i. Zametki. Suzhdeniia sovremennikov* (Moscow: Kremlin Multimedia, 2012), 271–272. >

69. RGALI f. 962, op. 3, ed. khr. 1685, ll. 22–32.

70. RGALI f. 962, op. 3, ed. khr. 1685, l. 166.

71. RGASPI f. 17, op. 125, d. 299, ll. 24–38.

72. GARF f. R7523, op. 11, d. 131, ll. 11–14.

73. RGALI f. 962, op. 3, ed. khr. 183, l. 17.

74. Jochen Hellbeck, "Fashioning the Stalinist Soul: The Diary of Stepan Podlubnyi (1931–1939)," *Jahrbücher für Geschichte Osteuropas* 44, no. 3 (1996): 348.

75. Sergei Zmeul, "Arkhitektura pamiatnikov Velikoi Otechestvennoi voiny" (Kandidat dissertation, Akademiia arkhitektury SSSR, 1950), 72.

76. GARF f. R5446, op. 51, d. 3096, l. 53.

77. Zmeul, "Arkhitektura pamiatnikov," 73; also see Tat'iana Malinina and Elena Ogarkova, *Pamiat' i vremia: iz khudozhestvennogo arkhiva Velikoi Otechestvennoi voiny 1941–1945 gg.* (Moscow: Galart, 2011), 215.

78. RGALI f. 962, op. 3, ed. khr. 1367, ll. 30–31.

79. This Committee for the Affairs of Monuments to the Great Patriotic War was to hold design competitions and commission monuments, museums, and panoramas; organize production facilities; protect and restore of monuments; sponsor research on monument design; create heritage preserves at important battlefields; and manage military museums, GARF f. R7523, op. 61, d. 14969.

80. GARF f. R5446, op. 48, d. 2190, ll. 2–5.

81. Sergiusz Michalski, *Public Monuments: Art in Political Bondage, 1870–1997* (London: Reaktion Books, 1998), 131–132.

82. Zmeul, "Arkhitektura pamiatnikov," 58–60. Several albums of prefabricated graveside monument designs, approved by the Committee for Architectural Affairs, were published in the immediate postwar years. For example, see Nikolai Kolli, ed., *Tipovye proekty pamiatnikov bratskikh i individual'nykh mogil voinov Sovetskoi Armii, Voenno-Morskogo flota i partizan, pogibshikh v boiakh s nemetsko-fashistskimi zakhvatchikami v gody Velikoi Otechestvennoi voiny* (Moscow: Voennoe izdatel'stvo, 1947).

83. Adrienne Harris, "Memorializations of a Martyr and Her Mutilated Bodies: Public Monuments to Soviet War Hero Zoya Kosmodemyanskaya, 1942 to the Present," *Journal of War & Culture Studies* 5, no. 1 (2012): 77.

84. Khmel'nitskii, *Zodchii Stalin*, 215.

85. Ivan Zholtovskii, "Printsip zodchestva," *Arkhitektura SSSR*, no. 5 (1933): 28.

86. Vera Mukhina, *Literaturno-kriticheskoe nasledie* (Moscow: Iskusstvo, 1960), 145, 160.

87. RGALI f. 2942, op. 1, ed. khr. 132, l. 26. Capitalization in the original.

88. Korolev, "Skul'ptura Dvortsa Dovetov," 19.

89. Evgenii Lansere, *Dnevniki. Kniga pervaia. Vospitanie chuvstv* (Moscow: Iskusstvo-XXI vek, 2008), 23–24.

90. Lansere, *Dnevniki. Kniga pervaia*, 98.

91. Quoted in Sergei Razgonov, *Vysota: zhizn' i dela Pavla Korina* (Moscow: Sovetskiii khudozhnik, 1978), 141. Italics mine.

92. Aleksandr Deineka, "Aleksandr Aleksandrovich Deineka," in *Mastera sovetskogo izobrazitel'nogo iskusstva: proizvedeniia i avtobiograficheskie ocherki*, ed. P. Sysoev and Viacheslav Shkvarikov (Moscow: Iskusstvo, 1951), 230.

93. See Andrew Bennett, *Romantic Poets and the Culture of Posterity* (Cambridge: Cambridge University Press, 1999), 2; Heather Jackson, *Those Who Write for Immortality: Romantic Reputations and the Dream of Lasting Fame* (New Haven, CT: Yale University Press, 2015).

94. RGALI f. 2458, op. 2, ed. khr. 1526, l. 256.

95. RGALI f. 3024, op. 1, ed. khr. 20, l. 1. Italics mine.

96. RGASPI f. 17, op. 125, d. 466, l. 93.

97. Hans Gunther, "Zhiznennye fazy sotsrealisticheskogo kanona," in *Sotsrealisticheskii kanon*, ed. Evgenii Dobrenko and Hans Gunther (St. Petersburg: Akademicheskii proekt, 2000), 281.

98. Jan Plamper, "Abolishing Ambiguity: Soviet Censorship Practices in the 1930s," *Russian Review* 60, no. 4 (2001): 531.

99. Katerina Clark, *The Soviet Novel: History as Ritual* (Bloomington: Indiana University Press, [1981] 2000), 13.

100. Quoted in Christina Kiaer, "Was Socialist Realism Forced Labour? The Case of Aleksandr Deineka in the 1930s," *Oxford Art Journal* 28, no. 3 (2005): 338.

101. Matvei Manizer, *Skul'ptor o svoei rabote. Tom 2* (Moscow: Iskusstvo, 1952), 50. Italics mine.

102. Respectively, Valentin Valev, "Skul'ptor V. Ts. Valev (Moskva)," in *Arkhitektura Dvortsa Sovetov. Materialy V plenuma Pravleniia SSA SSSR*, ed. I. Sushkevich (Moscow: Izdatel'stvo Akademii arkhitektury, 1939), 68–69; RGALI f. 2932, op. 1, ed. khr. 777, l. 21; RGAE f. 7857, op. 1ch3, d. 3789, ll. 34–35.

103. Lev Perchik, *Bol'shevistskii plan rekonstruktsii Moskvy* (Moscow: Partizdat, 1935), 98.

104. Boris Iofan, "Vosstanovlenie nashikh gorodov i zadachi arkhitektury," *Izvestiia*, September 12, 1944, 3.

105. Ivan Zholtovskii, "Klassika zhivet," *Sovetskoe iskusstvo*, March 15, 1932, 1.

106. Boris Iofan, "Ploshchad' i prospekt Dvotsa Sovetov," *Arkhitektura SSSR*, no. 11 (1935): 28.

107. Nikolai Kolli, "O nekotorykh osobennostiakh ansamblevoi zastroiki gorodov," in *Problema ansamblia v sovetskoi arkhitekture. Sbornik statei*, ed. K. Trapeznikov (Moscow: Gosudarstvennoe izdatel'stvo literatury po stroitel'stvu i arkhitekture, 1952), 30.

108. Grigorii Zakharov, "Arkhitekturnyi ansambl' v zastroike gorogov. Doklad sekretaria Pravleniia Soiuza sovetskikh arkhitektorov SSSR G. A. Zakharova," in *Arkhitekturnyi ansambl' v stroitel'stve gorodov: Materialy XIV plenuma Pravl. Soiuza sovetskikh arkhitektorov SSSR (2–5 iiunia 1952 g.)*, ed. G. Morozova (Moscow: Gosudarstvennoe izdatel'stvo literatury po stroitel'stvu i arkhitekture, 1952), 10.

109. The sheer resources that could be mobilized by state-commissioned monument construction were a definite draw to art professionals, not only in the Soviet context. The German architect Albert Speer spoke thus of the "truly staggering" monument commissions he received: "my execution of them, I was convinced, could make me one of the most famous architects of history," quoted in Alex Scobie, *Hitler's State Architecture: The Impact of Classical Antiquity* (University Park: Pennsylvania State University Press, 1990), 19.

110. Karo Alabian, "Perveishii dolg arkhitektorov," *Moskovskii stroitel'*, March 28, 1953, 2.

111. "O monumental'noi skul'pture," *Iskusstvo*, no. 4 (1952): 6; "Zhiznennye zadachi arkhitekturnoi praktiki," 1.

112. Lansere, *Dnevniki. Kniga tret'ia*, 454.

113. GARF f. R5446, op. 51, d. 3099, ll. 5–6; GARF f. R5446, op. 80, d. 3090, l. 9.

114. TsGAM f. 534, op. 1, d. 110, l. 164. The Committee also suggested acknowledging lead engineers on these plaques, TsGAM f. 534, op. 1, d. 110, l. 156.

115. Soiuz Arkhitektorov SSSR, *Tvorcheskie voprosy*, 6.

116. RGALI f. 2942, op. 1, ed. khr. 104, l. 3.

117. Lansere, *Dnevniki. Kniga tret'ia*, 685.

118. RGASPI f. 17, op. 125, d. 572, l. 64.

119. TsGAM f. 694, op. 1, d. 44, l. 80.

120. Merkurov, *Vospominania. Pis'ma. Stat'i*, 405.

121. TsGAM f. 534, op. 1, d. 40, l. 94.

122. TsGAM f. 534, op. 1, d. 157, ll. 38, 43.

123. Quoted in Plamper, *The Stalin Cult*, 144, 150.
124. Aleksandr Deineka, "K voprosu o monumental'nom iskusstve," *Iskusstvo*, no. 4 (1934): 5.
125. Mukhina, *Literaturno-kriticheskoe nasledie*, 106.
126. RGALI f. 962, op. 3, ed. khr. 583, ll. 49–51.

5. The Cultural Foundations of Stalinist Monument Building

1. Quoted in Ol'ga Voronova, *Vera Ignatievna Mukhina* (Moscow: Iskusstvo, 1976), 124.
2. Arkadii Mordvinov, *Khudozhestvennye problemy sovetskoi arkhitektury. Doklad vitse-prezidenta Akademii Arkhitektury SSSR A. G. Mordvinova* (Moscow: Gosudarstvennoe arkhitekturnoe izdatel'stvo, 1944), 6–7.
3. Respectively, Iuliia Kosenkova, *Sovetskii gorod 1940-kh—pervoi poloviny 1950-kh godov: ot tvorcheskikh poiskov k praktike stroitel'stva* (Moscow: Editorial URSS, 2000), 36; Ol'ga Zinov'eva, *Simvoly stalinskoi' Moskvy* (Moscow: Tonchu, 2009), 18; Andrei Ikonnikov, *Istorizm v arkhitekture* (Moscow: Stroiizdat, 1997), 459.
4. Charles Horton Cooley, *Social Process* (New York: Charles Scribner's Sons, 1918), 123–124.
5. Anthony Smith, *The Ethnic Origins of Nations* (Oxford: Blackwell Publishers, 1993), 176.
6. Erik van Ree, *The Political Thought of Joseph Stalin: A Study in Twentieth Century Revolutionary Patriotism* (London: Routledge, 2003), 191–196.
7. See Kevin Platt and David Brandenberger, eds., *Epic Revisionism: Russian History and Literature as Stalinist Propaganda* (Madison: University of Wisconsin Press, 2006).
8. See Nicholas Timasheff, *The Great Retreat: The Growth and Decline of Communism in Russia* (New York: Dutton, 1946).
9. Zygmunt Bauman, *Mortality, Immortality and Other Life Strategies* (Cambridge: Polity Press, 1992), 55.
10. Julie Deschepper, "Entre trace et monument. Le patrimoine soviétique en Russie: acteurs, discours et usages (1917–2017)" (PhD dissertation, Institut National des Langues et Civilisations Orientales, 2019), 147–156, 179–181.
11. GARF f. R1235, op. 76, d. 117, ll. 10–11.
12. GARF f. R10010, op. 1, d. 203, l. 11; F. Manevskii and I. Kriazhin, *O sbore, uchete i obrabotke materialov o pamiatnikakh i pamiatnykh istoricheskikh mestakh Velikoi Otechestvennoi voiny. Metodicheskoe pis'mo* (Moscow: Muzeino-kraevedcheskoe otdelenie Narkomprosa RSFSR, 1942), 3–6.
13. Although recently built architectural monuments were not usually considered immediate candidates for protected status, Julie Deschepper argues that official discourse imbued them "with a heritage value beyond legal classifications," Deschepper, "Entre trace et monument," 161.
14. GARF f. R5446, op. 1, d. 348, ll. 284–296.
15. I extrapolate this from mid-1953 applications for the use and display of protected monuments, see TsGAM f. 429, op. 4, d. 7, l. 1.
16. RGALI f. 962, op. 3, ed. khr. 1973, ll. 83–84.
17. RGALI f. 962, op. 3, ed. khr. 2300, l. 120.
18. TsGAM f. 150, op. 1, d. 1245, l. 346; RGALI f. 962, op. 11, ed. khr. 57, ll. 59–64.

19. TsGAM f. 429, op. 4, d. 7, ll. 3–6.
20. RGALI f. 674, op. 3, ed. khr. 1893, ll. 4–5.
21. Vladislav Tukanov, "Monumenty v sovetskom gradostroitel'stve" (Kandidat dissertation, Moskovskii arkhitekturnyi institut, 1953), 122. Other proposals included restoring the obelisk and rebuilding the battlefield monument dedicated to the twenty-eight Panfilov guardsmen (the heroized defenders of Moscow, fallen in late 1941) (RGALI f. 2075, op. 7, ed. khr. 283, l. 2) and replacing two dilapidated wooden monuments to Aleksandr Matrosov with a single stone one in Ufa (GARF f. R5446, op. 51, d. 3096, l. 50).
22. Marta Poliakova, *Okhrana kul'turnogo naslediia Rossii* (Moscow: Drofa, 2005), 82.
23. RGAE f. 7857, op. 1ch3, d. 3793, ll. 70–71; GARF f. R5446, op. 25, d. 3432, ll. 3–4, 6.
24. Quoted in Timothy Colton, *Moscow: Governing the Socialist Metropolis* (Cambridge, MA: Harvard University Press, 1995), 353.
25. Richard Stites, *Revolutionary Dreams: Utopian Vision and Experimental Life in the Russian Revolution* (Oxford: Oxford University Press, 1989), 244.
26. Mark Edele, *Stalinist Society: 1928–1953* (Oxford: Oxford University Press, 2011), 4.
27. Moshe Lewin, *The Making of the Soviet System* (London: Methuen, 1985), 221.
28. Stites, *Revolutionary Dreams*, 244.
29. Aleida Assmann, *Is Time out of Joint?: On the Rise and Fall of the Modern Time Regime*, trans. Sarah Clift (Ithaca, NY: Cornell University Press, 2020), 99.
30. Ernest Gellner, *Nations and Nationalism* (Ithaca, NY: Cornell University Press, 1983), 46.
31. Gellner, *Nations and Nationalism*, 57.
32. Zygmunt Bauman, *Liquid Modernity* (Cambridge: Polity, [2000] 2019).
33. Karl Deutsch, "Nation and World," in *Contemporary Political Science: Toward Empirical Theory*, ed. Ithiel de Sola Pool (New York: McGraw-Hill, 1967), 217; see discussion in Bauman, *Mortality, Immortality*, 113–114.
34. Iosif Stalin, "Rech' na prieme rukovodiashchikh rabotnikov i stakhanovtsev metallurgicheskoi i ugol'noi promyshlennosti 29 oktiabria 1937 goda," *Pravda*, October 31, 1937, 1.
35. Eric Hobsbawm, introduction to *The Invention of Tradition*, ed. Eric Hobsbawm and Terence Ranger (Cambridge: Cambridge University Press, 1983).
36. David Brandenberger, *Propaganda State in Crisis: Soviet Ideology, Indoctrination, and Terror under Stalin, 1927–1941* (New Haven, CT: Yale University Press, 2011), 139.
37. James Von Geldern, "Epic Revisionism and the Crafting of a Soviet Public," in *Epic Revisionism: Russian History and Literature as Stalinist Propaganda*, ed. David Brandenberger and Kevin Platt (Madison: University of Wisconsin Press, 2006), 329–330.
38. Paul Connerton, *How Modernity Forgets* (Cambridge: Cambridge University Press, 2009), 27.
39. Henri Lefebvre, *The Production of Space*, trans. Donald Nicholson-Smith (Oxford: Blackwell, 1974), 221.
40. Pierre Nora, "General Introduction: Between Memory and History," in *Realms of Memory: Rethinking the French Past. Volume 1: Conflicts and Divisons*, ed. Pierre Nora and Lawrence Kritzman (New York: Columbia University Press, 1996), 2, 7, 15.
41. Anatolii Lunacharskii, "Dvorets Sovetov. Tov. A. V. Lunacharskii ob arkhitekturnykh proektakh," *Sovetskoe iskusstvo*, January 26, 1932, 1.

42. Aleksandr Gabrichevskii, "Vvedenie k monografii 'Memorial'naia arkhitektura'," in *Pamiat' i vremia. Iz khudozhestvennogo arkhiva Velikoi Otechestvennoi voiny 1941–1945 gg*, ed. Tat'iana Malinina and Elena Ogarkova (Moscow: Galart, [1943–1946] 2011), 304. Italics mine.

43. See Yuri Slezkine, *The House of Government: A Saga of the Russian Revolution* (Princeton, NJ: Princeton University Press, 2017), 109–219.

44. Jonathan Brooks Platt, "Pushkin Now and Then: Images of Temporal Paradox in the 1937 Pushkin Jubilee," *The Russian Review* 67, no. 4 (2008): 640; also see Stites, *Revolutionary Dreams*, 47.

45. Boris Groys, *The Total Art of Stalinism: Avant-Garde, Aesthetic Dictatorship, and Beyond*, trans. Charles Rougle (Princeton, NJ: Princeton University Press, 1992), 72.

46. For a discussion of the concept, which originated in social psychology, see Robert Lifton and Eric Olson, *Living and Dying* (New York: Praeger Publishers, 1974). To the authorities, immortalization was a more appropriate strategy of death transcendence, substituting for belief in a transcendental afterlife, a key target in the antireligious and anticlerical campaigns of the 1920s and 1930s.

47. Lisa Kirschenbaum, *The Legacy of the Siege of Leningrad, 1941–1995: Myth, Memories, and Monuments* (Cambridge: Cambridge University Press, 2006), 80–81.

48. RGASPI f. 17, op. 125, d. 572, l. 34.

49. Soiuz Sovetskikh Arkhitektorov, "Zadachi arkhitektorov v dni Velikoi Otechestvennoi voiny. Rezoliutsiia X Plenuma Soiuza sovetskikh arkhitektorov SSSR, 22–25 aprelia 1942 goda," in *Zadachi arkhitektorov v dni Velikoi Otechestvennoi voiny: Materialy X Plenuma Soiuza sovetskikh arkhitektorov SSSR, 22–25 aprelia 1942 g*, ed. T. Sushkevich (Moscow: Izdatel'stvo Akademii arkhitektury, 1942), 57–58.

50. RGALI f. 962, op. 6, ed. khr. 1052, l. 3.

51. Tat'iana Malinina and Elena Ogarkova, *Pamiat' i vremia: iz khudozhestvennogo arkhiva Velikoi Otechestvennoi voiny 1941–1945 gg*. (Moscow: Galart, 2011), 191–192.

52. Malinina and Ogarkova, *Pamiat' i vremia*, 187.

53. Malinina and Ogarkova, *Pamiat' i vremia*, 190–193.

54. See, for instance, Akademiia arkhitektury SSSR, *Konkurs na sostavlenie proektov monumentov geroiam Velikoi Otechestvennoi voiny* (Moscow: Izdatel'stvo Akademii arkhitektury, 1942), 5.

55. Alexei Tarkhanov and Sergei Kavtaradze, *Architecture of the Stalin Era* (New York: Rizzoli, 1992), 114.

56. Iosif Stalin, "Rech predsedatelia Gosudarstvennogo komiteta oborony i Narodnogo komissara oborony tov. I. V. Stalina na Krasnoi ploshchadi v den' XXIV godovshchiny Velikoi Oktiabr'skoi sotsialisticheskoi revoliutsii," *Pravda*, November 8, 1941, 1.

57. David Brandenberger, *National Bolshevism: Stalinist Mass Culture and the Formation of Modern Russian National Identity, 1931–1956* (Cambridge, MA: Harvard University Press, 2002), 115–132.

58. For a classic account, see Brandenberger, *National Bolshevism*, 160–180.

59. See Anthony Smith, "War and Ethnicity: The Role of Warfare in the Formation, Self-images and Cohesion of Ethnic Communities," *Ethnic and Racial Studies* 4, no. 4 (1981); John Hutchinson, *Nationalism and War* (Oxford: Oxford University Press, 2017).

60. Oleg Khlevniuk, *Stalin: New Biography of a Dictator*, trans. Nora Favorov (New Haven: Yale University Press, 2015), 263.

61. For example, see GARF f. R7523, op. 61, d. 14969, ll. 3–4; RGASPI f. 17, op. 125, d. 368, ll. 77–78; also see Aaron Cohen, *War Monuments, Public Patriotism, and Bereavement in Russia, 1905–2015* (Lanham, MD: Lexington Books, 2020), 106–107.

62. GARF f. R5446, op. 51, d. 3096, l. 41.

63. Nikolai Vukov, "Death and Vitality in Monumental Art in Eastern Europe After the Second World War," *New Europe College Yearbook*, no. 9 (2001).

64. TsGAM f. 534, op. 1, d. 40, l. 96.

65. TsGAM f. 534, op. 1, d. 132, ll. 106, 109.

66. Nikolai Krementsov, *Revolutionary Experiments: The Quest for Immortality in Bolshevik Science and Fiction* (Oxford: Oxford University Press, 2014), 27.

67. Alexander Etkind, "Beyond Eugenics: The Forgotten Scandal of Hybridizing Humans and Apes," *Studies in History and Philosophy of Biological and Biomedical Sciences* 39, no. 2 (2008): 207–208; Mikhail Zolotonosov, "Masturbanizatsiia: 'Erogennye zony' sovetskoi kul'tury 1920–1930-kh godov," in *Erotika v russkoi literature: ot Barkova do nashikh dnei*, ed. I. Prokhorova and et al. (Moscow: Literaturnoe obozrenie, 1992), 97–98.

68. Dmitry Shlapentokh, "Bolshevism as a Fedorovian Regime," *Cahiers du monde russe* 37, no. 4 (1996).

69. Anja Kirsch, "From Biological to Moral Immortality: The Utopian Dimensions of Socialist Work Ethics," in *Imaginations of Death and the Beyond in India and Europe*, ed. Günter Blamberger and Sudhir Kakar (Singapore: Springer, 2018), 69–72.

70. Boris Groys, *Aleksander Deyneka* (Moscow: Ad Marginem Press, 2014), 62–63.

71. This process was paralleled in artistic life by what Boris Gasparov has called "avant-garde fatigue," quoted in Jonathan Brooks Platt, *Greetings, Pushkin!: Stalinist Cultural Politics and the Russian National Bard* (Pittsburgh, PA: University of Pittsburgh Press, 2016), 309.

72. Dmtrii Shostakovich, *Testimony*, trans. Antonina Bouis, ed. Solomon Volkov (New York: Limelight Editions, [1979] 1984), 183. The poignancy of this description is not diminished by the disputed authorship of the composer's memoir.

6. Self-Commemoration and the Interwar Culture of Time

1. Although, as mentioned, neo-totalitarian approaches lean toward functionalist interpretations of monument building, they do acknowledge (if in passing) dictators' megalomaniacal obsession with going down in history.

2. Igor Golomstock, *Totalitarian Art: In the Soviet Union, the Third Reich, Fascist Italy, and the People's Republic of China*, trans. Robert Chandler (London: Collins Harvill, [1990] 2011), 283.

3. Golomstock, *Totalitarian Art*, 170.

4. After the fact, Erenburg and Aleksei Tolstoi were asked to inspect the quality of the wine; it had, incidentally, gone sour, Il'ia Erenburg, *Sobranie sochinenii v deviati tomakh. Tom 8* (Moscow: Khudozhestvennaia literatura, 1966), 11.

5. M. Klimov, "Ideino-khudozhestvennye problemy arkhitektury Moskovskogo metropolitena (3–4 ocheredi)" (Kandidat dissertation, Akademiia obshchestvennykh nauk pri TsK VKP(b), 1952), 53.

6. Edwin Heathcote, *Monument Builders: Modern Architecture and Death* (Chichester, UK: Academy Editions, 1999), 47.

7. Zygmunt Bauman, *Liquid Modernity* (Cambridge: Polity, [2000] 2019), 132.

8. François Hartog, "The Modern Regime of Historicity in the Face of Two World Wars," in *Breaking up Time: Negotiating the Borders between Present, Past and Future*, ed. Berber Bevernage and Chris Lorenz (Göttingen: Vandenhoeck & Ruprecht, 2013), 125.

9. Hartog, "The Modern Regime of Historicity," 125.

10. Hartog, "The Modern Regime of Historicity," 129.

11. François Hartog, *Regimes of Historicity: Presentism and Experiences of Time*, trans. Saskia Brown (New York: Columbia University Press, 2015), xviii.

12. Vladimir Paperny, *Architecture in the Age of Stalin: Culture Two*, trans. John Hill and Roann Barris (Cambridge: Cambridge University Press, 2002), 18.

13. Reinhart Koselleck, *Futures Past: On the Semantics of Historical Time*, trans. Keith Tribe (Cambridge, MA: MIT Press, 1985), 202–212.

14. Aleida Assmann, *Is Time out of Joint?: On the Rise and Fall of the Modern Time Regime*, trans. Sarah Clift (Ithaca, NY: Cornell University Press, 2020), xviii.

15. Koselleck, *Futures Past*, 251–252.

16. For Hartog's "weaving" metaphor, see Hartog, *Regimes of Historicity*, 106.

17. Craig Calhoun, "Nationalism and the Contradictions of Modernity," *Berkeley Journal of Sociology* 42 (1997): 1. In Koselleck's terms, nations were the fundamental units for measuring comparative advancement, in a world characterized by the "contemporaneity of the noncontemporaneous," Koselleck, *Futures Past*, 247–249, 279.

18. Benedict Anderson, *Imagined Communities: Reflections on the Origin and Spread of Nationalism* (London: Verso, [1983] 2006), 11–12.

19. Zygmunt Bauman, *Mortality, Immortality and Other Life Strategies* (Cambridge: Polity Press, 1992), 120.

20. Anthony Smith, *The Ethnic Origins of Nations* (Oxford: Blackwell Publishers, 1993), 182.

21. Elizabeth Grossman, "Architecture for a Public Client: The Monuments and Chapels of the American Battle Monuments Commission," *The Journal of the Society of Architectural Historians* 43, no. 2 (1984): 143.

22. Antoine Prost, "Monuments to the Dead," in *Realms of Memory: The Construction of the French Past. Volume 2: Traditions*, ed. Pierre Nora and Lawrence Kritzman (New York: Columbia University Press, 1997), 309.

23. Stefan Goebel, *The Great War and Medieval Memory: War, Remembrance and Medievalism in Britain and Germany, 1914–1940* (Cambridge: Cambridge University Press, 2007).

24. Alex King, *Memorials of the Great War in Britain: The Symbolism and Politics of Remembrance* (Oxford: Berg, 1998), 195.

25. Quoted in, respectively, Philip Longworth, *The Unending Vigil: A History of the Commonwealth War Graves Commission, 1917–1967* (London: Constable, 1967), 54; Thomas Conner, *War and Remembrance: The Story of the American Battle Monuments Commission* (Lexington: University Press of Kentucky, 2018), 221.

26. Longworth, *The Unending Vigil*, 136, 144–148.

27. Barbara Miller Lane, "Architects in Power: Politics and Ideology in the Work of Ernst May and Albert Speer," *The Journal of Interdisciplinary History* 17, no. 1 (1986): 307.

28. Lois Craig, *The Federal Presence: Architecture, Politics, and Symbols in United States Government Building* (Cambridge: MIT Press, 1978), 281.

29. Quoted in Elizabeth Grossman, *The Civic Architecture of Paul Cret* (Cambridge: Cambridge University Press, 1996), 185. Italics mine.

30. Marlene Park and Gerald Markowitz, *Democratic Vistas: Post Offices and Public Art in the New Deal* (Philadelphia, PA: Temple University Press, 1984), 112.

31. Craig, *The Federal Presence*, 283.

32. Oskar J. W. Hansen, *The Sculptures at Boulder Dam* (Washington, DC: US GPO, 1942), 7.

33. Anthony Arrigo, *Imaging Hoover Dam: The Making of a Cultural Icon* (Reno: University of Nevada Press, 2014), 75, 157, 219.

34. George Mosse, *The Nationalization of the Masses: Political Symbolism and Mass Movements in Germany from the Napoleonic Wars through the Third Reich* (Ithaca, NY: Cornell University Press, [1975] 1991), 212–213.

35. Roger Griffin, *The Nature of Fascism* (London: Pinter, 1991).

36. Roger Griffin, *Modernism and Fascism: The Sense of a Beginning under Mussolini and Hitler* (Basingstoke, UK: Palgrave Macmillan, 2007), 225.

37. See Eric Michaud, "National Socialist Architecture as an Acceleration of Time," *Critical Inquiry* 19, no. 2 (1993): 227, 231; Roger Griffin, "Building the Visible Immortality of the Nation: The Centrality of 'Rooted Modernism' to the Third Reich's Architectural New Order," *Fascism* 7, no. 1 (2018): 43–44.

38. Albert Speer, *Inside the Third Reich: Memoirs*, trans. Richard Winston and Clara Winston (New York: Macmillan, 1970), 55–56.

39. Christopher Clark, "Time of the Nazis: Past and Present in the Third Reich," *Geschichte und Gesellschaft* 25 (2015): 180.

40. Eric Michaud, *The Cult of Art in Nazi Germany* (Stanford, CA: Stanford University Press, 2004), 119; also see Peter Adam, *Art of the Third Reich* (New York: Harry N. Abrams, 1992), 179.

41. Adolf Hitler, *Mein Kampf*, trans. Ralph Manheim (Boston, MA: Houghton Mifflin, [1927] 1971), 264.

42. Albert Speer, "The Fuhrer's Buildings," German Propaganda Archive, [1936] 1998, accessed October 24, 2020, http://research.calvin.edu/german-propaganda-archive/ahbuild.htm. Italics mine.

43. Speer, *Inside the Third Reich*, 127.

44. Fernando Esposito and Sven Reichardt, "Revolution and Eternity. Introductory Remarks on Fascist Temporalities," *Journal of Modern European History* 13, no. 1 (2015): 38, 41.

45. Quoted in Roger Griffin, "'I Am No Longer Human. I Am a Titan. A God!': The Fascist Quest to Regenerate Time," in *A Fascist Century. Essays by Roger Griffin*, ed. Matthew Feldman (Basingstoke, UK: Palgrave Macmillan, 2008), 14.

46. Quoted in Berthold Hinz, *Art in the Third Reich*, trans. Robert Kimber and Rita Kimber (New York: Pantheon Books, 1979), 197.

47. Hitler, *Mein Kampf*, 166.

48. Sergiusz Michalski, *Public Monuments: Art in Political Bondage, 1870–1997* (London: Reaktion Books, 1998), 83.

49. Adam, *Art of the Third Reich*, 249–250.

50. Dietmar Schirmer, "State, Volk, and Monumental Architecture in Nazi-Era Berlin," in *Berlin-Washington, 1800–2000: Capital Cities, Cultural Representation, and National*

Identities, ed. Andreas Daum and Chistof Mauch (Cambridge: Cambridge University Press, 2005), 148.

51. Gunnar Brands, "From WWI Cemeteries to the Nazi 'Fortresses of the Dead'," in *Places of Commemoration: Search for Identity and Landscape Design*, ed. Joachim Wolschke-Bulhmahn (Washington, DC: Dumbarton Oaks Research Library and Collection, 2001).

52. Roger Griffin, "Fixing Solutions: Fascist Temporalities as Remedies for Liquid Modernity," *Journal of Modern European History* 13, no. 1 (2015): 18.

53. Holger Herwig, "The Cult of Heroic Death in Nazi Architecture," in *War Memory and Popular Culture: Essays on Modes of Remembrance and Commemoration*, ed. Michael Keren and Holger Herwig (Jefferson, NC: McFarland, 2009), 108–109.

54. See Adam Tooze, *The Wages of Destruction: The Making and Breaking of the Nazi Economy* (London: Allen Lane, 2006).

55. Quoted in Michaud, *The Cult of Art in Nazi Germany*, 207.

56. Quoted in Jochen Thies, *Hitler's Plans for Global Domination: Nazi Architecture and Ultimate War Aims*, trans. Ian Cooke and Mary-Beth Friedrich (New York: Berghahn Books, 2012), 74.

57. Paul Jaskot, *The Architecture of Oppression. The SS, Forced Labor and the Nazi Monumental Building Economy* (London: Routledge, 2000), 114.

58. Julia Hell, "Imperial Ruin Gazers, Or Why Did Scipio Weep," in *Ruins of Modernity*, ed. Julia Hell and Andreas Schönle (Durham, NC: Duke University Press, 2010), 186–188.

59. Golomstock, *Totalitarian Art*, 170.

60. Frederic Spotts, *Hitler and the Power of Aesthetics* (Woodstock, NY: The Overlook Press, 2003), 322.

61. Lisbet Koerner, "Nazi Medievalist Architecture and the Politics of Memory," in *Medievalism in Europe*, ed. Leslie Workman (Cambridge, UK: D. S. Brewer, 1994), 58–59.

62. Jochen Thies, "Hitler's European Building Programme," *Journal of Contemporary History* 13, no. 3 (1978): 419–420.

63. Spotts, *Hitler and the Power of Aesthetics*, 377–378.

64. Petr Vail' and Aleksandr Genis, *60-e. Mir sovetskogo cheloveka* (Ann Arbor, MI: Ardis Publishers, 1989), 5.

65. Hartog, "The Modern Regime of Historicity," 133.

66. Sabina Tanović, *Designing Memory: The Architecture of Commemoration in Europe, 1914 to the Present* (Cambridge: Cambridge University Press, 2019), 37.

67. Alan Borg, *War Memorials: From Antiquity to the Present* (London: Leo Cooper, 1991), 82–83.

68. Hermann Lübbe, "The Contraction of the Present," in *High-Speed Society: Social Acceleration, Power, and Modernity*, ed. Hartmut Rosa and William Scheuerman (University Park: Pennsylvania State University Press, 2009), 159–162.

69. Bauman, *Liquid Modernity*, 137.

70. Boris Groys, *The Total Art of Stalinism: Avant-Garde, Aesthetic Dictatorship, and Beyond*, trans. Charles Rougle (Princeton, NJ: Princeton University Press, 1992), 75, 110.

71. Hartog, *Regimes of Historicity*, 159.

72. See Aleida Assmann, *Cultural Memory and Western Civilization: Functions, Media, Archives* (Cambridge: Cambridge University Press, 2011), 39.

73. Pierre Nora, "General Introduction: Between Memory and History," in *Realms of Memory: Rethinking the French Past. Volume 1: Conflicts and Divisons*, ed. Pierre Nora and Lawrence Kritzman (New York: Columbia University Press, 1996), 8–9.

74. Lübbe, "The Contraction of the Present," 161–162.

75. Andreas Huyssen, *Twilight Memories: Marking Time in a Culture of Amnesia* (London: Routledge, 1995), 34.

76. Zygmunt Bauman, *Retrotopia* (Cambridge: Polity Press, 2017), 62.

77. See Fredric Jameson, *Postmodernism, or the Cultural Logic of Late Capitalism* (Durham, NC: Duke University Press, 1991), 16–25.

78. Andreas Huyssen, "Present Pasts: Media, Politics, Amnesia," *Public Culture* 12, no. 1 (2000): 27.

79. Paul Connerton, *How Modernity Forgets* (Cambridge: Cambridge University Press, 2009), 79.

80. Bauman, *Mortality, Immortality*, 85–86.

81. Nora, "General Introduction," 12.

82. Andrew Hoskins, "Memory of the Multitude: The End of Collective Memory," in *Digital Memory Studies: Media Pasts in Transition*, ed. Andrew Hoskins (New York: Routledge, 2017), 86.

83. Bauman, *Liquid Modernity*, 37.

84. Assmann, *Is Time out of Joint?*, 222.

85. Mariia Romashova, "'The Heart of a Remarkable Communist Has Ceased to Beat': Grief in the Emotional Repertoire of Elderly Soviet Activists of the 1960s–1980s," (Paper presentation, 50th ASEEES Annual Convention, Boston, MA, December 8, 2018).

86. Hans Gumbrecht, *Our Broad Present: Time and Contemporary Culture* (New York: Columbia University Press, 2014), xiii.

Epilogue

1. Sergei Kruk, "Semiotics of Visual Iconicity in Leninist 'Monumental' Propaganda," *Visual Communication* 7, no. 1 (2008): 48.

2. Hana Pichova, *The Case of the Missing Statue: A Historical and Literary study of the Stalin Monument in Prague* (Prague: Arbor vitae, 2014).

3. Igor Golomstock, *Totalitarian Art: In the Soviet Union, the Third Reich, Fascist Italy, and the People's Republic of China*, trans. Robert Chandler (London: Collins Harvill, [1990] 2011), 281. For this observation, in relation to the Ukrainian context, see Serhy Yekelchyk, "Symbolic Plasticity and Memorial Environment: The Afterlife of Soviet Monuments in Post-Soviet Kyiv," *Canadian Slavonic Papers* 63, no. 1–2 (2021): 212.

4. Aleksei Shchusev, "Arkhitektura epokhi," *Kommunististicheskaia molodezh* no. 1 (1935): 46. Italics mine.

5. Robert Musil, *Posthumous Papers of a Living Author*, trans. Peter Wortsman (New York: Archipelago Books, [1936] 2012), 64, 67.

6. Musil, *Posthumous Papers of a Living Author*, 62–63.

7. Graeme Gill, *Symbolism and Regime Change in Russia* (Cambridge: Cambridge University Press, 2013), 211.

8. Galina Ptichnikova, "Osobennosti arkhitektury poslevoennogo perioda v Stalingrade," in *Arkhitektura Stalinskoi epokhi: opyt istoricheskogo osmysleniia*, ed. Iuliia Kosenkova (Moscow: KomKniga, 2010), 249–250.

9. Marina Dmitrieva, "Moscow Architecture between Stalinism and Modernism," *International Review of Sociology* 16, no. 2 (2006): 433.

10. Natal'ia Shashkova, "Istoriia, istoriko-kul'turnoe znachenie i sovremennoe ispol'zovanie naslediia sovetskoi arkhitektury: gostinitsa 'Leningradskaia'," *Prostranstvo i vremia* 15, no. 1 (2014): 176.

11. Elena Dzhandzhugazova, "Moskovskoe metro: puteshestvie vo vremeni i prostranstve," *Sovremennye problemy servisa i turizma* 1 (2010): 70–71.

12. Dmitrii Khmel'nitskii, "Mif o klassitsizme," February 5, 2014, accessed December 14, 2019, https://archi.ru/russia/52978/mif-o-klassicizme.

13. Ol'ga Zinov'eva, *Simvoly stalinskoi' Moskvy* (Moscow: Tonchu, 2009), 10.

14. "O proekte," Alcontower (website), accessed November 24, 2021, https://alcontower.com/about.html.

15. Alena Kuznetsova, "Obratnyi otschet," Archi, accessed November 25, 2020, https://archi.ru/russia/86421/obratnyi-otschet.

16. Lewis Mumford, *The Culture of Cities* (San Diego, CA: Harcourt Brace Jovanovich, [1938] 1970), 435.

17. Anthony Giddens, "Living in a Post-Traditional Society," in *Reflexive Modernization: Politics, Tradition and Aesthetics in the Modern Social Order*, ed. Ulrich Beck, Anthony Giddens, and Scott Lash (Cambridge: Polity Press, 1994), 104.

18. James Young, "Memory, Counter-Memory and the End of the Monument," in *Image and Remembrance: Representation and the Holocaust*, ed. Shelley Hornstein and Florence Jacobowitz (Bloomington: Indiana University Press, 2003), 62; James Young, "Memory/ Monument," in *Critical Terms for Art History*, ed. Robert Nelson and Richard Shiff (Chicago: University of Chicago Press, 2003), 244.

19. Magdalena Banaszkiewicz, "The 'Embodiments' of Stalin in the Tourism Landscape of Moscow," *International Journal of Tourism Anthropology* 5, no. 3–4 (2016): 229.

20. For a discussion of the path-dependence of postsocialist mnemonic discourses, see the special issue "The Commemorative Legacies of State Socialism," *Canadian Slavonic Papers* 63, no. 1 (2021).

21. Maria Ferretti, "Raskolotaia pamiat': Rossiia i voina," *Rossiia XXI*, no. 2 (2010).

22. For an overview of the literature exploring the commemoration of Stalinism in contemporary Russia, see Antony Kalashnikov, "Stalinist Crimes and the Ethics of Memory," *Kritika: Explorations in Russian and Eurasian History* 19, no. 3 (2018).

23. Nikolai Borytko and Irina Vlasiuk, "Potentsial arkhitektury Stalinskogo ampira g. Volgograda kak sredstvo patrioticheskogo vospitaniia sovremennogo shkol'nika," *Grani poznaniia* 41, no. 7 (2015): 129.

24. Maria Engström, "Re-Imagining Antiquity: The Conservative Discourse of 'Russia as the True Europe' and the Kremlin's New Cultural Policy," in *Russia as Civilization: Ideological Discourses in Politics, Media and Academia*, ed. Kare Johan Mjor and Sanna Turoma (Abingdon, UK: Routledge, 2020), 148.

25. Andreas Schönle, "Appropriating Stalinist Heritage: State Rhetoric and Urban Transformation in the Repurposing of VDNKh," in *Re-Centring the City: Global Mutations of Socialist Modernity*, ed. Jonathan Bach and Michal Murawski (London: UCL Press, 2020), 48, 54–56.

26. Julie Deschepper, "Le 'patrimoine soviétique' de l'URSS à la Russie contemporaine: généalogie d'un concept," *Vingtième Siècle. Revue d'histoire* 137, no. 1 (2018): 19.

27. Julie Deschepper, "Mémoires plurielles et patrimoines dissonants: l'héritage architectural soviétique dans la Russie poutinienne," *Le Mouvement Social*, no. 260 (2017): 39.

28. Schönle, "Appropriating Stalinist Heritage," 60.

29. Dmitrieva, "Moscow Architecture between Stalinism and Modernism," 445.

30. Henri Lefebvre, *The Production of Space*, trans. Donald Nicholson-Smith (Oxford: Blackwell, 1974), 222.

31. Elena Bykova, "Modul'nyi memorial'nyi tekst kak monumental'naia propaganda," *Izvestiia Rossiiskogo gosudarstvennogo pedagogicheskogo universiteta*, no. 131 (2011): 133.

32. Reuben Fowkes, "Soviet War Memorials in Eastern Europe, 1945–74," in *Figuration/ Abstraction: Strategies for Public Sculpture in Europe 1945–1968*, ed. Charlotte Benton (Aldershot, UK: Ashgate, 2004), 16–17.

33. Paul Connerton, *How Modernity Forgets* (Cambridge: Cambridge University Press, 2009), 29–30.

34. Dietmar Neutatz, *Moskovskoe metro: ot pervykh planov do velikoi stroiki stalinizma (1897–1935)*, trans. Iu. Petrov (Moscow: ROSSPEN, 2013), 167–168. Cemetery marble and bronze were also used in metro construction, Catherine Merridale, "Revolution among the Dead: Cemeteries in Twentieth-Century Russia," *Mortality* 8, no. 2 (2003): 181.

35. Valery Lazarev, conclusion to *The Economics of Forced Labor: The Soviet Gulag*, ed. Paul Gregory and Valery Lazarev (Stanford, CA: Hoover Institution Press, 2003), 196.

36. Serguei Oushakine, "Second-Hand Nostalgia: On Charms and Spells of the Soviet Trukhliashechka," in *Post-Soviet Nostalgia: Confronting the Empire's Legacies*, ed. Otto Boele, Boris Noordenbos, and Ksenia Robbe (New York: Routledge, 2019), 39.

37. Oushakine, "Second-Hand Nostalgia," 67.

38. Vera Mukhina, "Tema i obraz v monumental'noi skul'pture," *Sovetskoe iskusstvo*, November 14, 1944, 2.

39. Anna Sorokina, "Syndrome of Soviet Nostalgia among the Younger Generation of Russians," (Paper presentation, IX ICCEES Congress, Makuhari, Japan, August 8, 2015).

40. For a discussion of common practices, see Håkan Hökerberg, "Difficult Heritage: Various Approaches to Twentieth-Century Totalitarian Architecture," in *From Postwar to Postmodern: 20th Century Built Cultural Heritage*, ed. Maria Rossipal (Stockholm: Riksantikvarieämbetet, 2017).

41. Gabi Dolff-Bonekämper, "Sites of Memory and Sites of Discord: Historic Monuments as a Medium for Discussing Conflict in Europe," in *The Heritage Reader*, ed. Graham Fairclough et al. (London: Routledge, 2008).

42. Beverley James, *Imagining Postcommunism: Visual Narratives of Hungary's 1956 Revolution* (College Station: Texas A&M University Press, 2005), 32.

43. See Svetlana Boym, *The Future of Nostalgia* (New York: Basic Books, 2001), 83–91.

44. Iuliia Pirozhkova, "Gostinitsa 'Ukraina'," Uznai Moskvu, accessed March 15, 2019, https://um.mos.ru/houses/gostinitsa_ukraina/?sphrase_id=438088.

45. Evgeniia Stakhanova, "Vysotka na Kotel'nicheskoi naberezhnoi," Uznai Moskvu, accessed March 15, 2019, https://um.mos.ru/houses/vysotka_na_kotelnicheskoy_naberezhnoy/?sphrase_id=438088.

46. Tat'iana Vorontsova and Irina Trubetskaia, "VSKhV-VDNKh," Uznai Moskvu, accessed March 15, 2019, https://um.mos.ru/places/vskhv_vdnkh/?sphrase_id=438090; Irina Trubetskaia, "Arka severnogo vkhoda na VDNKh," Uznai Moskvu, accessed

March 15, 2019, https://um.mos.ru/houses/arka_severnogo_vkhoda_na_vdnkh/?sphrase_.

47. "Pavil'on stantsii metro 'Novokuznetksaia'," Uznai Moskvu, accessed March 15, 2019, https://um.mos.ru/houses/pavilon_stantsii_metro_novokuznetskaya/?sph; Tat'iana Vorontsova, "Stantsiia metro 'Kropotkinskaia'," Uznai Moskvu, accessed March 15, 2019, https://um.mos.ru/houses/stantsiya-metro-kropotkinskaya/?sphrase_id=4.

48. Cynthia Ruder, *Building Stalinism: The Moscow Canal and the Creation of Soviet Space* (London: I. B. Tauris, 2018), 176.

Bibliography

Archives (and key to cited *fondy*):

GARF, *Gosudarstvennyi arkhiv Rossiiskoi Federatsii* (State Archive of the Russian Federation)
  f. 10010. Cultural Research Institute of the Ministry of Culture of the RSFSR
  f. A259. Council of Ministers of the RSFSR (SM RSFSR)
  f. R1235. All-Russian Central Executive Soviet of Worker, Peasant, and Red Army Deputies (VTsIK)
  f. R3316. Central Executive Committee of the USSR (TsIK SSSR)
  f. R5325. Main Archival Directorate of the Council of Ministers of the USSR (GLAVARKhIV SSSR)
  f. R5446. Council of Ministers of the USSR (SM SSSR)
  f. R7523. Supreme Soviet of the USSR
  f. R8300. Ministry of State Audits of the USSR
RGAE, *Rossiiskii gosudarvennyi arkhiv ekonomiki* (Russian State Archive of the Economy)
  f. 339. State Committee of the Council of Ministers of the USSR for Construction Affairs (Gosstroi)
  f. 552. Construction Directorate of the Palace of the Soviets
  f. 4372. State Planning Committee of the Council of Ministers of the USSR (Gosplan)
  f. 7857. All-Union Agricultural Exhibition (VSKhV) of the Ministry of Agriculture of the USSR
  f. 9432. Committee for Architectural Affairs of the Council of Ministers of the USSR
RGALI, *Rossiiskii gosudarvennyi arkhiv literatury i iskusstva* (Russian State Archive of Literature and Art)
  f. 619. Editorial Office of the Journal *Oktiabr'*
  f. 674. Union of the Architects of the USSR
  f. 962. Committee for Arts Affairs of the Council of the Ministers of the USSR
  f. 2075. Committee for Arts Affairs of the Council of Ministers of the RSFSR
  f. 2329. Ministry of Culture of the USSR
  f. 2458. Directorate for Art Exhibitions and Panoramas of the Ministry of Culture of the USSR
  f. 2932. Central House for Art Professionals of the USSR (TsDRI)
  f. 2942. Art organizations—predecessors of the Moscow branch of the Union of Artists of the RSFSR (amalgamated *fond*)

f. 2943. Moscow branch of the Union of Artists of the RSFSR (MOSKh)
f. 3024. Zelenskaia Nina Germanovna (1898–1986), Ivanova Zinaida Grigor'evna (1897–1979)—sculptor

RGASPI, *Rossiiskii gosudarvennyi arkhiv sotsial'no-politicheskoi istorii* (Russian State Archive of Social and Political History)
f. 17. Central Committee of the Communist Party of the Soviet Union (TsK KPSS)

TsGAM, *Tsentral'nyi arkhiv goroda Moskvy* (Central State Archive of Moscow)
f. 150. Moscow City Soviet (Mossovet)
f. 278. Directorate of the Moscow Metro
f. 429. Directorate of Culture of the Moscow City Executive Committee (Mosgorispolkom)
f. 534. Main Architectural-Planning Directorate of the Moscow City Executive Committee
f. 694. Construction Directorate of the Palace of the Soviets of the Council of Ministers of the USSR

Newspapers and magazines

Arkhitektura SSSR
Arkhitekturnaia gazeta
Arkhitektura i stroitel'stvo
Arkhitektura i stroitel'stvo Moskvy
Dvorets Sovetov
Iskusstvo
Izvestiia
Kommunisticheskaia molodezh
LEF
Literaturnaia gazeta
Moskovskii stroitel'
Planirovka i stroitel'stvo gorodov
Pravda
Sovetskaia arkhitektura
Sovetskoe iskusstvo
Stroitel'naia gazeta
Stroitel'stvo Moskvy

Published primary materials

Akademiia arkhitektury SSSR. *Konkurs na sostavlenie proektov monumentov geroiam Velikoi Otechestvennoi voiny.* Moscow: Izdatel'stvo Akademii arkhitektury, 1942.
Alabian, Karo. "Perveishii dolg arkhitektorov." *Moskovskii stroitel'*, March 28, 1953, 2.
Alabian, Karo, and Vasilii Simbirtsev. "Arkhitekturnyi pamiatnik Krasnoi Armii." *Planirovka i stroitel'stvo gorodov*, no. 10 (1934): 22–25.
Anagarov, Aleksei. "O nekotorykh voprosakh sovetskoi arkhitektury. Stennogramma vystupleniia tov. Angarova na obshchemoskovskom sobranii arkhitektorov 27 fevralia 1936 g." *Arkhitektura SSSR*, no. 4 (1936): 7–11.

Arkin, David. "Arkhitektura i problema sinteza iskusstv." In *Voprosy sinteza iskusstv. Materialy pervogo tvorcheskogo soveshchania arkhitektorov, skul'ptorov i zhivopistsev (o kadrakh khudozhnikov-monumentalistov)*, edited by M. Zhitomirskii, 9–21. Moscow: IZOGIZ, 1936.
———. "Monumenty geroiam Velikoi Otechestvennoi voiny. Zametki o konkurse." *Arkhitektura SSSR*, no. 5 (1944): 3–11.
Atarov, Nikolai. *Dvorets Sovetov.* Moscow: Moskovskii rabochii, 1940.
Balashov, Sergei, and Aleksei Voronkov. *Dvorets nauki*. Moscow: Moskovskii rabochii, 1954.
Beriia, Lavrentii. "Velichaishii chelovek istorii." In *Stalin. K 60-letiiu so dnia rozhdeniia. Sbornik statei "Pravdy"*. Moscow: Pravda, 1940.
Beskin, Osip. "O monumental'nom iskusstve." *Iskusstvo*, no. 1 (1939): 54–82.
Blokhin, B. "K voprosu o monumental'nom iskusstve." *Iskusstvo*, no. 4 (1934): 2–3.
Borisovskii, Georgii. "Narodnoe tvorchestvo, klassicheskii order i sovremennyi standart." *Arkhitektura SSSR*, no. 13 (1946): 30–33.
Bunin, Andrei, and Mariia Kruglova. *Arkhitekturnaia kompozitsiia gorodov.* Moscow: Izdatel'stvo Akademii arkhitektury SSSR, 1940.
Chechulin, Dmitrii. "Arkhitektura Moskvy." *Arkhitektura i stroitel'stvo*, no. 11 (1947): 7–12.
———. *Zhizn' i zodchestvo*. Moscow: Molodaia gvardiia, 1978.
Cherkasskii, I. "Zhilye doma, a ne korpusa-kazarmy. Tsentralizovannyi fond Mossoveta v 1932 g.". *Stroitel'stvo Moskvy*, no. 7 (1932): 7–13.
Chernyshev, Nikolai. "Problemy monumental'noi zhivopisi." *Iskusstvo*, no. 1–2 (1933): 43–56.
———. "O rabotakh nashikh monumentalistakh." *Iskusstvo*, no. 4 (1934): 21–34.
———. "Mastera iskusstva o Moskovskom metro." *Iskusstvo*, no. 4 (1935): 14–27.
Chernyshev, Sergei. *General'nyi plan rekonstruktsii Moskvy i voprosy planirovki gorodov SSSR. Doklad prof. S. E. Chernysheva na Vsesoiuznom s"ezde sovetskikh arkhitektorov.* Moscow: Izdatel'stvo Vsesoiuznoi akademii arkhitektury, 1937.
Chubar', Vlas. "Rech' zamestitelia Predsedatelia Soveta Narodnykh Komissarov SSSR tov. V. Ia. Chubaria." In *Postanovleniia i materialy. Pervyi vsesoiuznyi s"ezd sovetskikh arkhitektorov*, edited by A. Barkhudarian and N. Kirsanova, 26–38. Moscow: Izdatel'stvo Akademii arkhitektury, 1937.
Davies, Robert, Oleg Khlevniuk, Arfon Rees, Liudmila Kosheleva, and Larisa Rogovaya, eds. *The Stalin-Kaganovich Correspondence, 1931–36*. New Haven, CT: Yale University Press, 2008.
Deineka, Aleksandr. "K voprosu o monumental'nom iskusstve." *Iskusstvo*, no. 4 (1934): 3–5.
———. "Khudozhniki v metro." *Iskusstvo*, no. 6 (1938): 75–80.
———. "Zhivopis' v inter'ere." *Arkhitektura SSSR*, no. 6 (1939): 24–25.
———. "Aleksandr Aleksandrovich Deineka." In *Mastera sovetskogo izobrazitel'nogo iskusstva: proizvedeniia i avtobiograficheskie ocherki*, edited by P. Sysoev and Viacheslav Shkvarikov, 221–230. Moscow: Iskusstvo, 1951.
Dinamov, Sergei. "O stile sovetskogo iskusstva." *Iskusstvo*, no. 4 (1935): 1–4.
Durov, B. "Obelisk konstitutsii." *Izvestiia*, December 18, 1936, 4.
Dushkin, Aleksei. "Iz poiasnitel'noi zapiski k proektu stantsii 'Maiakovskaia.'" In *Aleksei Nikolaevich Dushkin. Arkhitektura 1930–1950-kh godov. Katalog vystavki*, edited by Natal'ia Dushkina, 173. Moscow: A-Fond, 2004.

———. "Stantsiia 'Ploshchad' Revoliutsii'. 1935–1938." In *Aleksei Nikolaevich Dushkin. Arkhitektura 1930–1950-kh godov. Katalog vystavki*, edited by Natal'ia Dushkina, 150–167. Moscow: A-Fond, 2004.

———. "Stantsiia metro 'Zavod imeni Stalina'. 1939–1943. Stantsiia metro 'Paveletskaia-radial'naia'. 1941–1943." In *Aleksei Nikolaevich Dushkin. Arkhitektura 1930–1950-kh godov. Katalog vystavki*, edited by Natal'ia Dushkina, 194–205. Moscow: A-Fond, 2004.

Erenburg, Il'ia. *Sobranie sochinenii v deviati tomakh. Tom 8*. Moscow: Khudozhestvennaia literatura, 1966.

Fomin, Ivan. "Tvorcheskie puti sovetskoi arkhitektury i problema arkhitekturnogo nasledstva. I. A. Fomin." *Arkhitektura SSSR*, no. 3–4 (1933): 15–16.

Frolov, Vladimir. "Mozaika v arkhitekture." *Arkhitketurnaia gazeta*, February 8, 1935, 3.

———. "Mozaika Dvortsa Sovetov." *Dvorets Sovetov*, January 11, 1940, 3.

Gabrichevskii, Aleksandr. "Vvedenie k monografii 'Memorial'naia arkhitektura'." In *Pamiat' i vremia. Iz khudozhestvennogo arkhiva Velikoi Otechestvennoi voiny 1941–1945 gg*, edited by Tat'iana Malinina and Elena Ogarkova, 302–307. Moscow: Galart, [1943–1946] 2011.

Gaposhkin, Vladimir. "Eshche o monumental'noi zhivopisi." *Sovetskoe iskusstvo*, June 8, 1945, 2.

Gel'freikh, Vladimir, and Mikhail Minkus. "Vystonye zdaniia v ansamble goroda." *Sovetskoe iskusstvo*, December 12, 1951, 2.

Genin, Robert. "Nastennaia zhivopis' i ee tekhnika." *Arkhitektura SSSR*, no. 6 (1939): 26–27.

Gerasimov, Aleksandr. "A. M. Gerasimov." In *Voprosy razvitiia sovetskoi skul'ptury. Nauchnaia konferentsiia. 28–30 maia 1952 g*, edited by Matvei Manizer, 150–157. Moscow: Izdatel'stvo Akademii khudozhestv SSSR, 1953.

Ginzburg, Moisei. "Organicheskoe v arkhitekture i prirode." *Arkhitektura SSSR*, no. 3 (1939): 76–80.

Gol'ts, Georgii. "Ob ideinosti v arkhitekture." *Stroitel'naia gazeta*, March 8, 1940, 3.

———. "O pamiatnikakh." In *Mastera sovetskoi arkhitektury ob arkhitekture. Tom 2*, edited by Mikhail Barkhin et al., 340–341. Moscow: Iskusstvo, 1975.

Golosov, Il'ia. "O bol'shoi arkhitekturnoi forme." *Arkhitektura SSSR*, no. 5 (1933): 34.

Gor'kii, Maksim. "Istoriia fabrik i zavodov." *Pravda*, September 7, 1931, 2.

Hitler, Adolf. *Mein Kampf*. Translated by Ralph Manheim. Boston, MA: Houghton Mifflin, [1927] 1971.

———. *Hitler's Table Talk, 1941–44: His Private Conversations*. Translated by Norman Cameron and R. H. Stevens. London: Weidenfeld and Nicolson, 1973.

Il'in, Lev. "Ansambl' v arkhitekture goroda." *Arkhitektura SSSR*, no. 5 (1935): 41–50.

Iofan, Boris. "Ploshchad' i prospekt Dvotsa Sovetov." *Arkhitektura SSSR*, no. 11 (1935): 25–28.

———. "Stroitel'stvo Dvortsa Sovetov i sodruzhestvo iskusstv. Doklad akademika arkhitektury B. M. Iofana." In *Arkhitektura Dvortsa Sovetov. Materialy V plenuma Pravleniia SSA SSSR*, edited by I. Sushkevich, 7–23. Moscow: Izdatel'stvo Akademii arkhitektury, 1939.

———. "O novatorstve v arkhitekture." *Stroitel'naia gazeta*, May 24, 1940, 2.

———. "Vosstanovlenie nashikh gorodov i zadachi arkhitektury." *Izvestiia*, September 12, 1944, 3.

———. "Novyi siluet stolitsy." *Sovetskoe iskusstvo*, July 18, 1947, 2.

Iofan, Boris, and Vladimir Gel'freikh. "Nekotorye problemy stroitel'stva Dvortsa Sovetov." *Stroitel'stvo Moskvy*, no. 5 (1939): 4–7.

"Iz predstavlennoi v SNK SSSR i TsK VKP(b) dokladnoi zapiski Moskovskogo oblastnogo i gorodskogo komitetov VKP(b) i Moskovskogo soveta RK i KD o general'nom plane rekonstruktsii g. Moskvy." In *General'nyi plan rekonstruktsii goroda Moskvy. Postanovleniia i materialy*, edited by Ia. Tsvankin, 43–134. Moscow: Moskovskii rabochii, 1936.

Kaganovich, Lazar'. *Za sotsialisticheskuiu rekonstruktsiiu Moskvy i gorodov SSSR. Pererabotannaia stenogramma doklada na iun'skom plenume TsK VKP(b)*. Moscow: OGIZ "Moskovskii Rabochii," 1931.

Kalinin, Mikhail. "Bol'shaia obshenarodnaia zadacha." *Izvestiia*, December 10, 1943, 2.

"Kamen' v arkhitekture." *Sovetskoe iskusstvo*, October 12, 1945, 4.

Katsen, Il'ia, and Konstantin Ryzhkov. *Moskovskii Metropoliten*. Moscow: Izdatel' stvo Akademii Arkhitektury SSSR, 1948.

Kholodkovskii, Vladimir. *Moskovskie vstrechi*. Moscow: Moskovskii rabochii, 1948.

Klimov, M. "Ideino-khudozhestvennye problemy arkhitektury Moskovskogo metropolitena (3–4 ocheredi)." Kandidat dissertation, Akademiia obshchestvennykh nauk pri TsK VKP(b), 1952.

Kolli, Nikolai. "Arkhitektura metro." In *Kak my stroili metro*, edited by Aleksandr Kosarev, 174–207. Moscow: Istoriia fabrik i zavodov, 1935.

———. "O nekotorykh osobennostiakh ansamblevoi zastroiki gorodov." In *Problema ansamblia v sovetskoi arkhitekture. Sbornik statei*, edited by K. Trapeznikov, 29–44. Moscow: Gosudarstvennoe izdatel'stvo literatury po stroitel'stvu i arkhitekture, 1952.

———, ed. *Tipovye proekty pamiatnikov bratskikh i individual'nykh mogil voinov Sovetskoi Armii, Voenno-Morskogo flota i partizan, pogibshikh v boiakh s nemetsko-fashistskimi zakhvatchikami v gody Velikoi Otechestvennoi voiny*. Moscow: Voennoe izdatel'stvo, 1947.

Kolokolov, G. "Metrostroevskaia moral'." In *Metro: Sbornik posviashchaetsia pusku moskovskogo metropolitena*, edited by Leonid Kovalev, 237–241. Moscow: Rabochaia Moskva, 1935.

Kornfel'd, Iakov. *Laureaty Stalinskoi premii v arkhitekture. 1941–1950*. Moscow: GILSA, 1953.

Korolev, Boris. "Skul'ptury Dvotsa. Doklad skul'ptora B. D. Koroleva (Moskovskii Soiuz sovetskikh khudozhnikov-skul'ptorov)." In *Arkhitektura Dvortsa Sovetov. Materialy V plenuma Pravleniia SSA SSSR.*, edited by I. Sushkevich, 38–41. Moscow: Izdatel'stvo Akademii arkhitektury, 1939.

———. "Skul'ptura Dvortsa Sovetov. Gruppy i barel'efy." *Arkhitektura SSSR*, no. 6 (1939): 18–19.

Kruglova, Mariia. *Monumenty v arkhitekture gorodov*. Moscow: Gosudarstvennoe izdatel'stvo literatury po stroitel'stvu i arkhitekture, 1952.

Lansere, Evgenii. "Monumental'naia zhivopis'." *Izvestiia*, June 30, 1939, 3.

———. "O monumental'noi zhivopisi." *Sovetskoe iskusstvo*, April 19, 1945, 3.
———. *Dnevniki. Kniga pervaia. Vospitanie chuvstv.* Moscow: Iskusstvo-XXI vek, 2008.
———. *Dnevniki. Kniga tret'ia. Khudozhnik i gosudarstvo.* Moscow: Iskusstvo-XXI vek, 2009.
Lunacharskii, Anatolii. "Dvorets Sovetov. Tov. A. V. Lunacharskii ob arkhitekturnykh proektakh." *Sovetskoe iskusstvo*, January 26, 1932, 1.
———. "Lenin o monumental'noi propagande." *Literaturnaia gazeta*, January 29, 1933, 1.
———. "Sotsialisticheskii arkhitekturnyi monument." *Stroitel'stvo Moskvy*, no. 5–6 (1933): 3–10.
———. "Ob arkhitekturno-khudozhestvennom oformlenii Moskvy." *Stroitel'stvo Moskvy*, no. 6 (1934): 32–33.
———. "Monumental'naia agitatsiia." In *A. V. Lunacharkii ob iskusstve. Tom 2*, edited by Igor' Sats and A. Ermakov, 51–52. Moscow: Iskusstvo, [1918] 1982.
Manevskii, F., and I. Kriazhin. *O sbore, uchete i obrabotke materialov o pamiatnikakh i pamiatnykh istoricheskikh mestakh Velikoi Otechestvennoi voiny. Metodicheskoe pis'mo.* Moscow: Muzeino-kraevedcheskoe otdelenie Narkomprosa RSFSR, 1942.
Manizer, Matvei. *Skul'ptor o svoei rabote. Tom 1*. Moscow: Iskusstvo, 1940.
———. *Skul'ptor o svoei rabote. Tom 2.* Moscow: Iskusstvo, 1952.
Mashkovtsev, Nikolai. "Proekty novykh pamiatnikov." *Iskusstvo*, no. 3 (1947): 32–39.
Matsa, Ivan. "Traditsii i sovremennost'." *Sovetskoe iskusstvo*, March 29, 1946, 2.
Mayakovsky, Vladimir. *Poems.* Translated by Dorian Rottenberg. Moscow: Progress, 1972.
Merkurov, Sergei. "Monumenty Lenina i Stalina." *Arkhitekturnaia gazeta*, August 12, 1937, 1.
———. "Osnovnaia skul'ptura Dvortsa Sovetov—statuia V. I. Lenina." In *Arkhitektura Dvortsa Sovetov. Materialy V plenuma Pravleniia SSA SSSR*, edited by I. Sushkevich, 33–36. Moscow: Izdatel'stvo Akademii arkhitektury, 1939.
———. "Simvol epokhi." *Pravda*, January 20, 1939, 4.
———. *Vospominania. Pis'ma. Stat'i. Zametki. Suzhdeniia sovremennikov.* Moscow: Kremlin Multimedia, 2012.
Miliutin, N. "N. A. Miliutin (nachal'nik khudozhestvennoi chasti stroitel'stva Dvortsa Sovetov)." In *Arkhitektura Dvortsa Sovetov. Materialy V plenuma Pravleniia SSA SSSR*, edited by I. Sushkevich, 43–44. Moscow: Izdatel'stvo Akademii arkhitektury, 1939.
"Monumental'noe iskusstvo." In *Bol'shaia sovetskaia entsikolopediia. Tom 28*, edited by B. Vvedenskii. Moscow: Gosudarstvennoe nauchnoe izdatel'stvo 'Bol'shaia sovetskaia entsiklopedia', 1954.
"Monumental'nost'." In *Bol'shaia sovetskaia entsikolopediia. Tom 40*, edited by O. Shmidt. Moscow: Gosudarstvennyi Institut 'Sovetskaia entsiklopedia', 1938.
Mordvinov, Arkadii. *Khudozhestvennye problemy sovetskoi arkhitektury. Doklad vitse-prezidenta Akademii Arkhitektury SSSR A. G. Mordvinova.* Moscow: Gosudarstvennoe arkhitekturnoe izdatel'stvo, 1944.
Morgan, Dzhodzh. "Luchshyi v mire." In *Rasskazy stroitelei metro*, edited by Aleksandr Kosarev, 495–502. Moscow: Istoriia fabrik i zavodov, 1935.
Mukhina, Vera. "Skul'ptor V. I. Mukhina (Moskva)." In *Arkhitektura Dvortsa Sovetov. Materialy V plenuma Pravleniia SSA SSSR*, edited by I. Sushkevich, 44–45. Moscow: Izdatel'stvo Akademii arkhitektury, 1939.

———. "Tema i obraz v monumental'noi skul'pture." *Sovetskoe iskusstvo*, November 14, 1944, 2.

———. "Zametki khudozhnika." *Pravda*, September 19, 1951, 3–4.

———. "Monumental'no dekorativnoe iskusstvo v ansamble goroda." In *Problema ansamblia v sovetskoi arkhitekture. Sbornik statei*, edited by K. Trapeznikov, 83–96. Moscow: Gosudarstvennoe izdatel'stvo literatury po stroitel'stvu i arkhitekture, 1952.

———. "'Rabochii i kolkhoznitsa': Otryvok iz ustnykh vospominanii V. I. Mukhinoi, zapisannykh v 1939–1940 godakh, zapisannykh pisateliami L. Toom i A. Bekom." *Iskusstvo*, no. 8 (1957): 36–40.

———. *Literaturno-kriticheskoe nasledie*. Moscow: Iskusstvo, 1960.

"Narodnoe tvorchestvo." *Arkhitektura SSSR*, no. 1 (1937): 12–14.

"Ne torguite Leninym!". *LEF*, no. 5 (1924): 3–4.

"Novye temy i starye atributy." *Sovetskoe iskusstvo*, June 29, 1945, 4.

Oltarzhevskii, Viacheslav. *Stroitel'stvo vysotnykh zdanii v Moskve*. Moscow: Gosudarstvennoe izdatel'stvo literatury po stroitel'stvu i arkhitekture, 1953.

"O monumental'noi skul'pture." *Iskusstvo*, no. 4 (1952): 3–6.

"O pamiatnikakh respubliki." *Izvestiia*, April 14, 1918, 3.

Opochinskaia, Anna. "Ansambl' vysotnykh zdanii Moskvy i natsional'nye traditsii russkikh zodchikh." *Sovetskaia arkhitektura*, no. 5 (1954): 60–69.

"Pamiatnik Pavliku Morozovu." *Pravda*, July 24, 1935, 6.

Parshin, Iu. "Pod golubym kupolom." In *Dvorets nauki. Rasskazy stroitelei novogo zdaniia Moskovskogo gosudarstvennogo universiteta*, edited by V. Pospelov, 50–55. Moscow: Izdatel'stvo VTsSPS Profizdat, 1952.

Pavlenko, Oksana. "Radost' tvorchestva." In *Voprosy sinteza iskusstv. Materialy pervogo tvorcheskogo soveshchaniia arkhitektorov, skul'ptorov i zhivopistsev (o kadrakh khudozhnikov-monumentalistov)*, edited by M. Zhitomirskii, 112–115. Moscow: IZOGIZ, 1936.

Peganov, A. "A. A. Peganov (Moskva)." In *Arkhitektura Dvortsa Sovetov. Materialy V plenuma Pravleniia SSA SSSR*, edited by I. Sushkevich, 69–70. Moscow: Izdatel'stvo Akademii arkhitektury, 1939.

Perchik, Lev. *Bol'shevistskii plan rekonstruktsii Moskvy*. Moscow: Partizdat, 1935.

Posokhin, Mikhail. *Arkhitektura okruzhaiushchei sredy*. Moscow: Stroiizdat, 1989.

"Postanovlenie Soveta Narodnykh Komissarov ob uvekovechenii pamiati professora Kirsha." *Izvestiia*, August 3, 1920, 2.

"Postanovlenie tsentral'nogo Komiteta Kommunisticheskoi partii Sovetskogo Soiuza i Soveta Ministrov Soiuza SSSR o sooruzhenii Panteona—pamiatnika vechnoi slavy velikikh liudei Sovetskoi strany." *Pravda*, March 7, 1953, 2.

Radek, Karl. "Zodchii sotsialisticheskogo obshchestva." *Pravda*, January 1, 1934, 3–4.

Rakhmanov, Ivan. "Skul'ptura i gorod. Zadachi tresta skul'ptury." *Sovetskoe iskusstvo*, April 2, 1933, 1.

———. "Skul'ptor I. F. Rakhmanov (Moskva)." In *Arkhitektura Dvortsa Sovetov. Materialy V plenuma Pravleniia SSA SSSR*, edited by I. Sushkevich, 53–54. Moscow: Izdatel'stvo Akademii arkhitektury, 1939.

Rozhin, Igor'. "Iz moego opyta raboty v metro." In *Arkhitektura moskovskogo metro: 1935–1980-e gody*, edited by Ol'ga Kostina, 173–177. Moscow: BuksMArt, 2019.

BIBLIOGRAPHY

Rudnev, Lev. "Inter'ery Dvotsa nauki na Leninskikh gorakh." *Arkhitektura i stroitel'stvo Moskvy*, no. 1 (1953): 9–17.

———. "L. V. Rudnev." In *Voprosy razvitiia sovetskoi skul'ptury. Nauchnaia konferentsiia. 28–30 maia 1952 g.*, edited by Matvei Manizer, 75–78. Moscow: Izdatel'stvo Akademii khudozhestv SSSR, 1953.

———. "O formalizme i klassike." *Arkhitektura SSSR*, no. 11 (1954): 30–32.

Sar'ian, M. "Narodnyi khudozhnik Armenii M. S. Sar'ian (Erevan)." In *Arkhitektura Dvortsa Sovetov. Materialy V plenuma Pravleniia SSA SSSR*, edited by I. Sushkevich, 60–61. Moscow: Izdatel'stvo Akademii arkhitektury, 1939.

Savitskii, Iulii. "Ansambl' v sovetskom gradostroitel'stve." In *Problema ansamblia v sovetskoi arkhitekture. Sbornik statei*, edited by K. Trapeznikov, 5–14. Moscow: Gosudarstvennoe izdatel'stvo literatury po stroitel'stvu i arkhitekture, 1952.

Shantyko, Nina. *Evgenii Evgen'evich Lansere*. Moscow: Sovetskii khudozhnik, 1952.

Shaposhnikov, Iu. "Dostoinstva i nedostatki arkhitektury novykh stantsii metropolitena." *Arkhitektura SSSR*, no. 4 (1952): 1–20.

Shchusev, Aleksei. "Arkhitektura epokhi." *Kommunististicheskaia molodezh* no. 1 (1935): 46–49.

———. "Klassiki i my." *Izvestiia*, May 9, 1937, 3.

———. "Natsional'naia forma v arkhitekture." *Arkhitektura SSSR*, no. 10 (1940): 53–57.

Shchusev, Aleksei, and V. Lavrov. "General'nyi plan Novgoroda." *Arkhitektura i stroitel'stvo*, no. 5 (1946): 3–5.

Shkvarikov, Viacheslav. "Planirovka i stroitel'stvo russkikh gorodov." In *Russkaia arkhitektura: doklady, prochitannye v sviazi s dekadnikom po russkoi arkhitekture v Moskve v aprele 1939 g*, edited by Viacheslav Shkvarikov, 7–23. Moscow: Gosudarstvennoe izdatel'stvo Akademii arkhitektury SSSR, 1940.

Shostakovich, Dmtrii. *Testimony*. Translated by Antonina Bouis. Edited by Solomon Volkov. New York: Limelight Editions, [1979] 1984.

Soiuz Sovetskikh Arkhitektorov. "Zadachi arkhitektorov v dni Velikoi Otechestvennoi voiny. Rezoliutsiia X Plenuma Soiuza sovetskikh arkhitektorov SSSR, 22–25 aprelia 1942 goda." In *Zadachi arkhitektorov v dni Velikoi Otechestvennoi voiny: Materialy X Plenuma Soiuza sovetskikh arkhitektorov SSSR, 22–25 aprelia 1942 g*, edited by T. Sushkevich, 52–59. Moscow: Izdatel'stvo Akademii arkhitektury, 1942.

Soiuz Arkhitektorov SSSR. *Tvorcheskie voprosy sovetskoi arkhitektury i zadachi Soiuza sovetskikh arkhitektorov. Postanovlenie Prezidiuma Sovetskikh arkhitektorov SSSR 23 oktiabria 1946 goda*. Moscow: Izdatel'stvo Akademii arkhitektury SSSR, 1946.

Sokolov, Nikolai. "Klassika i sovremennost'." *Sovetskoe iskusstvo*, June 8, 1945, 2.

Sosfenov, Il'ia. "Problema sinteza v metro. Sintez v oformlenii stantsii 'Ploshchad' revoliutsii' Moskovskogo metro." *Iskusstvo*, no. 2 (1938): 29–42.

Sovet stroitel'stva Dvortsa Sovetov. "Ob organizatsii rabot po okonchatel'nomu sostavleniiu proekta Dvortsa sovetov SSSR v gor. Moskve." *Stroitel'stvo Moskvy*, no. 3 (1932): 15–16.

Speer, Albert. *Inside the Third Reich: Memoirs*. Translated by Richard Winston and Clara Winston. New York: Macmillan, 1970.

———. "The Fuhrer's Buildings." German Propaganda Archive, [1936] 1998, accessed 24 October 2020, http://research.calvin.edu/german-propaganda-archive/ahbuild.htm.

"Spisok lits koim predlozheno postavit' monumenty v g. Moskve i v drugikh gorodakh RSFSR, predstavlennyi v Sovet Narodnykh Komissarov Otdelom izobrazitel'nykh iskusstv Narodnogo komissariata po prosveshcheniiu." *Izvestiia*, August 2, 1918.

Stalin, Iosif. "Rech' na prieme rukovodiashchikh rabotnikov i stakhanovtsev metallurgicheskoi i ugol'noi promyshlennosti 29 oktiabria 1937 goda." *Pravda*, October 31, 1937, 1.

———. "Rech predsedatelia Gosudarstvennogo komiteta oborony i Narodnogo komissara oborony tov. I. V. Stalina na Krasnoi ploshchadi v den' XXIV godovshchiny Velikoi Oktiabr'skoi sotsialisticheskoi revoliutsii." *Pravda*, November 8, 1941, 1.

Steinbeck, John. *A Russian Journal*. New York: The Viking Press, 1948.

Sushkevich, I., ed. *Arkhitektura Dvortsa Sovetov. Materialy V plenuma Pravleniia SSA SSSR*. Moscow: Izdatel'stvo Akademii arkhitektury, 1939.

Ternovets, Boris. "Zadachi skul'ptury." *Arkhitektura SSSR*, no. 6 (1939): 20–22.

Timasheff, Nicholas. *The Great Retreat: The Growth and Decline of Communism in Russia*. New York: Dutton, 1946.

Tolstoi, Aleksei. "Poiski monumental'nosti." *Izvestiia*, February 27, 1932, 2–3.

Tolstoi, Vladimir. "Leninskii plan monumental'noi propagandy v deistvii." *Iskusstvo*, no. 1 (1952): 57–65.

Tomskii, Nikolai. "Khudozhestvennoe oformlenie dvortsa nauki." In *Dvorets nauki. Rasskazy stroitelei novogo zdaniia Moskovskogo gosudarstvennogo universiteta*, edited by V. Pospelov, 123–127. Moscow: Izdatel'stvo VTsSPS Profizdat, 1952.

———. "Problemy sovetskoi monumental'noi skul'ptury." In *Voprosy razvitiia sovetskoi skul'ptury. Nauchnaia konferentsiia. 28–30 maia 1952 g*, edited by Matvei Manizer, 11–40. Moscow: Izdatel'stvo Akademii khudozhestv SSSR, 1953.

Tosunova, Margarita. "Arkhitekturnyi obraz stantsii Moskovskogo metropolitena." *Sovetskaia arkhitektura*, no. 3 (1952): 8–22.

Tsapenko, Mikhail. *O realisticheskikh osnovakh sovetskoi arkhitektury*. Moscow: Gosudarstvennoe izdatel'stvo literatury po stroitel'stvu i arkhitekture, 1952.

Tukanov, Vladislav. "Monumenty v sovetskom gradostroitel'stve." Kandidat dissertation, Moskovskii arkhitekturnyi institut, 1953.

"Tvorcheskie pobedy sovetskikh khudozhnikov." *Iskusstvo*, no. 3 (1947): 3–8.

"Uroki maiskoi arkhitekturnoi vystavki: tvorcheskaia diskussiia v Soiuze sovetskikh arkhitektorov." *Arkhitektura SSSR*, no. 6 (1934): 5.

Valev, Valentin. "Skul'ptor V. Ts. Valev (Moskva)." In *Arkhitektura Dvortsa Sovetov. Materialy V plenuma Pravleniia SSA SSSR*, edited by I. Sushkevich, 68–69. Moscow: Izdatel'stvo Akademii arkhitektury, 1939.

Vesnin, Viktor. "Iazyk epokhi." *Sovetskoe iskusstvo*, March 15, 1932, 1.

———. "Dvorets Sovetov i sotrudnichestvo iskusstv. Vstupitel'noe slovo akademika arkhitektury V. A. Vesnina." In *Materialy V plenuma Pravleniia SSA SSSR*, edited by I. Sushkevich, 4–6. Moscow: Izdatel'stvo Akademii arkhitektury, 1939.

Vladimirskii, A., ed. *Otdelochnye materialy dlia Dvortsa Sovetov*. Moscow: Izdatel'stvo akademii arkhitektury SSSR, 1945.

Vuchetich, Evgenii, and Iakov Belopol'skii. "Pamiatnik general-leitenantu Efremovu." *Iskusstvo*, no. 3 (1947): 29–31.
Wright, Frank Lloyd. "Architecture and Life in the USSR." *Architectural Record* 82, no. 4 (1937): 58–63.
Zakharov, Grigorii. "Arkhitekturnyi ansambl' v zastroike gorogov. Doklad sekretaria Pravleniia Soiuza sovetskikh arkhitektorov SSSR G. A. Zakharova." In *Arkhitekturnyi ansambl' v stroitel'stve gorodov: Materialy XIV plenuma Pravl. Soiuza sovetskikh arkhitektorov SSSR (2–5 iiunia 1952 g.)*, edited by G. Morozova, 3–32. Moscow: Gosudarstvennoe izdatel'stvo literatury po stroitel'stvu i arkhitekture, 1952.
Zhdanov, Andrei. "Soviet Literature—The Richest in Ideas, the Most Advanced Literature." In *Soviet Writers' Congress 1934: The Debate on Socialist Realism and Modernism in the Soviet Union*, edited by Maksim Gorkii, 15–26. London: Lawrence & Wishart, 1977.
"Zhiznennye zadachi arkhitekturnoi praktiki." *Arkhitektura SSSR*, no. 13 (1946): 1–2.
Zholtovskii, Ivan. "Klassika zhivet." *Sovetskoe iskusstvo*, March 15, 1932, 1.
———. "Printsip zodchestva." *Arkhitektura SSSR*, no. 5 (1933): 28–29.
Zmeul, Sergei. "Arkhitektura pamiatnikov Velikoi Otechestvennoi voiny." Kandidat dissertation, Akademiia arkhitektury SSSR, 1950.
Zotov, Aleksei. *Mukhina, Vera Ignat'evna, narodnyi khudozhnik SSSR*. Moscow: Iskusstvo, 1944.

Published secondary materials

Adam, Peter. *Art of the Third Reich*. New York: Harry N. Abrams, 1992.
Aman, Anders. *Architecture and Ideology in Eastern Europe during the Stalin Era: An Aspect of Cold War History*. Translated by Roger Tanner and Kerstin Tanner. Cambridge, MA: MIT Press, 1992.
Anderson, Benedict. *Imagined Communities: Reflections on the Origin and Spread of Nationalism*. London: Verso, [1983] 2006.
Anderson, Richard. "The Future of History: The Cultural Politics of Soviet Architecture, 1928–41." PhD dissertation, Columbia University, 2010.
Armstrong, Elizabeth, and Suzanna Crage. "Movements and Memory: The Making of the Stonewall Myth." *American Sociological Review* 71, no. 5 (2006): 724–751.
Arrigo, Anthony. *Imaging Hoover Dam: The Making of a Cultural Icon*. Reno: University of Nevada Press, 2014.
Assmann, Aleida. *Cultural Memory and Western Civilization: Functions, Media, Archives*. Cambridge: Cambridge University Press, 2011.
———. *Is Time out of Joint?: On the Rise and Fall of the Modern Time Regime*. Translated by Sarah Clift. Ithaca, NY: Cornell University Press, 2020.
Assmann, Jan. *Cultural Memory and Early Civilization: Writing, Remembrance, and Political Imagination*. Cambridge: Cambridge University Press, 2011.
Astrakhantseva, Tat'iana. "Stil' 'Pobeda' v dekorativno-ornamental'nom iskusstve 1940–1950-kh godov: k probleme definitsii v sovetskom iskusstve stalinskoi epokhi." In *Arkhitektura Stalinskoi epokhi: opyt istoricheskogo osmysleniia*, edited by Iuliia Kosenkova, 142–149. Moscow: KomKniga, 2010.

Azizian, Irina. "Inobytie ar-deco v otechestvennoi arkhitekture." In *Arkhitektura Stalinskoi epokhi: opyt istoricheskogo osmysleniia*, edited by Iuliia Kosenkova, 50–63. Moscow: KomKniga, 2010.
Banaszkiewicz, Magdalena. "The 'Embodiments' of Stalin in the Tourism Landscape of Moscow." *International Journal of Tourism Anthropology* 5, no. 3–4 (2016): 221–234.
Bauman, Zygmunt. *Mortality, Immortality and Other Life Strategies*. Cambridge, UK: Polity Press, 1992.
——. *Retrotopia*. Cambridge, UK: Polity Press, 2017.
——. *Liquid Modernity*. Cambridge, UK: Polity Press, [2000] 2019.
Becker, Ernest. *The Denial of Death*. New York: The Free Press, 1973.
Bennett, Andrew. *Romantic Poets and the Culture of Posterity*. Cambridge: Cambridge University Press, 1999.
Benton, Charlotte, ed. *Figuration/ Abstraction: Strategies for Public Sculpture in Europe 1945–1968*. Aldershot, UK: Ashgate, 2004.
Blomqvist, Lars. "Some Utopian Elements in Stalinist Art." *Russian History* 11, no. 2–3 (1984): 298–305.
Borg, Alan. *War Memorials: From Antiquity to the Present*. London: Leo Cooper, 1991.
Borytko, Nikolai, and Irina Vlasiuk. "Potentsial arkhitektury Stalinskogo ampira g. Volgograda kak sredstvo patrioticheskogo vospitaniia sovremennogo shkol'nika." *Grani poznaniia* 41, no. 7 (2015): 129–132.
Bown, Matthew. *Art under Stalin*. New York: Holmes & Meier, 1991.
Boym, Svetlana. *The Future of Nostalgia*. New York: Basic Books, 2001.
Brandenberger, David. *National Bolshevism: Stalinist Mass Culture and the Formation of Modern Russian National Identity, 1931–1956*. Cambridge, MA: Harvard University Press, 2002.
——. *Propaganda State in Crisis: Soviet Ideology, Indoctrination, and Terror under Stalin, 1927–1941*. New Haven, CT: Yale University Press, 2011.
Brands, Gunnar. "From WWI Cemeteries to the Nazi 'Fortresses of the Dead'." In *Places of Commemoration: Search for Identity and Landscape Design*, edited by Joachim Wolschke-Bulhmahn, 215–256. Washington, DC: Dumbarton Oaks Research Library and Collection, 2001.
Buchli, Victor. "Moisei Ginzburg's Narkomfin Communal House in Moscow: Contesting the Social and Material World." *The Journal of the Society of Architectural Historians* 57, no. 2 (1998): 160–181.
Buck-Morss, Susan. *Dreamworld and Catastrophe: The Passing of Mass Utopia in East and West*. Cambridge, MA: MIT Press, 2000.
Bykova, Elena. "Modul'nyi memorial'nyi tekst kak monumental'naia propaganda." *Izvestiia Rossiiskogo gosudarstvennogo pedagogicheskogo universiteta*, no. 131 (2011): 131–137.
Calhoun, Craig. "Nationalism and the Contradictions of Modernity." *Berkeley Journal of Sociology* 42 (1997): 1–30.
Castillo, Greg. "Peoples at an Exhibition: Soviet Architecture and the National Question." In *Socialist Realism without Shores*, edited by Thomas Lahusen and Evgeny Dobrenko, 715–746. Durham, NC: Duke University Press, 1997.
——. "Soviet Orientalism: Socialist Realism and Built Tradition." *Traditional Dwellings and Settlements Review* 8, no. 2 (1997): 33–47.

Clark, Christopher. "Time of the Nazis: Past and Present in the Third Reich." *Geschichte und Gesellschaft* 25 (2015): 156–187.
Clark, Katerina. *Petersburg, Crucible of Cultural Revolution*. Cambridge, MA: Harvard University Press, 1995.
——. "Sotsrealizm i sakralizatsiia prostranstva." In *Sotsrealisticheskii kanon*, edited by Evgenii Dobrenko and Hans Gunther, 119–128. St. Petersburg: Akademicheskii proekt, 2000.
——. *The Soviet Novel: History as Ritual*. Bloomington: Indiana University Press, [1981] 2000.
——. "The New Moscow and the New Happiness: Architecture as the Nodal Point in the Stalinist System of Value." In *Petrified Utopia: Happiness Soviet Style*, edited by Marina Balina and Evgeny Dobrenko, 189–200. London: Anthem Press, 2009.
——. *Moscow as Fourth Rome: Stalinism, Cosmopolitanism, and the Evolution of Soviet Culture, 1931–1941*. Cambridge, MA: Harvard University Press, 2011.
Cohen, Aaron. *War Monuments, Public Patriotism, and Bereavement in Russia, 1905–2015*. Lanham, MD: Lexington Books, 2020.
Colton, Timothy. *Moscow: Governing the Socialist Metropolis*. Cambridge, MA: Harvard University Press, 1995.
Conner, Thomas. *War and Remembrance: The Story of the American Battle Monuments Commission*. Lexington: University Press of Kentucky, 2018.
Connerton, Paul. *How Modernity Forgets*. Cambridge: Cambridge University Press, 2009.
Cooke, Catherine. "Beauty as a Route to 'the Radiant Future': Responses of Soviet Architecture." *Journal of Design History* 10, no. 2 (1997): 137–160.
Cooley, Charles Horton. *Social Process*. New York: Charles Scribner's Sons, 1918.
Craig, Lois. *The Federal Presence: Architecture, Politics, and Symbols in United States Government Building*. Cambridge, MA: MIT Press, 1978.
Davidson, Pamela. *Cultural Memory and Survival: The Russian Renaissance of Classical Antiquity in the Twentieth Century*. London: School of Slavonic and East European Studies, UCL, 2009.
Davies, Sarah, and James Harris. *Stalin's World: Dictating the Soviet Order*. New Haven, CT: Yale University Press, 2014.
Day, Andrew. "The Rise and Fall of Stalinist Architecture." In *Architectures of Russian Identity*, edited by James Cracraft and Daniel Rowland, 172–190. Ithaca, NY: Cornell University Press, 2003.
DeHaan, Heather. *Stalinist City Planning: Professionals, Performance, and Power*. Toronto: University of Toronto Press, 2012.
Denno, Theodore. *The Communist Millennium: The Soviet View*. The Hague: Martinus Nijhoff, 1964.
Deschepper, Julie. "Mémoires plurielles et patrimoines dissonants: l'héritage architectural soviétique dans la Russie poutinienne." *Le Mouvement Social*, no. 260 (2017): 35–52.
——. "Le 'patrimoine soviétique' de l'URSS à la Russie contemporaine: généalogie d'un concept." *Vingtième Siècle. Revue d'histoire* 137, no. 1 (2018): 77–98.

———. "Entre trace et monument. Le patrimoine soviétique en Russie: acteurs, discours et usages (1917–2017)." PhD dissertation, Institut National des Langues et Civilisations Orientales, 2019.
Deutsch, Karl. "Nation and World." In *Contemporary Political Science: Toward Empirical Theory*, edited by Ithiel de Sola Pool, 204–227. New York: McGraw-Hill, 1967.
Devlin, Judith. "Soviet Power and Its Images: Celebrating Stalin's Seventieth Birthday." In *War of Words: Culture and the Mass Media in the Making of the Cold War in Europe*, edited by Judith Devlin and Christoph Muller, 30–47. Dublin: University College Dublin Press, 2013.
Dmitrieva, Marina. "Moscow Architecture between Stalinism and Modernism." *International Review of Sociology* 16, no. 2 (2006): 427–450.
Dobrenko, Evgenii. *Politiekonomiia sotsrealizma*. Moscow: Novoe literaturnoe obozreniie, 2007.
———. *Stalinist Cinema and the Production of History: Museum of the Revolution*. Edinburgh: Edinburgh University Press, 2008.
———. "Socialist Realism and Stasis." In *Utopian Reality: Reconstructing Culture in Revolutionary Russia and Beyond*, edited by Christina Lodder, Maria Kokkori and Maria Mileeva, 193–202. Leiden: Brill, 2013.
Dolff-Bonekämper, Gabi. "Sites of Memory and Sites of Discord: Historic Monuments as a Medium for Discussing Conflict in Europe." In *The Heritage Reader*, edited by Graham Fairclough, Rodney Harrison, John Jameson, *et al.*, 134–138. London: Routledge, 2008.
Doronina, Liudmila. *Skul'ptura stalinskoi epokhi (1930–1950-e gody)*. Moscow: Moskovskii gorodskoi pedagogicheskii universitet, 2013.
Dzhandzhugazova, Elena. "Moskovskoe metro: puteshestvie vo vremeni i prostranstve." *Sovremennye problemy servisa i turizma* 1 (2010): 65–72.
Edele, Mark. *Stalinist Society: 1928–1953*. Oxford: Oxford University Press, 2011.
Eigel', Isaak. *Boris Iofan*. Moscow: Stroiizdat, 1978.
Engström, Maria. "Re-Imagining Antiquity: The Conservative Discourse of 'Russia as the True Europe' and the Kremlin's New Cultural Policy." In *Russia as Civilization: Ideological Discourses in Politics, Media and Academia*, edited by Kare Johan Mjor and Sanna Turoma, 142–163. Abingdon, UK: Routledge, 2020.
Ennker, Benno. *Formirovanie kul'ta Lenina v Sovetskom Soiuze*. Translated by Aslan Gadzhikurbanov. Moscow: ROSSPEN, 2011.
Esposito, Fernando, and Sven Reichardt. "Revolution and Eternity. Introductory Remarks on Fascist Temporalities." *Journal of Modern European History* 13, no. 1 (2015): 24–43.
Etkind, Alexander. "Beyond Eugenics: The Forgotten Scandal of Hybridizing Humans and Apes." *Studies in History and Philosophy of Biological and Biomedical Sciences* 39, no. 2 (2008): 205–210.
Ferretti, Maria. "Raskolotaia pamiat': Rossiia i voina." *Rossiia XXI*, no. 2 (2010): 68–97.
Fitzpatrick, Sheila. "Supplicants and Citizens: Public Letter-Writing in Soviet Russia in the 1930s." *Slavic Review* 55, no. 1 (1996): 78–105.
———. *The Russian Revolution*. Oxford: Oxford University Press, 2017 [1982].

Fowkes, Reuben. "Soviet War Memorials in Eastern Europe, 1945–74." In *Figuration/ Abstraction: Strategies for Public Sculpture in Europe 1945–1968*, edited by Charlotte Benton, 11–32. Aldershot, UK: Ashgate, 2004.

Friedrich, Thomas. *Hitler's Berlin: Abused City*. Translated by Stewart Spencer. New Haven, CT: Yale University Press, 2012.

Gellner, Ernest. *Nations and Nationalism*. Ithaca, NY: Cornell University Press, 1983.

Gerchuk, Iurii. "The Aesthetics of Everyday Life in the Khrushchev Thaw in the USSR (1954–1964)." In *Style and Socialism: Modernity and Material Culture in Post-War Eastern Europe*, edited by Susan Reid and David Crowley, 81–100. Oxford: Berg, 2000.

Gerin, Annie. "Stories from Mayakovskaya Metro Station: The Production/ Consumption of Stalinist Monumental Space, 1938." PhD dissertation, University of Leeds, 2000.

Giddens, Anthony. "Living in a Post-Traditional Society." In *Reflexive Modernization: Politics, Tradition and Aesthetics in the Modern Social Order*, edited by Ulrich Beck, Anthony Giddens and Scott Lash. Cambridge, UK: Polity Press, 1994.

Gill, Graeme. "Building the Communist Future: Legitimation and the Soviet City." In *Russian Politics from Lenin to Putin*, edited by Stephen Fortescue, 76–100. Basingstoke, UK: Palgrave Macmillan, 2010.

———. *Symbolism and Regime Change in Russia*. Cambridge: Cambridge University Press, 2013.

Goebel, Stefan. *The Great War and Medieval Memory: War, Remembrance and Medievalism in Britain and Germany, 1914–1940*. Cambridge: Cambridge University Press, 2007.

Golomstock, Igor. *Totalitarian Art: In the Soviet Union, the Third Reich, Fascist Italy, and the People's Republic of China*. Translated by Robert Chandler. London: Collins Harvill, [1990] 2011.

Griffin, Roger. *The Nature of Fascism*. London: Pinter, 1991.

———. *Modernism and Fascism: The Sense of a Beginning under Mussolini and Hitler*. Basingstoke, UK: Palgrave Macmillan, 2007.

———. "'I Am No Longer Human, I Am a Titan, A God!': The Fascist Quest to Regenerate Time." In *A Fascist Century. Essays by Roger Griffin*, edited by Matthew Feldman, 3–23. Basingstoke, UK: Palgrave Macmillan, 2008.

———. "Fixing Solutions: Fascist Temporalities as Remedies for Liquid Modernity." *Journal of Modern European History* 13, no. 1 (2015): 5–23.

———. "Building the Visible Immortality of the Nation: The Centrality of 'Rooted Modernism' to the Third Reich's Architectural New Order." *Fascism* 7, no. 1 (2018): 9–44.

Grossman, Elizabeth. "Architecture for a Public Client: The Monuments and Chapels of the American Battle Monuments Commission." *The Journal of the Society of Architectural Historians* 43, no. 2 (1984): 119–143.

———. *The Civic Architecture of Paul Cret*. Cambridge: Cambridge University Press, 1996.

Groys, Boris. *The Total Art of Stalinism: Avant-Garde, Aesthetic Dictatorship, and Beyond*. Translated by Charles Rougle. Princeton, NJ: Princeton University Press, 1992.

———. *Aleksander Deyneka*. Moscow: Ad Marginem Press, 2014.

Gumbrecht, Hans. *Our Broad Present: Time and Contemporary Culture*. New York: Columbia University Press, 2014.
Gunther, Hans. "Zhiznennye fazy sotsrealisticheskogo kanona." In *Sotsrealisticheskii kanon*, edited by Evgenii Dobrenko and Hans Gunther, 281–288. St. Petersburg: Akademicheskii proekt, 2000.
Hansen, Oskar J. W. *The Sculptures at Boulder Dam*. Washington, DC: US GPO, 1942.
Harris, Adrienne. "Memorializations of a Martyr and Her Mutilated Bodies: Public Monuments to Soviet War Hero Zoya Kosmodemyanskaya, 1942 to the Present." *Journal of War & Culture Studies* 5, no. 1 (2012): 73–90.
Harris, Steven. *Communism on Tomorrow Street: Mass Housing and Everyday Life after Stalin*. Washington, DC: Woodrow Wilson Center Press, 2013.
Hartog, François. "The Modern Regime of Historicity in the Face of Two World Wars." In *Breaking up Time: Negotiating the Borders between Present, Past and Future*, edited by Berber Bevernage and Chris Lorenz, 124–133. Göttingen: Vandenhoeck & Ruprecht, 2013.
———. *Regimes of Historicity: Presentism and Experiences of Time*. Translated by Saskia Brown. New York: Columbia University Press, 2015.
Heathcote, Edwin. *Monument Builders: Modern Architecture and Death*. Chichester, UK: Academy Editions, 1999.
Hell, Julia. "Imperial Ruin Gazers, Or Why Did Scipio Weep." In *Ruins of Modernity*, edited by Julia Hell and Andreas Schönle, 169–192. Durham, NC: Duke University Press, 2010.
Hellbeck, Jochen. "Fashioning the Stalinist Soul: The Diary of Stepan Podlubnyi (1931–1939)." *Jahrbücher für Geschichte Osteuropas* 44, no. 3 (1996): 344–373.
Herwig, Holger. "The Cult of Heroic Death in Nazi Architecture." In *War Memory and Popular Culture: Essays on Modes of Remembrance and Commemoration*, edited by Michael Keren and Holger Herwig, 105–119. Jefferson, NC: McFarland, 2009.
Hinz, Berthold. *Art in the Third Reich*. Translated by Robert Kimber and Rita Kimber. New York: Pantheon Books, 1979.
Hobsbawm, Eric. "Introduction: Inventing Traditions." In *The Invention of Tradition*, edited by Eric Hobsbawm and Terence Ranger, 1–14. Cambridge: Cambridge University Press, 1983.
Hobsbawm, Eric, and Terence Ranger, eds. *The Invention of Tradition*. Cambridge: Cambridge University Press, 1983.
Hoffmann, David. "Was There a 'Great Retreat' from Soviet Socialism? Stalinist Culture Reconsidered." *Kritika: Explorations in Russian and Eurasian History* 5, no. 4 (2004): 651–674.
Hökerberg, Håkan. "Difficult Heritage: Various Approaches to Twentieth-Century Totalitarian Architecture." In *From Postwar to Postmodern: 20th Century Built Cultural Heritage*, edited by Maria Russipal, 64–70. Stockholm: Riksantikvarieämbetet, 2017.
Hoskins, Andrew. "Memory of the Multitude: The End of Collective Memory." In *Digital Memory Studies: Media Pasts in Transition*, edited by Andrew Hoskins, 85–109. New York: Routledge, 2017.
Hutchinson, John. *Nationalism and War*. Oxford: Oxford University Press, 2017.

Huyssen, Andreas. *Twilight Memories: Marking Time in a Culture of Amnesia*. London: Routledge, 1995.
———. "Present Pasts: Media, Politics, Amnesia." *Public Culture* 12, no. 1 (2000): 21–38.
Ikonnikov, Andrei. *Istorizm v arkhitekture*. Moscow: Stroiizdat, 1997.
Jackson, Heather. *Those Who Write for Immortality: Romantic Reputations and the Dream of Lasting Fame*. New Haven, CT: Yale University Press, 2015.
James, Beverley. *Imagining Postcommunism: Visual Narratives of Hungary's 1956 Revolution*. College Station: Texas A&M University Press, 2005.
Jameson, Fredric. *Postmodernism, or the Cultural Logic of Late Capitalism*. Durham, NC: Duke University Press, 1991.
Jaskot, Paul. *The Architecture of Oppression. The SS, Forced Labor and the Nazi Monumental Building Economy*. London: Routledge, 2000.
Jenks, Andrew. "A Metro on the Mount: The Underground as a Church of Soviet Civilization." *Technology and Culture* 41, no. 4 (2000): 697–724.
Junyk, Ihor. "'Not Months but Moments': Ephemerality, Monumentality, and the Pavilion in Ruins." *Open Arts Journal*, no. 2 (2013–2014): 1–15.
Kalashnikov, Antony. "Stalinist Crimes and the Ethics of Memory." *Kritika: Explorations in Russian and Eurasian History* 19, no. 3 (2018): 599–626.
Kallis, Aristotle. *The Third Rome, 1922–1943: The Making of the Fascist Capital*. Basingstoke, UK: Palgrave Macmillan, 2014.
Kelly, Catriona. *Comrade Pavlik: The Rise and Fall of a Soviet Boy Hero*. London: Granta Books, 2014.
Khalturin, A. *Monumenty SSSR*. Moscow: Sovetskii khudozhnik, 1969.
Khlevniuk, Oleg. *Stalin. Zhizn' odnogo vozhdia*. Moscow: Corpus, 2005.
———. *Stalin: New Biography of a Dictator*. Translated by Nora Favorov. New Haven, CT: Yale University Press, 2015.
Khmel'nitskii, Dmitrii. *Arkhitektura Stalina. Psikhologiia i stil'*. Moscow: Progress-Traditsiia, 2007.
———. *Zodchii Stalin*. Moscow: Novoe literaturnoe obozrenie, 2007.
———. "Miff o klassitsizme." February 5, 2014, accessed December 14, 2019, https://archi.ru/russia/52978/mif-o-klassicizme.
Kiaer, Christina. "Was Socialist Realism Forced Labour? The Case of Aleksandr Deineka in the 1930s." *Oxford Art Journal* 28, no. 3 (2005): 321–345.
King, Alex. *Memorials of the Great War in Britain: The Symbolism and Politics of Remembrance*. Oxford: Berg, 1998.
Kirsch, Anja. "From Biological to Moral Immortality: The Utopian Dimensions of Socialist Work Ethics." In *Imaginations of Death and the Beyond in India and Europe*, edited by Günter Blamberger and Sudhir Kakar, 59–82. Singapore: Springer, 2018.
Kirschenbaum, Lisa. *The Legacy of the Siege of Leningrad, 1941–1995: Myth, Memories, and Monuments*. Cambridge: Cambridge University Press, 2006.
Koerner, Lisbet. "Nazi Medievalist Architecture and the Politics of Memory." In *Medievalism in Europe*, edited by Leslie Workman, 48–75. Cambridge, UK: D. S. Brewer, 1994.
Kopp, Anatole. *Town and Revolution: Soviet Architecture and City Planning, 1917–1935*. Translated by Thomas Burton. New York: Braziller, 1970.

Koselleck, Reinhart. *Futures Past: On the Semantics of Historical Time.* Translated by Keith Tribe. Cambridge, MA: MIT Press, 1985.
Kosenkova, Iuliia. *Sovetskii gorod 1940-kh—pervoi poloviny 1950-kh godov: ot tvorcheskikh poiskov k praktike stroitel'stva.* Moscow: Editorial URSS, 2000.
Kotkin, Stephen. *Magnetic Mountain: Stalinism as Civilization.* Berkeley: University of California Press, 1995.
Krasil'nikova, Ekaterina. "Memorializatsiia S. M. Kirova v zapadnoi sibiri (1934 g.—pervaia polovina 1941 g.)." *Vestnik Tomskogo gosudarstvennogo universiteta* 36, no. 4 (2015): 21–28.
Krementsov, Nikolai. *Revolutionary Experiments: The Quest for Immortality in Bolshevik Science and Fiction.* Oxford: Oxford University Press, 2014.
Kruk, Sergei. "Semiotics of Visual Iconicity in Leninist 'Monumental' Propaganda." *Visual Communication* 7, no. 1 (2008): 27–56.
Kucher, Katharina. *Park Gor'kogo. Kul'tura dosuga v stalinskuiu epokhu. 1928–1941.* Moscow: ROSSPEN, 2012.
Kutseleva, Anna. "Mesto moskovskogo metropolitena v sovetskom kul'turnom prostranstve." In *Arkhitektura Stalinskoi epokhi: opyt istoricheskogo osmysleniia,* edited by Iuliia Kosenkova, 174–182. Moscow: KomKniga, 2010.
Kuznetsova, Alena, "Obratnyi otschet." Archi.ru, accessed November 25, 2020, https://archi.ru/russia/86421/obratnyi-otschet.
Lampard, Marie. "Larger Than Life: Soviet Monumental Sculpture in the Stalin Period." *Experiment* 18, no. 1 (2012): 209–239.
Lane, Barbara Miller. "Architects in Power: Politics and Ideology in the Work of Ernst May and Albert Speer." *The Journal of Interdisciplinary History* 17, no. 1 (1986): 283–310.
Lazarev, Valery. "Conclusions." In *The Economics of Forced Labor: The Soviet Gulag,* edited by Paul Gregory and Valery Lazarev, 189–198. Stanford, CA: Hoover Institution Press, 2003.
Lefebvre, Henri. *The Production of Space.* Translated by Donald Nicholson-Smith. Oxford: Blackwell, 1974.
Lewin, Moshe. *The Making of the Soviet System.* London: Methuen, 1985.
Lifton, Robert, and Eric Olson. *Living and Dying.* New York: Praeger Publishers, 1974.
Lodder, Christina. "Lenin's Plan for Monumental Propaganda." In *Art of the Soviets: Painting, Sculpture and Architecture in a One-Party State,* edited by Matthew Bown and Brandon Taylor, 16–32. Manchester: Manchester University Press, 1993.
Longworth, Philip. *The Unending Vigil: A History of the Commonwealth War Graves Commission, 1917–1967.* London: Constable, 1967.
Lübbe, Hermann. "The Contraction of the Present." In *High-Speed Society: Social Acceleration, Power, and Modernity,* edited by Hartmut Rosa and William Scheuerman, 159–178. University Park: Pennsylvania State University Press, 2009.
———. *V nogu so vremenem. Sokrashchennoe prebyvanie v nastoiashchem.* Translated by Aleksei Grigor'ev and Vitalii Kurennoi. Moscow: Izdatel'skii dom Vysshei shkoly ekonomiki, 2016.
Maddox, Steven. *Saving Stalin's Imperial City: Historic Preservation in Leningrad, 1930–1950.* Bloomington: Indiana University Press, 2014.

Malinina, Tat'iana, and Elena Ogarkova. *Pamiat' i vremia: iz khudozhestvennogo arkhiva Velikoi Otechestvennoi voiny 1941–1945 gg.* Moscow: Galart, 2011.
Margalit, Avishai. *The Ethics of Memory.* Cambridge, MA: Harvard University Press, 2002.
Martin, Terry. *The Affirmative Action Empire: Nations and Nationalism in the Soviet Union, 1923–1939.* Ithaca, NY: Cornell University Press, 2001.
Medvedev, Roy, and Zhores Medvedev. *The Unknown Stalin.* New York: IB Tauris, 2003.
Merridale, Catherine. *Night of Stone: Death and Memory in Russia.* London: Granta, 2000.
———. "Revolution among the Dead: Cemeteries in Twentieth-Century Russia." *Mortality* 8, no. 2 (2003): 176–188.
Michalski, Sergiusz. *Public Monuments: Art in Political Bondage, 1870–1997.* London: Reaktion Books, 1998.
Michaud, Eric. "National Socialist Architecture as an Acceleration of Time." *Critical Inquiry* 19, no. 2 (1993): 220–233.
———. *The Cult of Art in Nazi Germany.* Stanford, CA: Stanford University Press, 2004.
Mosse, George. *The Nationalization of the Masses: Political Symbolism and Mass Movements in Germany from the Napoleonic Wars through the Third Reich.* Ithaca, NY: Cornell University Press, [1975] 1991.
Mumford, Lewis. *The Culture of Cities.* San Diego, CA: Harcourt Brace Jovanovich, [1938] 1970.
Murawski, Michal. *The Palace Complex: A Stalinist Skyscraper, Capitalist Warsaw, and a City Transfixed.* Bloomington: Indiana University Press, 2019.
Musil, Robert. *Posthumous Papers of a Living Author.* Translated by Peter Wortsman. New York: Archipelago Books, [1936] 2012.
Neimark, Anna. "The Infrastructural Monument: Stalin's Water Works under Construction and in Representation." *Future Anterior* 9, no. 2 (2013): 1–14.
Nekhezina, Margarita. *Russkii Mikelandzhelo: o tvorchestve Evgeniia Vucheticha.* Volgograd: Izdatel', 2011.
Neutatz, Dietmar. *Moskovskoe metro: ot pervykh planov do velikoi stroiki stalinizma (1897–1935).* Translated by Iu. Petrov. Moscow: ROSSPEN, 2013.
Nora, Pierre. "General Introduction: Between Memory and History." Translated by Arthur Goldhammer. In *Realms of Memory: Rethinking the French Past. Volume 1: Conflicts and Divisons*, edited by Pierre Nora and Lawrence Kritzman, 1–20. New York: Columbia University Press, 1996.
O'Mahony, Mike. "Archaeological Fantasies: Constructing History on the Moscow Metro." *The Modern Language Review* 98, no. 1 (2003): 138–150.
"O proekte." Alcontower.com, accessed November 24, 2021, https://alcontower.com/about.html.
Oushakine, Serguei. "Remembering in Public: On the Affective Management of History." *Ab Imperio* 2013, no. 1 (2013): 269–302.
———. "Second-Hand Nostalgia: On Charms and Spells of the Soviet Trukhliashechka." In *Post-Soviet Nostalgia: Confronting the Empire's Legacies*, edited by Otto Boele, Boris Noordenbos and Ksenia Robbe, 38–69. New York: Routledge, 2019.

Paperny, Vladimir. *Architecture in the Age of Stalin: Culture Two.* Translated by John Hill and Roann Barris. Cambridge: Cambridge University Press, 2002.
Park, Marlene, and Gerald Markowitz. *Democratic Vistas: Post Offices and Public Art in the New Deal.* Philadelphia, PA: Temple University Press, 1984.
"Pavil'on stantsii metro 'Novokuznetksaia'." Uznai Moskvu, accessed March 15, 2019, https://um.mos.ru/houses/pavilon_stantsii_metro_novokuznetskaya/?sph.
Pavlinov, Pavel. "'Nu vot i voina . . .'. Evgenii Evgenievich Lansere. Tvorchstvo voennykh let." *Tret'iakovskaia gallereia* 47, no. 2 (2015): 70–79.
Petrone, Karen. *Life Has Become More Joyous, Comrades: Celebrations in the Time of Stalin.* Bloomington: Indiana University Press, 2000.
Pichova, Hana. *The Case of the Missing Statue: A Historical and Literary study of the Stalin Monument in Prague.* Prague: Arbor vitae, 2014.
Pirozhkova, Iuliia, "Gostinitsa 'Ukraina'." Uznai Moskvu, accessed March 15, 2019, https://um.mos.ru/houses/gostinitsa_ukraina/?sphrase_id=438088.
Plamper, Jan. "Abolishing Ambiguity: Soviet Censorship Practices in the 1930s." *Russian Review* 60, no. 4 (2001): 526–544.
———. *The Stalin Cult: A Study in the Alchemy of Power.* New Haven, CT: Yale University Press, 2012.
Platt, Jonathan Brooks. "Pushkin Now and Then: Images of Temporal Paradox in the 1937 Pushkin Jubilee." *The Russian Review* 67, no. 4 (2008): 638–660.
———. "Snow White and the Enchanted Palace: A Reading of Lenin's Architectural Cult." *Representations* 129, no. 1 (2015): 86–115.
———. *Greetings, Pushkin!: Stalinist Cultural Politics and the Russian National Bard.* Pittsburgh, PA: University of Pittsburgh Press, 2016.
Platt, Kevin, and David Brandenberger, eds. *Epic Revisionism: Russian History and Literature as Stalinist Propaganda.* Madison: University of Wisconsin Press, 2006.
Poliakova, Marta. *Okhrana kul'turnogo naslediia Rossii.* Moscow: Drofa, 2005.
Prost, Antoine. "Monuments to the Dead." In *Realms of Memory: The Construction of the French Past. Volume 2: Traditions,* edited by Pierre Nora and Lawrence Kritzman, 307–333. New York: Columbia University Press, 1997.
Ptichnikova, Galina. "Osobennosti arkhitektury poslevoennogo perioda v Stalingrade." In *Arkhitektura Stalinskoi epokhi: opyt istoricheskogo osmysleniia,* edited by Iuliia Kosenkova, 237–250. Moscow: KomKniga, 2010.
Razgonov, Sergei. *Vysota: zhizn' i dela Pavla Korina.* Moscow: Sovetskiii khudozhnik, 1978.
Reid, Susan. "In the Name of the People: The Manège Affair Revisited." *Kritika: Explorations in Russian and Eurasian History* 6, no. 4 (2006): 673–716.
Renfrew, Colin. *Prehistory: The Making of the Human Mind.* New York: Random House, 2008.
Rhoads, William. "Franklin D. Roosevelt and Washington Architecture." *Records of the Columbia Historical Society* 52 (1989): 104–162.
Riegl, Alois. "The Modern Cult of Monuments: Its Character and Its Origin." In *Oppositions Reader: Selected Readings from a Journal for Ideas and Criticism in Architecture, 1973–1984,* edited by Kenneth Michael Hays, 621–653. Princeton, NJ: Princeton Architectural Press, 1998.

Romashova, Mariia. "'The Heart of a Remarkable Communist Has Ceased to Beat': Grief in the Emotional Repertoire of Elderly Soviet Activists of the 1960s–1980s." Paper presented at the 50th ASEEES Annual Convention, Boston, USA, December 8, 2018.

Ruder, Cynthia. *Building Stalinism: The Moscow Canal and the Creation of Soviet Space*. London: I. B. Tauris, 2018.

Ruthers, Monica. "Sovetskaia rodina kak prostranstvo gorodskoi arkhitektury." *Ab Imperio* 2 (2006): 193–231.

Schirmer, Dietmar. "State, Volk, and Monumental Architecture in Nazi-Era Berlin." In *Berlin-Washington, 1800–2000: Capital Cities, Cultural Representation, and National Identities*, edited by Andreas Daum and Chistof Mauch, 127–153. Cambridge: Cambridge University Press, 2005.

Schönle, Andreas. "Appropriating Stalinist Heritage: State Rhetoric and Urban Transformation in the Repurposing of VDNKh." In *Re-Centring the City: Global Mutations of Socialist Modernity*, edited by Jonathan Bach and Michal Murawski, 44–62. London: UCL Press, 2020.

Scobie, Alex. *Hitler's State Architecture: The Impact of Classical Antiquity*. University Park: Pennsylvania State University Press, 1990.

Selivanova, Aleksandra. *Postkonstruktivizm. Vlast' i arkhitektura v 1930-e gody v SSSR*. Moscow: BuksMArt, 2020.

Shashkova, Natal'ia. "Istoriia, istoriko-kul'turnoe znachenie i sovremennoe ispol'zovanie naslediia sovetskoi arkhitektury: gostinitsa 'Leningradskaia'." *Prostranstvo i vremia* 15, no. 1 (2014): 176–186.

Shevtsov, Ivan. *Evgenii Viktorovich Vuchetich*. Leningrad: Khudozhnik RSFSR, 1960.

Shlapentokh, Dmitry. "Bolshevism as a Fedorovian Regime." *Cahiers du monde russe* 37, no. 4 (1996): 429–465.

Silina, Mariia. *Istoriia i ideologiia: monumental'no-dekorativnyi rel'ef 1920–1930-kh godov v SSSR*. Moscow: BuksMArt, 2014.

Simpson, Pat. "The Nude in Soviet Socialist Realism: Eugenics and Images of the New Person in the 1920s–1940s." *Australian and New Zealand Journal of Art* 5, no. 1 (2004): 113–137.

Slezkine, Yuri. *The House of Government: A Saga of the Russian Revolution*. Princeton, NJ: Princeton University Press, 2017.

Smith, Anthony. "War and Ethnicity: The Role of Warfare in the Formation, Self-images and Cohesion of Ethnic Communities." *Ethnic and Racial Studies* 4, no. 4 (1981): 375–397.

——. *The Ethnic Origins of Nations*. Oxford: Blackwell Publishers, 1993.

Solzhenitsyn, Aleksandr. *The Gulag Archipelago, 1918–1956. An Experiment in Literary Investigation. III-IV*. Translated by Thomas Whitney. New York: Harper & Row, 1975.

Sorokina, Anna. "Syndrome of Soviet Nostalgia among the Younger Generation of Russians." Paper presented at IX ICCEES Congress, Makuhari, Japan, August 8, 2015.

Spotts, Frederic. *Hitler and the Power of Aesthetics*. Woodstock, NY: The Overlook Press, 2003.

Stakhanova, Evgeniia, "Vysotka na Kotel'nicheskoi naberezhnoi." Uznai Moskvu, accessed March 15, 2019, https://um.mos.ru/houses/vysotka_na_kotelniches koy_naberezhnoy/?sphrase_id=438088.

Starostenko, Iuliia. "Problema ansamblia v sovetskom gradostroitel'stve 1920–1930-kh gg." In *Sovetskoe gradostroitel'stvo, 1917–1941. Kniga pervaia*, edited by Iuliia Kosenkova, 327–366. Moscow: Progress-Traditsiia, 2018.

Stern, Robert. *Modern Classicism*. New York: Rizzoli, 1988.

Stites, Richard. *Revolutionary Dreams: Utopian Vision and Experimental Life in the Russian Revolution*. Oxford: Oxford University Press, 1989.

——. "Stalinism and the Restructuring of Revolutionary Utopianism." In *The Culture of the Stalin Period*, edited by Hans Gunther, 78–94. London: Macmillan, 1990.

Tanović, Sabina. *Designing Memory: The Architecture of Commemoration in Europe, 1914 to the Present*. Cambridge: Cambridge University Press, 2019.

Tarkhanov, Alexei, and Sergei Kavtaradze. *Architecture of the Stalin Era*. New York: Rizzoli, 1992.

Thies, Jochen. "Hitler's European Building Programme." *Journal of Contemporary History* 13, no. 3 (1978): 413–431.

——. *Hitler's Plans for Global Domination: Nazi Architecture and Ultimate War Aims*. Translated by Ian Cooke and Mary-Beth Friedrich. New York: Berghahn Books, 2012.

Tolstoi, Vladimir. *Monumental'noe iskusstvo SSSR*. Moscow: Sovetskii khudozhnik, 1978.

Tooze, Adam. *The Wages of Destruction: The Making and Breaking of the Nazi Economy*. London: Allen Lane, 2006.

Trubetskaia, Irina, "Arka severnogo vkhoda na VDNKh." Uznai Moskvu, accessed March 15, 2019, https://um.mos.ru/houses/arka_severnogo_vkhoda_na _vdnkh/?sphrase_.

Tucker, Robert. *Stalin in Power: The Revolution from Above, 1928–1941*. New York: WW Norton & Company, 1992.

Tumarkin, Nina. *Lenin Lives!: The Lenin Cult in Soviet Russia*. Cambridge, MA: Harvard University Press, 1983.

Vail', Petr, and Aleksandr Genis. *60-e. Mir sovetskogo cheloveka*. Ann Arbor, MI: Ardis Publishers, 1989.

van Ree, Erik. *The Political Thought of Joseph Stalin: A Study in Twentieth-Century Revolutionary Patriotism*. London: Routledge, 2003.

Volkogonov, Dmitrii. *Stalin: Triumph and Tragedy*. Translated by Harold Shukman. New York: Grove Weidenfeld, 1991.

Von Geldern, James. "Epic Revisionism and the Crafting of a Soviet Public." In *Epic Revisionism: Russian History and Literature as Stalinist Propaganda*, edited by David Brandenberger and Kevin Platt, 325–340. Madison: University of Wisconsin Press, 2006.

Voronov, Nikita. *Sovetskaia monumental'naia skul'ptura*. Moscow: Znanie, 1976.

——. *Monumental'noe iskusstvo vchera i segodnia*. Moscow: Znanie, 1988.

Voronova, Ol'ga. *Vera Ignatievna Mukhina*. Moscow: Iskusstvo, 1976.

Vorontsova, Tat'iana, "Stantsiia metro 'Kropotkinskaia'." Uznai Moskvu, accessed March 15, 2019, https://um.mos.ru/houses/stantsiya-metro-kropotkinskaya/?sphrase_id=4.

Vorontsova, Tat'iana, and Irina Trubetskaia, "VSKhV-VDNKh." Uznai Moskvu, accessed March 15, 2019, https://um.mos.ru/places/vskhv_vdnkh/?sphrase_id=438090.

Vukov, Nikolai. "Death and Vitality in Monumental Art in Eastern Europe After the Second World War." *New Europe College Yearbook*, no. 9 (2001): 251–298.

Vyazemtseva, Anna. "Soviet Fascination for Fascist Rome, or The International Style of Regimes." In *Blickwendungen: Architektenreisen nach Italien in Moderne und Gegenwart*, edited by Kai Kappel and Erik Wegerhoff, 113–132. Munich: Hirmer, 2019.

Yampolsky, Mikhail. "In the Shadow of Monuments: Notes on Iconoclasm and Time." In *Soviet Hieroglyphics: Visual Culture in Late Twentieth-Century Russia*, edited by Nancy Condee, 93–112. Bloomington: Indiana University Press, 1995.

Yekelchyk, Serhy. "Symbolic Plasticity and Memorial Environment: The Afterlife of Soviet Monuments in Post-Soviet Kyiv." *Canadian Slavonic Papers* 63, no. 1–2 (2021): 207–228.

Young, James. "Memory, Counter-Memory and the End of the Monument." In *Image and Remembrance: Representation and the Holocaust*, edited by Shelley Hornstein and Florence Jacobowitz, 59–78. Bloomington: Indiana University Press, 2003.

———. "Memory/ Monument." In *Critical Terms for Art History*, edited by Robert Nelson and Richard Shiff, 234–250. Chicago: University of Chicago Press, 2003.

Zinov'ev, Aleksandr. *Stalinskoe metro. Istoricheskii putevoditel' po Moskovskomu metropolitenu.* Moscow: A. N. Zinov'ev, 2011.

Zinov'eva, Ol'ga. *Simvoly stalinskoi' Moskvy.* Moscow: Tonchu, 2009.

Zolotonosov, Mikhail. "Masturbanizatsiia: 'Erogennye zony' sovetskoi kul'tury 1920–1930-kh godov." In *Erotika v russkoi literature: ot Barkova do nashikh dnei*, edited by I. Prokhorova and et al., 93–99. Moscow: Literaturnoe obozrenie, 1992.

———. *Gliptokratos. Issledovanie nemogo diskursa: annotirovannyi katalog sadovo-parkovoi skul'ptury stalinskogo vremeni.* St. Petersburg: Inopress, 1999.

Zubovich, Katherine. *Moscow Monumental: Soviet Skyscrapers and Urban Life in Stalin's Capital.* Princeton, NJ: Princeton University Press, 2021.

Index

Abrosimov, Pavel, 109
Academy of Architecture, USSR, 11, 28, 30, 40, 43, 93, 107
Academy of Arts, USSR, 11, 42
Academy of Sciences, USSR, headquarters of, 109
Agranov, Aleksei, 55
Agricultural Exhibition, All-Union, 4, 23, 26, 39–40, 81, 102, 132, 137–138, 142
Akulov, Ivan, 147n29
Alcon Tower, 134
Aleshin, Pavel, 53
allegory, 65, 140
All-Union Communist Party (Bolshevik). *See* Communist Party of the Soviet Union
American Battle Monuments Commission, 118
amnesia, cultural, 140–141
Andreev, Andrei, 147n29
Andreev, Nikolai, 56
Andrianov, Aleksei, 133
Architecture Institute, 43, 59
Arkin, David, 8, 54
art deco, 34, 133–134
Art Exhibition, All-Union, 85
atheism and anticlericalism, 65, 166n46
avant-garde, artistic and architectural, 4–5, 17–21, 30–34, 167n71

Baburin, Viktor, 85
Bell Tower of Ivan the Great, 42, 53
Belopol'skii, Iakov, 55
Beriia, Lavrenii, 79
Beskin, Osip, 63
Bogdanov, Aleksandr, 109–110
Bolshoi Theater, reconstruction of, 93–94
Borisovskii, Georgii, 36
Bulganin, Nikolai, 147n29
Burov, Andrei, 47

Campanella, Tommaso, 16
Cathedral of Christ the Savior, 42, 140
Chaldymov, Andrei, 37
Château-Thierry, American war memorial at, 118
Chechulin, Dmitrii, 47, 51, 109
Cheliuskin Rescue, Monument to the, 87
Chernyshev, Boris, 95
Chernyshev, Nikolai, 22, 62
Chernyshev, Sergei, 51–52
Chkalov, Valerii, monuments and memorialization of, 55–56, 62, 73, 86–88
Chubar', Vlas, 7, 53
Churchill, Winston, 118
civil war, in the Soviet Union, 17–19, 109
Cold War, 6, 108
collectivization of agriculture, 2, 23, 25, 103, 110–111, 131
Committee for Architectural Affairs, All-Union, 10, 37, 58–59, 94
Committee for Arts Affairs, All-Union, 10, 24–25, 36, 55–56, 84, 88–89, 94, 97, 100–101, 107, 159n14, 162n82; council of experts of, 55–57, 67, 87, 91–92; RSFSR branch, 67
communist future. *See* utopianism: Bolshevik
Communist Party of the Soviet Union, 3, 36, 77, 131; Central Committee, 11, 26, 57–58, 67, 79, 159n14; Politburo, 7, 10–11, 53, 63, 73–74, 88, 109
conservatism, Stalinist cultural. *See* Great Retreat
Constitution of the USSR (1936), 61; monuments and memorialization of, 8, 57, 60, 96–97, 146n23, 161n60
constructivism. *See* avant-garde, artistic and architectural
Council of Labor and Defense complex, 23

INDEX

Council of Ministers (Council of People's Commissars), 16, 27, 53, 58, 67, 72–73, 76, 87–88, 94, 101, 158n3
countermonuments, 126, 143–144
Cultural Revolution, 103

Defenders of the Perekop, Monument to the, 102
Deineka, Aleksandr, 43, 91–92, 96, 110
de-Stalinization, 27, 125, 131–132, 142
Dinamov, Sergei, 77
disurbanism, 5
Dostoianie residential complex, 133
Douaumont, French ossuary at, 118
Dushkin, Aleksei, 43
Duvidzon, V., 95
Dvorets Sovetov metro station, 140
Dzerzhinskii, Feliks, bust of, 142

Egyptian revivalism. *See under* historicist (traditionalist) architecture
Eisenstein, Sergei, 99
Elektrozavodskaia metro station, 74
Encyclopedia, Great Soviet, 22, 41
end of history, under Stalinism, 2, 6, 34, 39, 46, 71, 106, 110
ensemble, architectural, 52–53, 93
epigraphy in monumental art, 57–60
Erenburg, Il'ia, 114, 167n4
Eternal Youth of Science sculpture, 51
excess, architecture of, 27–28, 44, 60, 70

Federal Reserve Building, Washington, 119
Fedorov, Nikolai, 109–110
First World War, 115, 120, 124–125; memorialization of, 9, 109, 118, 122–123, 126
Five-Year Plans: First, 2, 5, 30, 110; Third, 41
Fomin, Ivan, 34–35
forced labor, 23, 133, 140–141, 143, 148n29
forced-pace modernization, 72, 103–106, 124, 131
Friendship of the Peoples fountain, 137–138
Frolov, Vladimir, 43

Gabrichevskii, Aleksandr, 22, 58, 105
Gagarin, Iurii, monument to, 29
Gel'freikh, Vladimir, 47
generalized representations, 62–65, 157n79
Gerasimov, Aleksandr, 42
German War Graves Commission, 123

Germany, Nazi, monument building in, 7, 13–14, 47, 115, 120–125. *See also entries for individual monuments*
Ginzburg, Moisei, 30, 35–36
Glukhovskii, Dmitrii, 133
Golikov, Filipp, 64, 157n83
Golosov, Il'ia, 35
Gol'ts, Georgii, 35, 68
Gor'kii, Maksim, 74, 83, 109–110; monuments to, 67, 88, 92, 102, 147n32
Gor'kii, monumental stairway in the city of, 24
Gor'kii Park statuary, 56, 74
Gorod gorki ski resort, 137
Great Break, 2, 97
Great Depression, 118–120, 122, 124–125
Great Patriotic War (1941–1945), 115, 124, 133; effect on monument design, 8, 24–25, 50–51, 109; grassroots and amateur memorialization of, 25, 87–90, 102, 106–107; heritage preservation during, 100–101; historical politics during, 108; mothballing of monument-building projects, 3, 24, 149n33; official memorialization of, 24–27, 56–58, 60–61, 63–64, 68, 79–80, 89–91, 102, 107–109, 114–115, 125–126, 131, 136–138, 162n79; postwar urban reconstruction, 25, 51–52. *See also* Second World War (1939–1945)
Great Retreat, 5, 33–34, 99
Gulag. *See* forced labor
Gundorov, Aleksandr, 26, 149n46

Hansen, Oskar J. W., 120
heritage preservation, 33–34, 41–42, 51–53, 100–102, 109, 137–138, 142–144, 164n13, 165n21
Hero of Socialist Labor, monuments to two-time recipients, 74, 159n14
Hero of the Soviet Union, monuments to two-time recipients, 57, 67, 74–76
hierarchy of commemorability, 73–76, 79–83
Himmler, Heinrich, 123
historicist (traditionalist) architecture, 30–34, 38–43, 44–51, 59, 61, 68–69, 115, 127, 133–134, 137, 151n35; Egyptian revivalism, 42, 51, 109, 119, 152n55; medieval revivalism, 36, 38, 51, 65–66, 137; neoclassicism, Graeco-Roman, 34–39, 42, 44, 50–51, 61, 143; neoclassicism, Russian, 33, 38, 44; Palladianism, 30, 33; stripped classicism, 46–48, 69, 119; vernacular architecture, 33, 36–39, 44, 51, 61, 137

INDEX   199

Hitler, Adolf, 13–14, 47, 120–124
Holden, Charles, 47
Holocaust, 89–90, 126
Hoover Dam, 119–120
Hotel Moscow, 136
House on the Embankment, 23, 136, 143

Iakovlev, Vasilii, 94
iconoclasm, 16, 131–132, 135, 140, 142
Il'in, Mikhail, 51, 61
immortalization decrees, 72–73, 100, 159n5
imperialism, Russian: aesthetics of, 5, 33–34, 38, 108, 137–138 (*see also* Tsarist monuments); politics of, 99, 111, 135, 137–138, 144
international style. *See* modernism, architectural
Iofan, Boris, 3, 11, 41, 47, 54, 93, 95, 109, 136, 143
Italy, fascist, monument building in, 7, 47. *See also entries for individual monuments*
Ivanova, Zinaida, 63, 67–68, 147n32

Kaganovich, Lazar', 11
Kalinin, Mikhail, 24, 61; monuments and memorialization of, 81
Kaluzhskaia metro station, 109
Katsman, Evgenii, 95
Khrapchenko, Mikhail, 89
Khrushchev, Nikita, 27–28, 147n29
Kievskaia-kol'tsevaia metro station, 61, 157n79
Kirov, Sergei, monuments and memorialization of, 67, 73, 95–96
Kirsh, Karl, 158n3
Kolli, Nikolai, 93
Kolpinskii, Dmitrii, 76
Komsomol'skaia-kol'tsevaia metro station, 137
Komsomol'skaia-radial'naia metro station, 59
Konenkov, Sergei, 91–92
Konev, Ivan, 89
Koretskii, Viktor, 77–78
Korin, Pavel, 91
Kornfel'd, Iakov, 61, 96
Korolev, Boris, 74, 91
Krasin, Leonid, 20, 109–110
Kremlin, Moscow, 28, 53, 102, 136; Hall of Victory, in the Great Kremlin Palace, 76; Wall Necropolis, 19, 21
Krupskaia, Nadezhda, 20
Kuibyshev, Valerian, 109, 147n29

Kulaga, Lev, 58
Kurskaia metro station, 61, 138–139

lacquering, 65
Langemarck Hall, Olympic complex in Berlin, 122
Lansere, Evgenii, 54–55, 63, 65–66, 91, 93–94
League of Time, 110
Lenin, Vladimir, 8, 40; Commission for the Immortalization of Memory of, 19–21; cult of personality, 20–22; mausoleum, 19–21, 131–132; monuments and memorialization of, 19–20, 23, 40, 67–68, 87, 131; Plan for Monumental Propaganda, 16–19, 22, 26, 29
Lenin library, 23, 53–54, 94, 133, 140
Liberation of Simferopol', Monument to the, 56
living memorials, 126
Lubianka metro station, 142
Lubianka square, secret police headquarters on, 143
Lunacharskii, Anatolii, 7, 17, 22, 41, 105, 109–110

Maiakovskaia metro station, 43, 59–60
Maiakovskii, Vladimir, 17, 20–21, 109–110
Manizer, Matvei, 76, 92
Marble Palace, 42
Mars Fields' Memorial to the Victims of the Revolution, 19
Marx-Engels-Lenin Institute, 79
Mashkovtsev, Nikolai, 63
mass housing campaign, 28
Matrosov, Aleksandr, monuments to, 165n21
Matsa, Ivan, 85
medieval revivalism. *See under* historicist (traditionalist) architecture
Mekhlis, Lev, 89
Mel'nikov, Konstantin, 109–110
memory boom, 127–128
Merkurov, Sergei, 40, 56, 64–65, 67–68, 79, 87, 95, 102
Metro 2033 (novel), 133
Michelangelo, 22, 61, 65, 92
Michurin, Ivan, monument to, 137
modernism, architectural, 17, 28, 33, 35, 119, 126, 133, 137. *See also* avant-garde, artistic and architectural
modern order of time, 115–117, 120–129
Mokhovaia street, residential building on, 31–33
Molotov, Viacheslav, 11

INDEX

Montfaucon, American war memorial at, 118
Montsec, American war memorial at, 118
Mordvinov, Arkadii, 97
Morozov, Pavlik, monument to, 73–74, 86
Moscow, 1, 23–25, 52–53, 100–102, 130, 132–134, 142–143; architectural and sculptural monuments (*see entries for individual monuments*); Architectural Council of the Municipal Executive Committee, 61, 95, 109, 134; bridges, 21, 53, 63; high-rises, 4, 21, 25, 28, 53, 93, 111, 132–134, 136–138, 143 (*see also* Moscow State University Main Building); metro, 4, 21–26, 58–61, 77, 83–84, 111, 114–115, 131, 133, 140–143, 173n34 (*see also entries for individual metro stations*); Plan for the Socialist Reconstruction of, 23, 51–52, 55, 59, 84
Moscow Brain Research Institute, 72
Moscow Soviet building, 52–53
Moscow State University Main Building, 44–46, 51, 53, 57, 81, 83, 141
Moscow-Volga Canal, 4, 21, 23, 67–68, 81, 143
Mount Rushmore, 119
Mukhina, Vera, 26, 53, 55–58, 62–65, 67, 91–92, 97, 137, 141–142, 147n32
Museum of Architecture, Shchusev State, 142
Museum of Moscow, 142
Museum of Soviet Socialist Culture, 8
Muzeon statue park, 142–143

Narkomfin (People's Commissariat of Finances), residential building for, 30–31
Nasledie residential complex, 133
National Gallery of Art, Washington, 119
nationalism, temporalities of, 98–100, 102–108, 111–112, 116–125, 128–129, 168n21
neoclassicism, Graeco-Roman. *See under* historicist (traditionalist) architecture
neoclassicism, Russian. *See under* historicist (traditionalist) architecture
neo-totalitarianism (historiographic school), 2, 5–7, 10, 13, 34, 38–39, 46, 71, 82, 113–114, 167n1
neo-traditionalism (historiographic school), 5, 99
new Soviet person, 5, 30, 63
Novokuznetskaia metro station, 114
Novoslobodskaia metro station, 60
nudity in monumental art, 56–57, 121
Nuremberg Congress Hall, 123

obelisks in Kerch and Chernovtsy, 102
October Revolution (1917), monuments and memorialization of, 16–17, 29, 53–54, 57–58, 125–126, 156n61
Okhotnyi riad metro station, 59, 140
Oltarzhevskii, Viacheslav, 47
Ordzhonikidze, Sergo, monuments and memorialization of, 61, 88
Orientalism, 33, 37–38
Oruzheinyi high-rise, 133

Palace of Congresses, 28
Palace of the Soviets, 2–4, 8, 17, 21, 28, 53, 57, 76, 83–84, 91, 93, 96, 111, 133, 155n22; construction council, 11, 30, 39, 41, 68; construction directorate, 44, 61, 93–94; design, 3–4, 8, 11, 49, 54–55, 74, 87, 95, 105; design competitions, 7, 30, 49–50, 86; materials and synthetic art for, 39–43
Palais de Chaillot, 46–47
Palazzo Littorio, 47
Palladianism. *See under* historicist (traditionalist) architecture
Panfilov guardsmen, Monument to the Twenty-Eight, 165n21
Pan-Slavic Committee, 26
Pantheon—A Monument to the Immortal Memory of Great People of the Soviet State. *See* Stalin: death and Pantheon project
Park Pobedy metro station, 133
Paveletskaia metro station, 60, 114
Peace mural, in Kazan' railway station, 65
Pentagon building, 119
Pershing, John, 118
Peter and Paul Fortress, 42
Platonov, Andrei, 109–110
Plekhanov, Georgii, monument to, 17
Ploshchad' revoliutsii metro station, 59–60, 156n61
Pokrovskii, Mikhail, 109–110
Popov, Georgii, 102
Poskrebyshev, Aleksandr, 88
presentism, 126–129
progress narrative, 5, 115–122, 124–129
props, sculptural, 55, 59, 62
prospective memorialization, definition and theory of, 7–9, 21–23, 26–27, 116, 119, 146n20

Radek, Karl, 79
realism, 65–67, 69–70
Red Army Theatre, 24

INDEX

Red Doric architecture, 35
Red Square, in Moscow, 20, 87, 131
Rokossovskii, Konstantin, 89
romanticism, 64–65, 69–70, 91
Roosevelt, Franklin, 46
Rozhin, Igor', 74
Rudnev, Lev, 45, 51, 65, 68
Russian Military-Historical Society, 136–137

Savitskii, Iulii, 53
Second World War (1939–1945), 123–124, 126; memorialization of, 123–125, 126. *See also* Great Patriotic War (1941–1945)
Senate House of the University of London, 47
Serpukhovskaia metro station, 25
Shadr, Ivan, 91–92
Shcherbakov, Aleksandr, 88
Shchuko, Vladimir, 47
Shchusev, Aleksei, 35, 37–38, 52, 63, 83, 94, 132, 137
Shervud, Leonid, 42
Sholokhov, Mikhail, 92
Shostakovich, Dmitrii, 111
Shurpin, Aleksandr, 149n36
Smolenskaia metro station, 82
Snegirev, Vladimir, monument to, 92
social condenser, 4, 30
socialist realism, 6, 92, 110, 145n13
Sokol'niki metro station, 59
Sokolov, Nikolai, 36
Soldatenhalle, 123
Solovetskii stone, 143
Sosfenov, Il'ia, 54
Speer, Albert, 14, 120–121, 163n109
Spy (film), 133
Stalin, Iosif, 2, 47, 92, 95, 97, 104, 107–108, 111, 131; cult of personality, 21, 27, 79–82, 131; curation of art and monument design, 11, 34, 81, 87, 89, 92, 106, 147n32; death and Pantheon project, 21, 27, 38, 68, 81–82, 86, 125, 161n62; interest in legacy-building, 1–2, 77, 79; monuments and memorialization of, 8, 39, 57–58, 60–61, 67–68, 79–81, 102, 131, 137–139, 143, 146n23
State Central Archive, 42
St. Isaac's Cathedral, 42
Stratonauts, Monument to Hero-, 62
stripped classicism. *See under* historicist (traditionalist) architecture
Supreme Soviet of the USSR, 28, 73, 88
Suslov, Mikhail, 159n14

Sverdlov, Iakov, grave of, 19
synthesis, theory of, 3, 8, 21–22, 54–55, 59, 61–62, 139–140

Taganskaia metro station, 60
Tank Crews, Monument to Soviet, 56
Tatlin, Vladimir, 17–19
Ternovets, Boris, 54
terror, 23, 79, 103–104, 110–111, 140–141, 143, 148n29
Thiepval, British war memorial at, 118
Third International, Monument to, 17–19
Tolstoi, Aleksei, 41, 99, 167n4
Tolstoi, Vladimir, 157n79
Tomskii, Nikolai, 45, 67, 75–76
Toropov, Sergei, 22
Tosunova, Margarita, 61
totalitarianism, historiographic school of. *See* neo-totalitarianism (historiographic school)
Totenburgen, 123–124
Transformation of Nature, Stalin Plan for the, 117
Triumph of Victory bridge-side monument, 24, 57, 101–102
Triumph-Palace high-rise, 133
Tsaplin, Dmitrii, 56
Tsarist monuments, 9, 16, 26
Tukai, Gabdulla, monument to, 86

Union of Soviet Architects, 10–11, 25, 33, 41, 50–51, 79, 93–94, 107; 1946 conference on monumentalism, 22, 51, 61; First Congress of, 7, 35
Union of Soviet Artists, 10–11, 30–31; Moscow branch, 22, 42, 95
United States of America, monument building in, 46–47, 115, 119–120. *See also entries for individual monuments*
urbanization, 103–104
utopianism: Bolshevik, 5, 16–18, 20–21, 106, 109–110, 116; after Stalin's death, 28–29, 125–126; in Nazi ideology, 120–122, 125; under Stalin, 2–3, 5–6, 30–31, 34, 103, 110–111, 124–125
Uzbek State Opera and Ballet Theater House, 37–38
Uznai Moskvu (interactive mobile app), 143

Vakhtangov Theater, reconstruction of, 95, 109
vernacular architecture. *See under* historicist (traditionalist) architecture
Vesnin, Viktor, 50, 94

Victory Arch, Baku, 102
Victory mural, in Kazan' railway station, 65
Vimy, Canadian National Memorial at, 118
Volga-Don Canal, 26, 58, 81
Volkshalle, 13, 122
Volodarskii, V., monument to, 17
Voroshilov, Kliment, 11, 63, 87, 95;
    monuments and memorialization of, 81
Vuchetich, Evgenii, 26, 55, 64–66, 157n83

War Memorial, Soviet, in Tiergarten Park, 56
War Memorial, Soviet, in Treptower Park, 78

wedding-cake architecture. *See* excess,
    architecture of
Worker and Kolkhoz Woman sculpture,
    56–57, 96, 137, 142

Young Transformers of Nature, Monument
    to the, 57

Zakharov, Grigorii, 93
Zelenskaia, Nina, 67, 147n32
Zholtovskii, Ivan, 31–33, 91
Zhukov, Georgii, 76, 89, 94

www.ingramcontent.com/pod-product-compliance
Lightning Source LLC
Chambersburg PA
CBHW032214230426
43672CB00011B/2553